Native Shrubs and Woody Vines of the Southeast

Native Shrubs and Woody Vines of the Southeast

LANDSCAPING USES AND IDENTIFICATION

Leonard E. Foote

Samuel B. Jones, Jr.

TIMBER PRESS
Portland, Oregon

ISBN 0-88192-128-9
Printed in Hong Kong

Timber Press, Inc.
9999 SW Wilshire
Portland, Oregon 97225

Library of Congress Cataloging-in-Publication Data

Foote, Leonard E.
    Native shrubs and woody vines of the Southeast : Landscaping uses
and identification / Leonard E. Foote, Samuel B. Jones, Jr.
        p.   cm.
    Bibliography: p.
    Includes index.
    ISBN 0-88192-128-9
    1. Native plants for cultivation--Southern States. 2. Shrubs-
-Southern States--Identification. 3. Climbing plants--Southern
States--Identification. 4. Native plant gardening--Southern States.
5. Landscape gardening--Southern States. 6. Ornamental shrubs-
-Southern States. 7. Ornamental climbing plants--Southern States.
I. Jones, Samuel B., 1933-   . II. Title.
SB439.24.S66F66   1989
715'.0975--dc19   88-38086
                                                          CIP

Contents

Acknowledgments

The preparation of a book on the shrubs and woody vines requires the use of information from the publications of many authors and from herbarium collections of many field botanists. The authors are grateful to all these persons. In addition, we wish to express our gratitude to those who have provided assistance, encouragement, and cooperation in the preparation of the manuscript and its color photographs. Special thanks are due Howard Miller, Fred Galle, Raleigh Bryans, Robert Platt, Lance Lowell, Mike Moore, Ann and Leo T. Barber, John Bozeman, Greg Krakow, Bill Houghton, Linda Chafin, Wayne Faircloth, and Ruth Bell. Unless otherwise credited, all photographs were taken by the authors.

Margarita and Eugene Cline permitted use of their extensive arboretum for photographs, helped in locating specific shrubs, and advised on optimum flowering and fruiting times. Nancy Coile provided support of the University of Georgia Herbarium, identifying many voucher specimens. Anna Baker located numerous references and patiently made copies of the manuscript. We were given every assistance by the University of Georgia Libraries and the Department of Botany.

The assistance of many individuals at Timber Press in preparing the manuscript for publication is acknowledged. We are especially indebted to Carol Krom for suggestions which improve the text and for careful editing. Richard Abel's advice on subject matter and content and its treatment was particularly helpful.

Gratitude is extended to our spouses, Grace Foote and Carleen Jones, for their patience with us while bringing this book to fruition as well as their companionship and aid during many years of field work in various parts of the Southeastern United States.

Leonard E. Foote
Samuel B. Jones, Jr.

Introduction

Native Shrubs and Woody Vines of the Southeast was written to increase the understanding and appreciation of this beautiful and valuable group of plants. More people are becoming interested in our native shrubs and woody vines, but no simple, yet complete and up-to-date treatment specifically for this geographic region has heretofore been available. This book brings together photographs, keys, descriptions, and other pertinent information for rapid identification of all native and naturalized shrubs and woody vines of the Southeast excluding those of peninsular Florida.

To promote preservation and enjoyment of these plants, information on those native shrubs and woody vines that can be used to create interesting and attractive southeastern landscapes also is included. The material has been designed to meet the needs of interested amateurs as well as students and professionals in the sciences.

Woody plants are perennials living from year to year in contrast to annuals which live for only one season. Many perennials are herbaceous, remaining alive only below ground and sending out new growth each year from roots, tubers, rhizomes, bulbs, or similar structures. However, the aboveground stems of woody plants remain alive from year to year. Some continue growth during the winter while others are in a state of dormancy. Some are dormant in the northern or higher parts of the Southeast but continue to grow in the lower or more southerly latitudes. This volume includes all native and naturalized shrubs and woody vines occurring in eastern Texas, Louisiana, Arkansas, Kentucky, West Virginia, Maryland, Delaware, extreme northern Florida, and states to the south and east. There are approximately 550 of these species representing 76 plant families. Many of the plants described also occur outside our region, extending the utility of this volume.

Woody vines are plants which climb by twining, use of aerial roots, or other means. Shrubs are woody plants usually growing to less than 7 meters (23 feet) in height, often arising from multiple stems. Several species are early-growth forms of small trees; the sourwood, for example, can flower and produce fruit when less than 2 meters tall yet may exceed 20 meters in height in forest stands. Some woody plants form a shrub habit on poor soils or in adverse microclimates but are trees where growth conditions are more suitable.

In the plant descriptions of this volume each plant is labeled first by its common or vernacular name and then by its scientific name. The common names used are those that are most descriptive and in popular use in at least part of the southeastern United States. Where no vernacular name is available, the plant's generic name is given.

The scientific names used have been established by rules of the *International Code of Botanical Nomenclature.* This code requires exact identification of a plant by use of a name that applies to one species of plant and no other, unlike a common name which might apply to several plants. A plant's scientific name consists of a generic name, a specific epithet, and the name of the author or authors of the plant name. Two similar, related, but differing plants carry the same generic name but different species names. Minor but consistent character differences may constitute a subspecies or variety.

The text describes each species and denotes its distinguishing characteristics and differences from those it most closely resembles. While some species are easily identified, others are so closely related it is difficult to determine whether they are distinct, and the problem becomes a technical one. Therefore, the volume contains a glossary which is helpful in defining technical plant taxonomy terms. Photographs are provided to aid in identification.

While emphasis is given to the commoner and more widely distributed species, those that are rare and/or endangered are included, as are shrubs and woody vines which have escaped from cultivation and become naturalized. Simple yet diagnostic keys for genera with three or more species aid identification.

This book supports the growing movement toward naturalistic landscaping and the desire of many persons to use native plant materials in their gardens. The southeastern United States has a wealth of native shrubs and woody vines with qualities desired by gardeners and landscapers. Many species are waiting to be discovered and utilized in the garden landscape. Information is presented on those native shrubs and woody vines most useful for landscape purposes in the Southeast, and principles for creating attractive and successful landscape designs using native plant materials are discussed. Many of the species are quite well known to gardeners; others, perhaps uncommon or of limited natural distribution, have not attracted the attention of horticulturists but have remained in the domain of the botanist.

Each species having value in the landscape is so noted and discussed in the text. Recommendations are made as to how and where the plants are best utilized in southern gardens. Lists are provided of plants having special uses or certain desirable features or qualities. For example, if native shrubs tolerant to salt spray are desired, a list of suitable species is provided, or if fall or spring flowers are needed to accent the garden, shrubs and woody vines are listed by these categories. Recommendations are given for species to enhance wildlife.

One reason for the increasing use of native plants in the landscape is the realization that the vigor and appearance of many of our native shrubs and vines improves dramatically in cultivation where competition for moisture, light, and nutrients is reduced by application of fertilizer, water, and organic matter to the soil. In addition, horticulturists now understand that certain attractive, low-maintenance, native ornamentals, if placed in the proper site, may require less cultural attention than many exotic shrubs. Catalysts for this change of attitude include the recent severe droughts in the Southeast, as well as extreme low temperatures which harmed many introduced ornamentals. Actually, where else would shrubs and vines be found with genetic adaptation to southeastern growing conditions but within this very region.

In this book, we scrutinize those species which are desirable and adaptable, hopefully encouraging the use of native plant material which will maintain itself over the years and which naturally belong in southeastern landscapes. Perpetual pleasures and satisfaction can come from landscaping our gardens as sanctuaries for native treasures which are our regional heritage. Growing the recommended shrubs and woody vines can make us aware of their great beauty and the desirability of preserving them in both the wild and in our gardens. We have included information on photographing and collecting specimens for herbaria for those so inclined; both activities are enriching experiences.

Caution in acquiring plants must be exercised as preservation is not encouraged by careless digging or ripping them up from roadsides and woods or ravaging natural stands. Constantly decreasing through habitat destruction, many native species now are making a last stand in the face of extermination. If some are to be saved, it must be through prompt action of horticulturists, botanists, and gardeners. We must learn how to propagate and grow all of the jeopardized species. By growing these plants, nurserymen and gardeners can become involved in conservation and enjoy the beauty of our native species, as well as having the satisfaction of perpetuating them. At one point, the native flora was best left untouched, but with increasing encroachment of highways, housing and commercial developments, and changing forest practices, some of our species will survive only in garden environments. We hope to encourage nurserymen and gardeners to seek genetically diverse native plants, to select cultivars with desirable characteristics, and stimulate commercial production serving conservation, the nursery industry, and the general public.

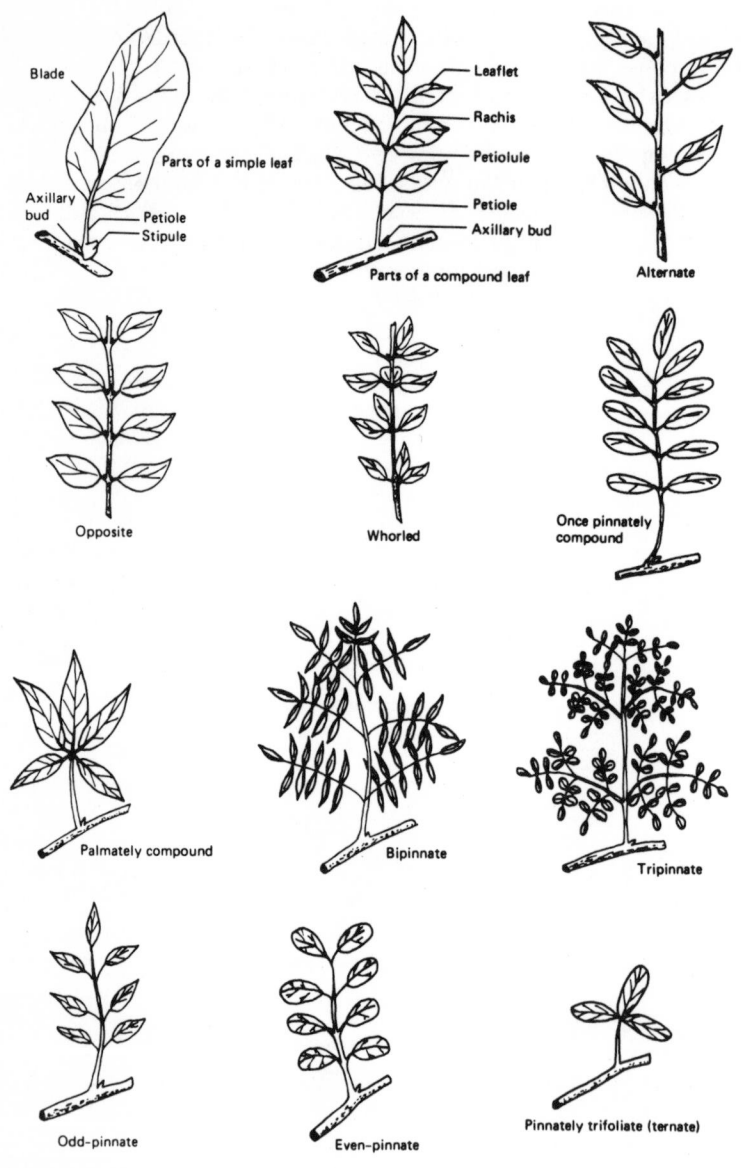

FIGURE 1. Leaf types and parts. (From Jones and Luchsinger, 1986. Used with permission of McGraw-Hill Book Company.)

Identification: Structure of Woody Shrubs and Vines

The ability to identify shrubs and vines is dependent upon recognizing differences in features between one species and another. As this ability develops, the effort to apply names for shrubs and vines diminishes rapidly and enjoyment increases. The important plant structures to help the amateur identify shrubs and vines are illustrated in the following pages. They may be considered in three categories: vegetative, floral, and fruiting. An inexpensive hand lens magnifying 10 diameters is helpful in identifying many plants. One is essential in examining very small flowers, useful in determining some vegetative characteristics such as pubescence and marginal structures of leaves and in discerning pits, sutures, ribs, or wings on very small seeds.

VEGETATIVE STRUCTURES

The vegetative parts of a shrub or vine are root, stem, and leaf or combinations of these. One important combination occurs in buds, which consist of small to minute leaves on an embryonic stem. Stems are usually above ground and bear leaves. When the leaves fall off, scars are left on the stem. Each circular section of the stem which bears a leaf or leaves is a *node* and the space between any two adjacent nodes is called an *internode.* Many shrubs, particularly the thicket-forming colonial ones, have underground stems called rhizomes, often rooting at the nodes.

Roots are usually underground, although some vines have aerial ones. Roots bear no leaves or leaf scars and have no nodes or internodes. Stems sometimes sprout from roots, and because they bear nodes, stems usually can be distinguished from roots.

Leaves almost always have an expanded part (the *blade*), usually a stalk (the *petiole*), and sometimes *stipules* where the leaf joins the stem. If the leaf has no stalk, it is termed *sessile.* This term may be applied to any stalkless structure, such as sessile flowers, sessile fruits, or sessile glands. Stipules are most often attached to the side of the petiole, but may arise from the petiole and stem, or the stem alone. They may be so conspicuous as to be mistaken for leaves, or may be only very small projections, or may be modified to thorns or spines. The blades of leaves are sometimes divided into smaller parts called leaflets. A leaf in which the blade is divided in this manner is termed a compound leaf; a leaf without a divided blade is said to be simple. Because some leaves are deeply notched it is often difficult to determine whether a leaf is simple or compound. Perhaps the single most important item in determining "what is a leaf" is to consider the position of leaves in respect to the axillary buds. A leaf will have an axillary bud where it joins the stem. Leaflets of a compound leaf will not have axillary buds at their base. Vines may be specialized for climbing either by the twining of stems or the modification of stems, stipules, or reduced leaflets into tendrils sometimes tipped by disks. Other vines climb by aerial roots. The diagrams below illustrate various vegetative characteristics. These and others are defined in the glossary.

11

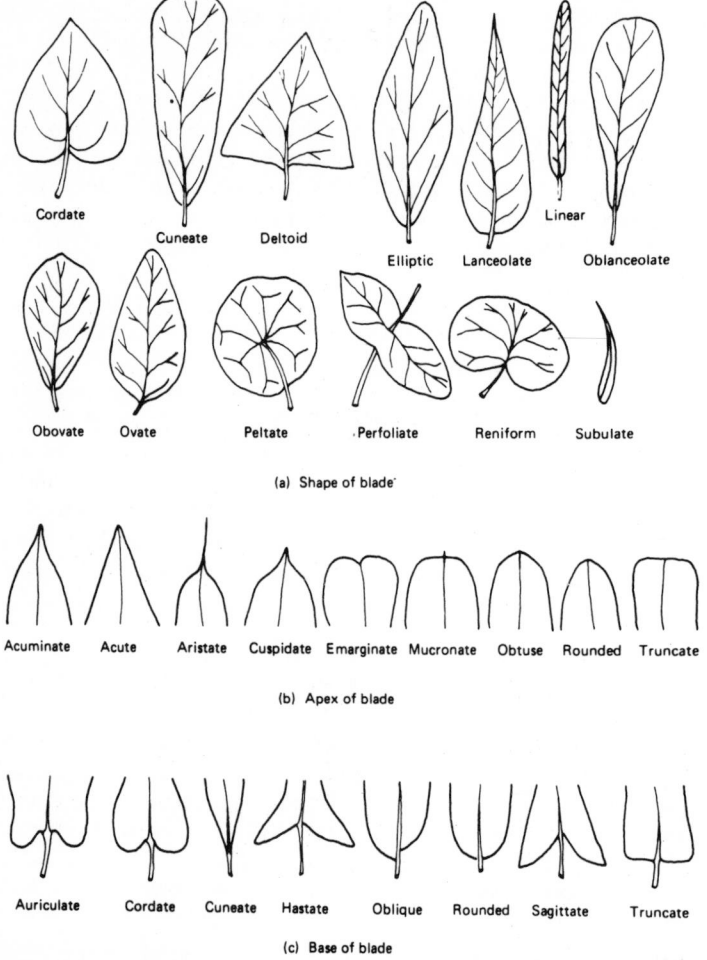

FIGURE 2. Leaf blades, (a) shape of blade; (b) shape of apex of blade; (c) shape of base of blade. (From Jones and Luchsinger, 1986. Used with permission of McGraw-Hill Book Company.)

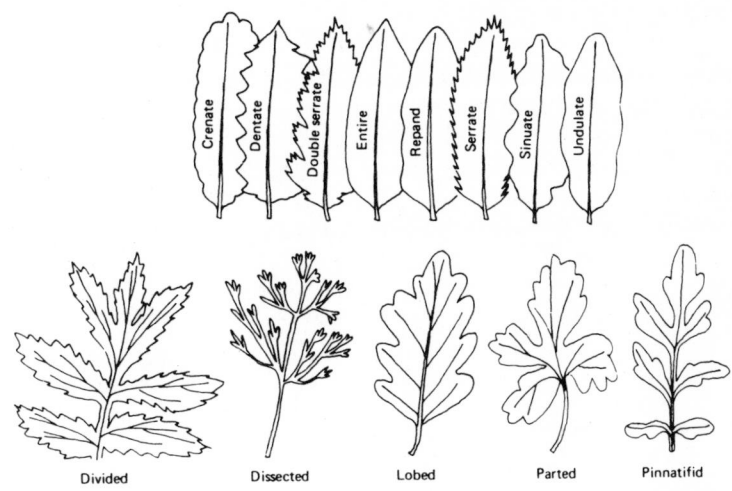

FIGURE 3. Leaf margins. (From Jones and Luchsinger, 1986. Used with permission of McGraw-Hill Book Company.)

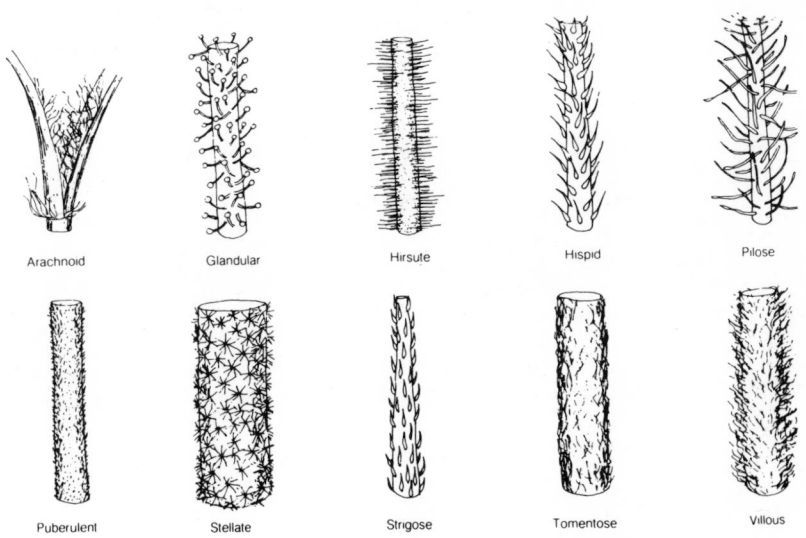

FIGURE 4. The more common types of pubescence on surface coverings. (From Jones and Luchsinger, 1986. Used with permission of McGraw-Hill Book Company.)

13

FLORAL STRUCTURES

A complete flower is made up of four sets of parts (calyx, corolla, stamens, pistil) attached to a special stem called a *pedicel.* That part of the pedicel to which the four sets are attached is called the *receptacle.* Each of the four sets is represented by one or more whorls. Members of each set may be completely separate, or partly or completely fused. The outermost set is the *calyx,* consisting of the *sepals,* which often are green. The *petals* are above these, and are collectively called the *corolla,* which usually is the most colorful part of the flower. *Stamens,* which bear the

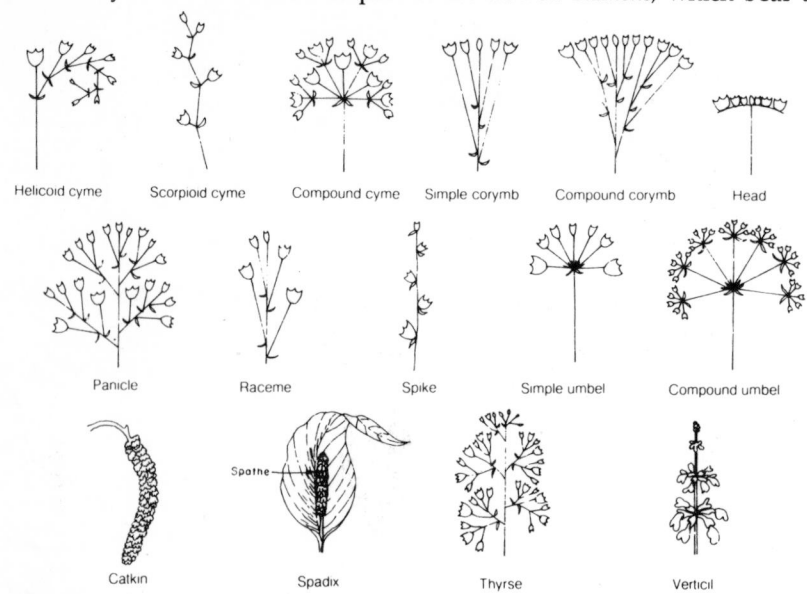

FIGURE 5. The major types of inflorescences. (From Jones and Luchsinger, 1986. Used with permission of McGraw-Hill Book Company.)

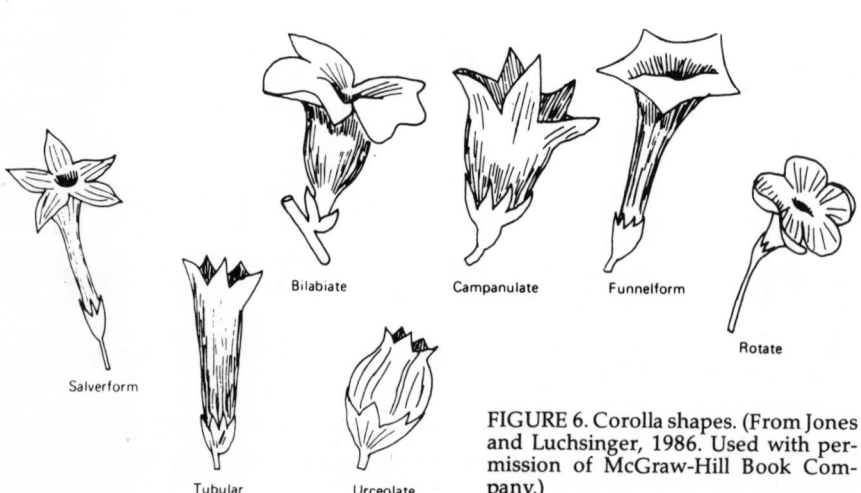

FIGURE 6. Corolla shapes. (From Jones and Luchsinger, 1986. Used with permission of McGraw-Hill Book Company.)

14

pollen, are the third set of parts. The final set is the *pistils,* varying from one to many and bearing the *ovules.* The pistils grow into fruits and the ovules into seeds in them. The *hypanthium* is a cup-, saucer-, or disk-shaped structure sometimes present that supports the sepals, petals, and stamens and lies between these parts and the receptacle.

FRUITING STRUCTURES

Fruits develop from pistils, together with any other structures that may adhere to the matured pistil. Often the hypanthium is an added part. In the apple, this structure forms the outer fleshy part that is eaten. In the raspberry, the receptacle is enlarged and is the major part of the fruit. A common shrub fruit is the drupe, which is fleshy or pulpy with the inner portion of the pericarp hard or stony and enclosing the seed.

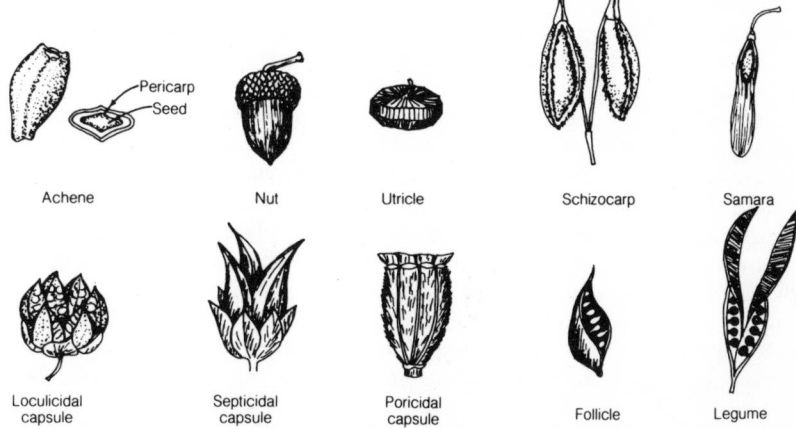

FIGURE 7. Types of fruits. (From Jones and Luchsinger, 1986. Used with permission of McGraw-Hill Book Gompany.)

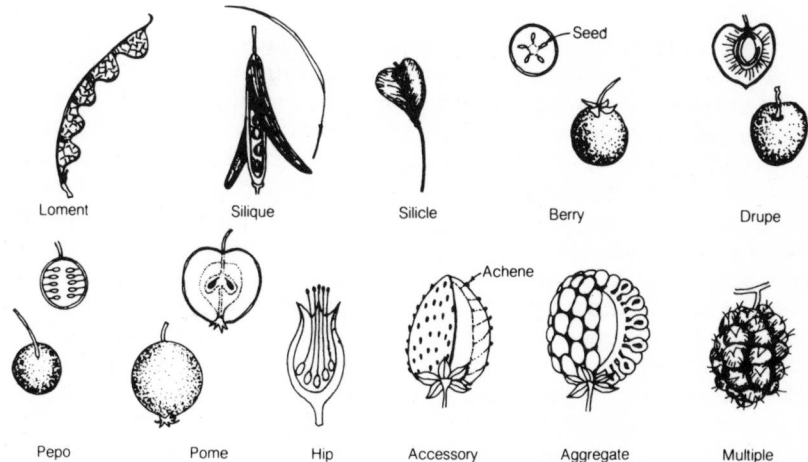

FIGURE 8. Types of fruits. (From Jones and Luchsinger, 1986. Used with permission of McGraw-Hill Book Company.)

Identification: Steps in Identifying a Woody Vine or Shrub

The foregoing section illustrates many of the common characters by which plants differ from one another. Other features used in identification are described in the text by words commonly used by botanists that have special applications to plants. These are defined in the Glossary in this volume as well as in most extensive popular dictionaries. Many of these words are used in the Keys to Families and Keys to Genera to describe the combination of diagnostic characters of each family or species of shrub or vine.

If you know the common name of a plant, begin identification by checking the index and examining the photographs of the plants bearing that common name. If there is a resemblance compare the plant with the description in the text of the pictured plant, consulting the glossary for definitions of unfamiliar words. If the plant differs slightly but still resembles the photograph, turn to the key to plants of that genus and "run" the specimen through the key, considering each descriptive alternate in turn. Usually this process will yield correct identification of any woody vine or shrub found in the southeastern states. An identification can be confirmed by sending a specimen to a university herbarium. The University of Georgia Herbarium will welcome specimens whether the plant is from Georgia or not.

If you do not know the common name, search through the photographs until a picture resembling the specimen is found. Take care, however, to avoid making an improper identification from an apparent likeness. Although all southeastern woody shrubs and vines are included in this volume, not all are pictured. Two shrubs may appear to be the same but differ in important, but not obvious, characteristics.

If the shrub cannot be identified readily from its common name and picture, consult the appropriate Keys to Families, and examine the plant for each set of key characters by proceeding through the key. Once the family has been established, consult the text or the appropriate key to the genus to complete the identification. The plant should "fit" the text characteristics, and ordinarily it will be found within the range and in the habitat listed in the text description.

As you become familiar with the native and introduced woody shrubs and vines, identification becomes easier and you often will be able to instantly identify a particular plant by its key features although fruit or flowers or both may be missing. These key features are included in both the keys and text. Some of these features are stems, branches, and branchlets that are green; thorns, spines, or bristles; glands; perfoliate leaves; bladderlike fruits; square stems; needlelike leaves; leaves that are aromatic when crushed; spicy-scented fruits; leaves with silvery scales; stems with milky sap; roots that are yellow; especially showy flowers; leaves that appear to be flower parts. There are many others.

For rapid identification, it usually is not necessary to start at the beginning of the Keys to Families because the keys are first divided into large groups. If the plant is a vine with compound leaves, for instance, only 5 character couplets need be considered to determine the family to which the vine belongs. So first examine the plant to determine if it is a vine or shrub, if the leaves are evergreen or deciduous, compound, or simple, and enter the key at the appropriate point.

Once familiar with the use of keys, you usually can identify a plant from the most fragmentary evidence. Detection sometimes is achieved by following both alternatives of a key couplet when the fragment does not have the discriminatory feature listed in the couplet. The possibility can be narrowed, in this fashion, to two alternative candidates. Consulting the text usually will yield a proper identity. If necessary, additional information may be obtained from other sources listed in the References cited in this volume.

Landscaping with Native Shrubs and Vines

Those of us who have spent time, energy, and money developing a garden are sometimes asked: Why do we do it?—Why make a garden? One might respond by answering that to know gardens intimately is a precious avocation. Gardens afford us an ever delightful and rewarding occupation. As time unfolds, our love of plants and gardening can prove to be a buffer against the stresses of life, and gardens a quiet place for reflection. Gardens can be a citadel where we can turn to unravel problems or to seek solace in the face of crisis or sorrow. But gardens are also rooms outside the home and can provide the background for great summer parties, where we enjoy the pleasure of friends, or a setting for happy family events like wedding celebrations. However, it is essentially the doing of a garden, rather than the seeing, which is dearest to the serious gardener.

Plants are alive—they impart a sense of grace and beauty to the environment, and a garden will enhance our lives if planned to complement our homes and other structures as well as the contours of the land. To be effective, design and selection of plant material must not be incidental to the site; nor should they reflect impulse buying of what is on "special" at the local discount garden store. If well planned, our gardens have aesthetic qualities, provide a sense of privacy, accent the qualities of our homes, soften physical surroundings and provide us with much pleasure.

THE ADVANTAGES OF USING NATIVE SHRUBS

Plant for plant, dollar for dollar, shrubs give more satisfaction over the years than any other group of plants. Once planted, a shrub can last a lifetime. In a southern garden, what are the advantages of using shrubs native to the southeastern United States? First of all, they are adapted to the local climates and soils of the Southeast. They are generally easy to grow here and most do not require constant care once they become established in a site where they are "happy." When compared with a garden composed of exotic plant materials, a garden consisting largely of native shrubs and vines requires little upkeep. For the property owner blessed with natural topography of slope, rock outcrop, depression, or stream, the native shrubs are an excellent choice to highlight these variations in the land.

Among our native shrubs and vines, a wide variety of heights, shapes, foliage colors and textures, flower colors, as well as fruit shapes and colors can be found. Landscapers and gardeners can choose from a broad palette of natives whose versatility, adaptability, and visual interest make them attractive landscape candidates. There are native shrubs and vines which will fit most needs and desires. If well sited and properly selected, native plant material can give your garden or landscape constant renewal, a shifting focus of attention from place to place during the season, and a lightness needed to soften the environment (Plate 1).

Once native shrubs are planted in an adequately designed space, they generally need relatively little pruning and are attacked by few maladies. In addition to requiring reduced maintenance (indeed often little at all), native shrubs and vines are designed by nature to bestow all kinds of favors. Together with our trees, they form the background or matrix to the whole scene or picture we are developing. They are essential for defining our gardens and landscape. Some native shrubs can be used to form magnificent hedges or screens either on a boundary or between one part of our property and the garden area. Others make splendid roadside plantings to beautify the site, reduce noise, and screen the lights of nearby traffic. They can create microhabitats by shading other plants; forming windbreaks for tender plants; and providing shelter, nesting sites, and food for birds.

Among our wonderful array of natives can be found small or large plants, fine or coarse in texture; plants luxuriant in flower and foliage; flowers impressive and sumptous or dainty and charming which are followed by sparkling, jewel-like fruit. In foliage alone, our native shrubs may rival the hues of the painter's palette. In fact, the leaves of shrubs should be an important consideration for they remain on the plant from spring to frost or even year-round on evergreen plants. The southeastern flora is so widely diversified, so wonderfully rich in beautiful and useful shrubs and woody vines, that there are abundant suitable species for most imaginable purposes or situations. In the southeastern United States, there are native shrubs which will prosper in wet bogs, in hot dry sands, in stiff red clay, in the highly acid humus soil of our coastal pinelands, or on the sweet soils formed over limestone.

The cultivation of native shrubs and vines in your garden can open new gardening horizons. A sense of satisfaction can come with the encouragement and reestablishment of plants that may have grown in the area prior to past development. It becomes increasingly likely that certain species of native plants will survive only in our gardens; one of the best methods of protecting and preserving our native plants is to bring them into cultivation. Native plant materials can be used to restore the charm of neglected woodlands in both suburban and rural environments. At the seashore, lake, or mountain retreat, natives can make the summer place look a part of the natural landscape. Native shrubs may be especially suited for parks and open spaces, and once mature, may spread their progeny nearby. Clearly, highway roadsides are best reclaimed by natives. When used in commercial and industrial settings, native shrubs can break up the harsh and ugly aspects of the site. Native shrubs have been used with great success in ecological restoration of disturbed sites to hasten natural plant succession. It is good common sense to consider the use of native plant material (Plate 2).

It is a common *but mistaken* belief that plants from the wild are inherently scraggly and unkempt in appearance. When our native shrubs and vines are relieved of the intense natural competition existing in native habitats and are given room, nutrients, and moisture in a congenial environment, they become compact and shapely, and produce better flowers and fruits in greater profusion. Contrary to popular belief, there is no real difference between the requirements for growing natives and those for growing exotics in the garden. Once introduced and established here, natives and exotics are on equal terms. In the long term, natives often exhibit advantages in cold and drought tolerance and in resistance to insect pests and diseases. However, the success of natives in the garden will be the result of good planning, proper judgment, gardening skill, and some luck.

On the negative side, native shrubs may be hard to locate at garden centers. But this problem is rapidly changing as the nursery trade slowly becomes aware of the advantages intrinsic to native plant material. Consumer demand increases production. Consumers should request that their garden centers carry a line of natives. If a nursery is unwilling to do so there are numerous mail order sources (*see* appendix for a list of sources). Additionally, there is the problem that many

19

landscape architects, professional horticulturists, and gardeners have not been educated about the value of natives as ornamentals. This situation is also changing as many educators and professionals become more attuned to the naturalistic landscape movement. However, a word of caution, plant material used in developing a garden should be nursery propagated and not dug in the wild; good conservation practices are a must. Additionally, nursery-grown shrubs are easier to establish and have better form than material collected in the wild.

Consideration should be given to the type of native shrubs and vines which will make good garden and landscape plants. Aesthetic appeal is primary! Other considerations include: the quality of plant form, foliage characteristics, flowering and fruiting capabilities, appropriate size, good garden temperament, the tendency not to become weedy, and the ease of propagation and nursery production. Some secondary traits include ability to attract wildlife, usefulness in erosion control, and reclamation potential. Native shrubs with some mix of these characteristics may be found in every part of the Southeast.

USING NATIVES IN OUR GARDENS

How do you best use natives in the landscape? Visit many gardens at various seasons of the year. Consider the general impression made by each garden; try to determine the picture presented by the garden design, then search out the details which brought the garden to fruition. Determine what plants were used; were natives among the plants included in the design? How were the plant materials integrated; how were textures and forms combined?

A design with a few native shrubs scattered about a property is not necessarily delightful. In fact, such an approach may create a cluttered feeling and cause the garden to seem smaller. A simple garden scheme will bring the shrubs together and make the garden appear larger than it actually is. Make sure that a garden is well designed with background and enclosure, that it has a setting and parameters. A garden or landscape planting must relate to other parts of the grounds and to physical structures such as buildings. It must have proportion, balance, rhythm, unity of composition, and accent. An attractive garden is not merely a botanical collection of unusual native plants but a practical and appealing artistic entity, effective for its purpose. In other words, avoid growing plants simply for the sake of having them but rather consider the overall picture you are developing. What do you wish the plants to do in the landscape? Do you wish them to screen an undesirable view, enclose a place for privacy, cover the ground to reduce maintenance, provide food and cover for wildlife, provide a background for wildflowers or perennials, or simply make a show themselves?

DESIGNING A GARDEN LANDSCAPE USING NATIVE PLANTS

It may be possible to go to your local garden center and ask their designer to prepare a plan for your garden, or you may retain a landscape architect. Before you contract with professional designers determine whether they are familiar with native plant materials. A third possibility is to prepare your own plan. Regardless of your approach, do not begin to plant in the absence of a plan.

To begin your own design on paper, obtain some grid paper and select a scale for the plan. You might wish to have one square on the paper equal one square foot on the ground or if the site is larger allow one square to equal five square feet on the ground. Proceed to measure off the area, noting any existing trees or physical structures and include terrain features. Note how many hours of sun each area in your yard receives. Transfer the information to the grid paper. By planning your design from a first rough idea, and getting that on paper, you can work and rework various ideas and concepts into a series of drawings. Attempt to develop the over-all concept that you would like your design to reflect. Have in mind the picture you would like to present. A well-thought-out plan will save a lot of useless effort and make planting easier.

At some point in the development of your plan, begin to consider possible plants of the proper height, color, texture, and form. Use the lists in the appendix of this book and read the descriptions and landscape comments of the species under consideration. When certain of your choices, make a circle on the grid paper to indicate where the center of the plant will be located and where you will dig the hole. The width of the circles should reflect the ultimate size of each plant. Then number the circles and key them to a plant list. When converting the plan to the ground, mark your flowing curves with a long flexible garden hose and remember that curves should be boldly executed. It may be necessary to make minor adjustments in the plan during construction and installation of the garden. Do not worry about making mistakes. Bear in mind there will be failures, and that ideas will change. Have a simple basic plan which must be firm but to which you can add minor modifications, refinements, and additions.

Although many gardens and landscapes no longer have the formality of yesterday, there are still garden design principles to be considered. Following are some basic principles:

1. Provide a background of trees, or, if the property is small, a border of large shrubs as a pleasing background.

2. Do not allow existing trees to dominate and control your garden scene; some trees may require removal to provide adequate light and reduce root competition. It may be desirable to plant trees to provide shade or background for the garden.

3. Strive for simplicity of design; avoid a complicated arrangement of bed and paths.

4. Do not use geometric shapes such as squares, rounds, and ovals; these shapes require professional skill in design application.

5. Determine the amount of available sun and shade when selecting plants.

6. Match the plants to the soil type and to the soil moisture levels by observing the species in the field or by examining the habitat information provided in this book.

7. Design shrub borders as wide as the setting and space will allow.

8. Consider foliage, flowers, and fruit when selecting native shrubs; foliage may be as important as flowers, so rely on plants that look well both in and out of bloom; emphasize the reliables; eliminate from consideration those which are difficult, or are unduly rampant, and those that flower briefly or tend to sulk.

9. Strive for emphasis: plants should be massed; if you have three plants group them together. Larger shrubs can be used singly for accent plants.

10. Plan the garden to have a physically defined beginning and end—it cannot go on forever.

When planning the use of natives adjacent to the home, choose plants to enhance the house, not smother it. Never plant shrubs which will hide doorways or cover windows. Generally, relatively few shrubs are needed for foundation plantings near the home. Examine the structure of the building and determine which features need to be enhanced with plants. The corner of a house or building may need accenting or it may need softening with a tall-growing shrub or small tree. Tall shrubs or small trees may be used to break roof lines and soften heavy masonry chimneys. It is often better to have a few large masses of several good species than a mixed collection about the home. Disharmonious plants purchased by impulse when they are on sale at the local discount store are no bargain.

Several southeastern native shrubs such as bottlebrush buckeye, smoketree, or *Torreya taxifolia*, are suitable as specimen plants, but do not place a specimen shrub in the middle of the front lawn; this is the poorest possible use. Site a specimen to show its form, foliage, or coloration (flowers, fruit or fall coloration) at the foreground of a border, by a gate, or at a focal point where you wish to draw the attention of the beholder. If a barrier or obstacle is needed to keep people or animals from cutting across your property, try using some of the native hawthorns, viburnums, or deciduous hollies. For windbreaks or screening consider the use of southern wax myrtle or some of the evergreen hollies. Use *Vaccinium vacillans* or a similar species as a very low understory shrub where the tree cover is thin to avoid mowing or to prevent the encroachment of undesirables.

Topographic features of the property such as gentle or moderate slopes offer great possibilities. Hummocks and banks open the way for dwarf or creeping native shrubs or to others that will drape over them. The natural features of the site, such as the contours of the ground, the distant overlooks, and the desirable indigenous trees and shrubs should be preserved and enhanced. By guiding and encouraging nature with a careful selection of native shrubs arranged in a satisfactory manner, you will create a delightful picture (Plate 3).

SELECTION OF PLANT MATERIAL

Much of the effectiveness of a garden or home landscape depends on how well the plant species selected serve as elements of the design scheme. Growing plants for the sake of having them may be fine in a botanical garden, but the successful development of a garden landscape depends much more on the effectiveness of the display rather than on the number of species included in the plan. There is danger in selecting too many species and also in developing a larger garden than you care to manage. It is reasonable to limit the selection to a few plants, placing and cultivating them wisely and well.

Dirty fingernails or the ability to recite the names of plants are not the only prerequisites for utilizing native shrubs and vines in the landscape. One must be willing to dig for information about a plant, such as where it grows naturally, under what conditions it can be cultivated, the value of the species in the landscape, and the flowering, fruiting, and coloration features of the plant under consideration. The garden and landscape value of a native shrub may be much more important than its rarity, or even beauty. Species with good garden value grow easily and lustily when their basic requirements are met in a reasonable sort of way. Landscape value is determined by the characteristics of the shrub that make it desirable in the garden picture that you are creating. Relate the plant to the type of character the garden will have and consider its seasonal appeal. For example, *Philadelphus* reaches its peak of attractiveness when in flower, but is less attractive the remainder of the year. Thus certain shrubs that flower only briefly should not be placed in a prominent position in the garden.

The diversity of shrubs and vines from the habitats of the Southeast require a variety of growing conditions. Plants from the bayheads or swamps of the Coastal Plain, woods of the Piedmont, or balds of the southern Appalachians can not necessarily be expected to grow equally well together. Beware of shrubs whose cultural directions include a phrase such as, "likes moisture but must be in well-drained soil." This is a good hint that such species are going to be difficult to place in a suitable site. Do not use plants that require pampering; if their requirements suggest they are difficult, discard the idea of using them. There are plenty of other species worthy of consideration. On the other hand, if a demanding species is especially appealing to you, you might find it worthwhile to give it those special conditions.

The descriptions in the text of this book provide information on the habitat requirements for native shrubs. The experienced person can observe the native plant in its own natural environment to learn the conditions that seem to best suit the plant. It is likely that most gardens will have a mix of sun, shade, temperature, moisture, fertility, and topography. Those gardens that have the advantage of a variety of exposures and terrain have several small-scale environments or microclimates, and each is suitable to certain native plant species. The cultivation of native shrubs is not a complicated process; quite the contrary, it is often a simple undertaking, comparable with ordinary gardening. Simply stated, the plants selected must be comfortable in the environment in which the conditions of soil, moisture, shade, or sun duplicate, as nearly as possible, those of their natural habitat.

It should be remembered that plants often respond to each other more noticeably than they do to the physical elements of the environment. Plants make shade, extract moisture and nutrients, and control local temperatures. The effect of an overtopping shrub or tree can adversely or positively influence nearby plants. It will pay to give shrubs plenty of elbow room both in spacing and in vertical stratification. In a woodland garden, it usually will be necessary to thin the over-story trees and to provide extra moisture and nutrients due to the competition provided by the roots of the overstory trees. Botanists use the term "allelopathy" to describe the adverse effect of one plant's chemistry on the growth of another plant. The allelopathic effect of black walnut is well known. Evidence is accumulating that other plants, such as sumac, mountain laurel, and the evergreen rhodo-dendrons, produce chemicals that inhibit the growth of nearby plants.

Consult the plant lists following this Chapter for help in selecting native shrubs and vines for your garden. But how to make your selection of the native shrubs to include in your own garden is no easy task. It is difficult to select the 10 best or even the 25 most popular natives. Personal preference certainly goes a long way in any selection, but landscape and garden value are important considera-tions. As discussed previously, the compatability of a plant with its place in the garden (a place where its requirements can be met) is a key issue. You should also remember that natives can coexist with exotics in a garden setting or that the garden may include only natives. Patience, time, practical gardening skills, con-tinued experimentation, discovery of species new to you, and constant garden work (there is no such thing as a no-maintenance garden) will give years of pleasure to you and to your friends.

PLANTING AND MANAGEMENT

Native shrubs can be obtained in several ways. Nursery stock can be purchased as field-grown, balled and burlapped plants, container-grown plants, or field-grown, bare-root plants. If time is not a factor, you can propagate your own plants. Plants can also be collected and dug from the wild. The latter is likely to be unsuccessful and is not desirable from a conservation standpoint.

Late fall and early winter are the best times of the year to plant throughout much of the Southeast since the plants are dormant and some species will make root growth over winter. Plants should be planted as soon as possible after they are obtained. If bare-root plants are purchased, soak the roots in water for a couple of hours prior to planting. Based upon the previously developed planting plan, prepare the holes twice as wide as the root mass and about 12 inches deeper. Many gardeners amend the backfill (soil that goes back into the hole) with ground pine bark; however, there is some evidence that organic amendments should not be used and that native soil is best for plant establishment. However, it is agreed that in the Southeast, pine bark is better than peat moss for soil amendment. Do not add any fertilizer at the time of planting but wait until new growth is about to appear in the spring.

Before replacing the backfill, spread out the roots of bare-root material; or remove the burlap, string, and wire on balled and burlapped nursery stock; or slide container-grown plants out of the nursery pot. In the Southeast, most container-grown shrubs are grown in pure pine bark. Recent research and experience has shown that it is usually best to remove most of this pine-bark potting mix. The idea is to get the roots in contact with and established in the native soil. If the container-grown plant is pot-bound, unwind the roots and spread them out prior to planting. If this is not possible, it may be advantagous to cut a few of the roots to promote lateral root growth. Plant shrubs in the hole at the same depth at which they had been growing. But azaleas, vacciniums, and rhododendrons should be planted slightly higher to ensure proper drainage. Fill the hole with the backfill to the soil line and then finish by firming the backfill and watering thoroughly. To aid in establishing the shrub, prune about one-third of the top growth and apply an organic mulch of pine straw, wood chips, leaves, or pine bark.

Top-heavy shrubs should be protected from wind damage by staking and tying with wire. Use pieces of old garden hose on the wire to protect the bark of the shrub. Once the plant is established in its new home, remove the wire to avoid girdling. It may be advisable to wrap the main stems of large, newly planted shrubs with commercial tree wrapping to prevent sunscald. Tie the tree wrapping to the stem at the top and bottom with cotton cord and remove it after a couple of years. There are plastic tree wraps which also help to prevent rodent damage to the stems of newly planted shrubs. Rodents are often attracted to nursery-produced plant material apparently because of nutrients present in the well-fertilized plants unlike others found on the site.

Once planted, management of a garden containing native shrubs and woody vines is similar to that for any other planting. During the first few growing seasons, newly planted shrubs and vines will need to be watered frequently if rain is lacking. In much of the Southeast, droughts of one to four weeks can occur during any month of the growing season, and additional water will always be helpful at those periods of stress. Each year in the early spring immediately prior to the appearance of new growth, a light application of a complete fertilizer such as 10-

10-10 will be helpful. Species that require a low pH, such as *Vaccinium,* and *Rhodo-dendron,* need an acid camellia/azalea fertilizer. Other species, such as *Cotinus,* will benefit from the addition of a bit of lime to sweeten the soil. Mulching will assist in controlling weeds in newly planted areas. It is important that weeds not be allowed to compete with the newly planted native species for moisture, light, and nutrients. Most shrubs and vines will benefit from occasional pruning to develop the desired form. By using good gardening common sense, you will find that natives are not difficult to grow and that they will reward you with years of pleasure.

SELECTED REFERENCES

Bean, W. J. 1981. *Trees and Shrubs Hardy in the British Isles.* 8th rev. ed., 4 vols. St. Martins. NY.

Durand, H. 1923. *Taming the Wildings.* G. P. Putnam's Sons. NY.

Floyd, J. A. et al. 1980. *Southern Living Gardening—Trees and Shrubs.* Oxmoor House. Birmingham, AL.

Halfacre, R. G., and A. R. Shawcroft. 1975. *Carolina Landscape Plants.* 2nd ed. Sparks Press. Raleigh, NC.

Hillier, H. G. 1981. *Hillier's Manual of Trees and Shrubs.* 5th ed. Van Nostrand Reinhold. NY.

Philips, C. E. L. and P. N. Barber. 1981. *Ornamental Shrubs.* Van Nostrand Reinhold. NY.

Whitcomb, D. E. 1986. *Landscape Plant Production, Establishment and Maintenance.* Lacebark Pub. Stillwater, OK.

Wigginton, B. E. 1963. *Trees and Shrubs for the Southeast.* University of Georgia Press. Athens, GA.

Wyman, D. 1969. *Shrubs and Vines for American Gardens.* rev. ed. Macmillan. NY.

Zucker, I. 1966. *Flowering Shrubs.* D. Van Nostrand Reinhold. Princeton, NJ.

SHRUBS FOR MOIST TO WET SITES OR ALONG STREAM BANKS

Aronia arbutifolia – Red Chokeberry
Cephalanthus occidentalis – Button Bush
Clethra alnifolia – Sweet Pepperbush
Cliftonia monophylla – Buckwheat-Bush
Cornus asperifolia – Cornel
Cornus foemina – Swamp Dogwood
Crataegus aestivalis – May Haw
Cyrilla racemiflora – Titi
Decodon verticillatus – Water Willow
Ilex cassine – Dahoon
Ilex coriacea – Large Gallberry
Ilex myrtifolia – Myrtle Holly
Illicium floridanum – Anise-stinkbush
Itea virginica – Virginia Willow
Kalmia angustifolia – Lamb-Kill
Kalmia cuneata – White-Wicky
Magnolia virginiana – Sweetbay
Nyssa ogeche – Ogeechee-Lime
Pieris phillyreifolia – Pieris
Pinckneya bracteata – Fevertree
Rhododendron arborescens – Sweet Azalea
Rhododendron canescens – Piedmont Azalea
Rosa palustris – Swamp Rose
Sambucus canadensis – Elderberry
Viburnum nudum – Swamp Haw
Xanthorhiza simplicissima – Yellow-root

SHRUBS TOLERANT OF SALT SPRAY

Baccharis halimifolia – Groundsel Tree
Borrichia frutescens – Sea Ox-Eye
Bumelia lycoides – Southern Buckthorn
Ceratiola ericoides – Sandhill Rosemary
Chrysoma pauciflosculosa – Bush Goldenrod
Conradina canescens – Wild Rosemary
Forestiera segregata
Ilex cassine – Dahoon
Ilex glabra – Inkberry
Ilex vomitoria – Yaupon
Myrica cerifera – Wax Myrtle
Myrica heterophylla – Bayberry
Myrica pensylvanica – Bayberry
Persea borbonia – Swamp Red Bay
Serenoa repens – Saw Palmetto
Smilax auriculata – Wild-Bamboo
Yucca aloifolia – Spanish Dagger
Yucca gloriosa – Spanish Bayonet
Zanthoxylum clava-herculis – Hercules' Club

SHRUBS WITH INTERESTING FRUIT

Aesculus spp. – Buckeye – leathery capsule, seeds brown
Amelanchier spp. – Shadbush-Serviceberry – purple-black pome
Aralia spinosa – Hercules' Club – clustered black, berrylike drupes
Aronia arbutifolia – Red Chokeberry – red or blue-black pome
Aronia melanocarpa – Black Chokeberry – blackish pome
Baccharis halimifolia – Groundsel Tree – heads with white pappus
Callicarpa americana – Beauty-berry – bright purple drupe
Castanea pumila – Allegheny Chinquapin – prickly bur
Celastrus scandens – Bittersweet – scarlet capsule, red seeds
Chionanthus virginicus – Grandsir-Graybeard – blue-black drupe
Cliftonia monophylla – Buckwheat-tree – winged yellow drupe
Cornus alternifolia – Pagoda Dogwood – blue-black drupe
Cornus amomum – Silky Cornel – pale blue drupe
Cornus florida – Flowering Dogwood – red drupe
Cornus foemina – Swamp Dogwood – bright blue drupe
Corylus americana – Beaked Hazel-nut – brownish acornlike
Corylus cornuta – Hazel-nut – brownish acornlike
Crataegus spp. – Hawthorn – red-green-brown-orange
Daubentonia spp. – Purple Sesban-Rattle Bush – brown 4-winged legume
Euonymous americanus – Strawberry Bush – warty red capsule, scarlet seed
Gaylussacia spp. – Huckleberry – black berries
Halesia spp. – Silverbell-Snowdrop Tree – winged yellow-brown
Ilex cassine – Dahoon – red drupe
Ilex coriacea – Large Gallberry – black drupe
Ilex decidua – Possum Haw – red drupe
Ilex glabra – Inkberry – black drupe
Ilex myrtifolia – Myrtle Holly – red drupe
Ilex verticillata – Winterberry – red drupe
Ilex vomitoria – Yaupon – red drupe
Lindera benzoin – Spice-bush – bright red drupe
Malus spp. – Crab-apple – greenish pome
Myrica cerifera – Wax Myrtle – gray
Nyssa ogeche – Ogeechee Lime – large plumlike rose-red drupes
Osmanthus americanus – Wild Olive – blue-black drupe
Oxydendrum arboreum – Sourwood – drooping racemes of capsules
Parthenocissus quinquefolia – Virginia Creeper – blue berries
Persea borbonia – Swamp Red Bay – dark blue drupe
Prunus americana – Wild Plum – red-blue drupe
Prunus angustifolia – Chickasaw Plum – red-yellow drupe
Prunus caroliniana – Carolina Cherry Laurel – black drupe
Prunus pensylvanica – Fire Cherry – red drupe
Prunus umbellata – Black Sloe Plum – black-red drupe
Prunus virginiana – Choke Cherry – dark red drupe
Ptelea trifoliata – Wafer Ash – large waferlike samara
Rhus copallina – Winged Sumac – clustered red drupes
Rhus glabra – Common Sumac – clustered red drupes
Rhus typhina – Staghorn Sumac – clustered red drupes
Rosa palustris – Swamp Rose – red hip

Rosa setigera – Prairie Rose – red hip
Rubus spp. – Raspberry-Blackberry – red-black druplet aggregate
Sambucus canadensis – Elderberry – purple-black berrylike drupe
Sorbus americana – Mountain Ash – orange-red pome
Staphylea trifolia – Bladdernut – large inflated capsule
Styrax spp. – Snowbell-Storax – globular greenish brown
Symphoricarpos orbiculatus – Coral Berry – red berrylike drupe
Vaccinium spp. – Blueberry – blue-black berries
Viburnum spp. – Arrowwoods-Haws – blue-black
Vitis rotundifolia – Muscadine – purple-greenish-gold berries

SHRUBS FOR DRY SITES OR DEEP SANDS
Ceratiola ericoides – Sandhill Rosemary
Chrysoma pauciflosculosa – Bush Goldenrod
Conradina canescens – Wild Rosemary
Leiophyllum buxifolium – Sand Myrtle
Rhus aromatica – Fragrant Sumac
Satureja coccinea – Red Basil
Satureja georgiana – Georgia Basil
Serenoa repens – Saw Palmetto
Xanthoxylum clava-herculis – Hercules' Club
Yucca aloifolia – Spanish Dagger
Yucca gloriosa – Spanish Bayonet

NATIVE WOODY VINES (D=Deciduous, E=Evergreen)
Ampelopsis arborea – D – Peppervine
Aristolochia macrophylla – D – Dutchman's Pipe
Aristolochia tomentosa – D – Wooley Pipe Vine
Berchemia scandens – D – Rattan-vine
Bignonia capreolata – E – Cross Vine
Brunnichia cirrhosa – D – Ladies Eardrops
Campsis radicans – D – Trumpet Creeper
Celastrus scandens – D – Bittersweet
Cocculus carolinus – D – Coralbeads
Decumaria barbara – D – Climbing Hydrangea
Gelsemium rankinii – E – Jasmine
Gelsemium sempervirens – E – Yellow Jasmine
Lonicera flava – D – Yellow Honeysuckle
Lonicera sempervirens – D – Red Trumpet Honeysuckle
Parthenocissus quinquefolia – D – Virginia Creeper
Schisandra coccinea – D – Star-vine
Smilax smallii – E – Sweet-scented Smilax
Vitis rotundifolia – D – Muscadine
Wisteria frutescens – D – Wisteria

SHRUBS FOR FALL COLOR

Acer leucoderme – Chalk Maple – yellow-deep red
Amelanchier spp. – Shadbush-Serviceberry – orange
Calycanthus floridus – Sweet-shrub – yellow
Cornus florida – Flowering Dogwood – red-purple
Cotinus americanus – Smoketree – red-orange
Diospyros virginiana – Persimmon – yellow-green
Dirca palustris – Leatherwood – yellow
Elliottia racemosa – Georgia Plume – reddish
Fothergilla gardenii – Dwarf Witch Alder – yellow-scarlet
Fothergilla major – Witch Alder – yellow-scarlet
Hamamelis vernalis – Springtime Witch Hazel – yellow
Hamamelis virginiana – Witch Hazel – yellow
Hydrangea quercifolia – Oak Leaf Hydrangea – red-purple
Leucothoe recurva – Mountain Fetterbush – scarlet
Lindera benzoin – Spice-bush – yellow
Nyssa ogeche – Ogeechee Lime – purple-scarlet
Oxydendrum arboreum – Sourwood – reddish
Ptelea trifoliata – Wafer-ash – yellowish
Rhus aromatica – Fragrant Sumac – reddish
Rhus copallina – Winged Sumac – reddish
Rhus glabra – Common Sumac – reddish
Rhus typhina – Staghorn Sumac – reddish
Vaccinium corymbosum – Highbush Blueberry – reddish

DECIDUOUS SHRUBS

Aesculus parviflora – Bottle-brush Buckeye
Aesculus pavia – Red Buckeye
Aesculus sylvatica – Buckeye
Alnus serulata – Tag Alder
Amelanchier arborea – Serviceberry
Amelanchier canadensis – Shadbush
Amelanchier obovalis – Shadbush
Amelanchier sanguinea – Round-leaved Shadbush
Amelanchier spicata – Shadbush
Amorpha fruticosa – False Indigo
Aralia spinosa – Hercules' Club
Aronia arbutifolia – Red Chokeberry
Aronia melanocarpa – Black Chokeberry
Asimina triloba – Pawpaw
Callicarpa americana – Beauty Berry
Calycanthus floridus – Sweet-shrub
Ceanothus americanus – New Jersey Tea
Ceanothus herbaceus – Red Root
Ceanothus microphyllus – Little Leaf Red Root
Cephalanthus occidentalis – Buttonbush
Chionanthus virginicus – Grandsir-Graybeard
Clethra acuminata – Mountain Pepperbush
Clethra alnifolia – Sweet Pepperbush

Cornus alternifolia – Pagoda Dogwood
Cornus amomum – Silky Dogwood
Cornus canadensis – Bunchberry
Cornus florida – Flowering Dogwood
Cornus stolonifera – Red Osier Dogwood
Corylus americana – Hazel-Nut
Corylus cornuta – Beaked Hazel-Nut
Cotinus obovatus – Smoke-tree
Crataegus aestivalis – May Haw
Crataegus marshallii – Parsley Hawthorn
Crataegus viridis – Green Hawthorn
Daubentonia longifolia – Rattlebush
Daubentonia punicea – Purple Sesban
Diervilla lonicera – Bush Honeysuckle
Dirca palustris – Leatherwood
Elliottia racemosa – Georgia Plume
Euonymus americanus – Strawberry Bush
Euonymus atropurpureus – Burning-bush
Fothergilla gardenii – Dwarf Witch Alder
Fothergilla major – Witch Alder
Gaylussacia baccata – Black Huckleberry
Halesia carolina – Silverbell
Halesia diptera – Snowdrop Tree
Halesia parviflora
Hamamelis virginiana – Witch Hazel
Hydrangea arborescens – Wild Hydrangea
Hydrangea quercifolia – Oak Leaf Hydrangea
Hypericum frondosum – Golden St. John's Wort
Ilex amelanchier – Sarvis Holly
Ilex decidua – Possum Haw
Ilex verticillata – Winterberry
Itea virginica – Virginia Willow
Leucothoe racemosa – Swamp Leucothoe
Leucothoe recurva – Mountain Fetterbush
Lyonia ligustrina – Maleberry
Lyonia mariana – Staggerbush
Magnolia ashei
Malus angustifolia – Southern Crab-apple
Malus coronaria – Wild Crab-apple
Neviusia alabamensis – Neviusia
Oxydendrum arboreum – Sourwood
Philadelphus hirsutus – Mock-Orange
Philadelphus inodorus – Philadelphus
Physocarpus opulifolius – Ninebark
Pinckneya bracteata – Fevertree
Ptelea trifoliata – Wafer Ash
Rhododendron alabamense – Alabama Azalea
Rhododendron arborescens – Sweet Azalea
Rhododendron atlanticum – Dwarf Azalea

Rhododendron austrinum – Florida Azalea
Rhododendron bakeri – Baker's Azalea
Rhododendron calendulaceum – Flame Azalea
Rhododendron canescens – Piedmont Azalea
Rhododendron flammeum – Oconee Azalea
Rhododendron periclymenoides – Pinxter Bloom
Rhododendron roseum – Roseshell Azalea
Rhododendron serrulatum – Hammock Sweet Azalea
Rhododendron vaseyi – Pinkshell Azalea
Rhododendron viscosum – Swamp Azalea
Rhus aromatica – Fragrant Sumac
Rhus copallina – Winged Sumac
Rhus glabra – Common Sumac
Rhus typhina – Staghorn Sumac
Robinia hispida – Bristly Locust
Robinia viscosa – Clammy Locust
Rosa carolina – Carolina Rose
Staphlea trifoliata – American Bladdernut
Stewartia malacodendron – Silky Camellia
Stewartia ovata – Mountain Camellia
Styrax americana – Snowbell
Styrax grandifolia – Storax
Symphoricarpos orbiculatus – Coral Berry
Vaccinium corymbosum – Highbush Blueberry
Vaccinium pallidum – Upland Low Blueberry
Vaccinium stamineum – Deerberry
Viburnum acerifolium – Maple-leaved Arrowwood
Viburnum dentatum – Southern Arrowwood
Xanthorhiza simplicissima – Yellow Root

EVERGREEN SHRUBS

Agarista populifolia – Fetterbush
Ceratiola ericoides – Sandhill Rosemary
Cliftonia monophylla – Buckwheat-tree
Croton alabamensis – Alabama Croton
Cyrilla racemiflora – Titi
Gaultheria procumbens – Checkerberry
Gordonia lasianthus – Loblolly Bay
Ilex cassine – Dahoon
Ilex glabra – Inkberry
Ilex myrtifolia – Myrtle Holly
Ilex vomitoria – Yaupon
Illicium floridanum – Anise-Stinkbush
Illicium parviflorum – Star-Anise
Juniperus communis var. *depressa* – Juniper
Kalmia angustifolia – Lambkill
Kalmia cuneata – White-Wicky
Kalmia latifolia – Mountain Laurel
Leiophyllum buxifolium – Sand Myrtle

Leucothoe axillaris – Doghobble
Leucothoe fontanesiana – Doghobble
Lyonia ferruginea – Stagger-bush
Lyonia fruticosa – Stagger-bush
Lyonia lucida – Fetterbush
Magnolia virginiana – Sweet Bay
Myrica cerifera – Wax Myrtle
Myrica heterophylla – Bayberry
Myrica inodora – Odorless Wax Myrtle
Myrica pensylvanica – Bayberry
Osmanthus americana – Wild Olive
Pachysandra procumbens – Alleghany Spurge
Paxistima canbyi – Mountain Lover
Persea borbonia – Swamp Red Bay
Pieris floribunda – Mountain Fetterbush
Pieris phillyreifolia – Pieris
Prunus caroliniana – Carolina Cherry Laurel
Rhapidophyllum hystrix – Needle Palm
Rhododendron catawbiense – Mountain Rose Bay
Rhododendron maximum – Rose Bay
Rhododendron minus – Dwarf Rhododendron
Rhododendron minus var. *chapmanii* – Chapman's Rhododendron
Sabal minor – Dwarf Palmetto
Serenoa repens – Saw Palmetto
Taxus canadensis – American Yew
Taxus floridana – Florida Yew
Torreya taxifolia – Stinking Cedar
Vaccinium arboreum – Sparkleberry
Vaccinium myrsinites – Evergreen Blueberry
Viburnum nudum – Swamp Haw
Viburnum prunifolium – Black Haw
Viburnum rufidulum – Blue Haw
Yucca aloifolia – Spanish Dagger
Yucca filamentosa – Bear Grass
Yucca gloriosa – Spanish Bayonet
Zenobia pulverulenta – Zenobia

SPRING-FLOWERING SHRUBS

Aesculus pavia – Red Buckeye–reddish
Aesculus sylvatica – Buckeye – greenish-yellow
Amelanchier arborea – Serviceberry – white
Amelanchier canadensis – Shadbush – white
Amelanchier obovalis – Shadbush – white
Amelanchier sanguinea – Shadbush – white
Amelanchier spicata – Shadbush – white
Amorpha fruticosa – False Indigo – violet-purple
Aronia arbutifolia – Red Chokeberry – white-pink
Aronia melanocarpa – Black Chokeberry – white-pink
Calycanthus floridus – Sweet-shrub – brown-purple

Some native plants, like the buttonbush, are ideal as planted borders to lakes or other wetlands.

Native plants like sassafras and sparkleberry are among many with luxuriant fall color.

Native shrubs may be used to enhance the entrance sign to a neighborhood development.

PLATE 1

Native shrubs are attractive and suitable to mark the entrance to a local "wild" area.

Plantings of native shrubs to frame buildings. They may also be used to hide undesirable structures.

Fences along drives or paths can be beautified by native shrub plantings in the fence corners, or by using vines such as the red trumpet honeysuckle vine trained to grow along fence rails.

PLATE 2

Yellow trumpet honeysuckle vine is here being trained to climb the house foundation and the porch rails.

Cecropia Moth on Azalea. Although they do not feed, adult moths may be attracted to flower color.

PLATE 3

Brown Thrasher, the some-
time voice of the Mockingbird, often nests in the crotch
of wild apple. This species is
omniverous and eats most
wild fruits and many kinds of
insects.

Female Cardinal nesting in a
thicket of Japanese
Honeysuckle. All the
honeysuckles are attractive to
nesting birds but are especially used by Mockingbirds,
Chats, Catbirds and others
that seek dense nesting cover.

Flowering Dogwood fruits
are a favorite food of many
kinds of wildlife, including
Robins, Cedar Waxwings, and
Gray Squirrels.

PLATE 4

Serenoa repens

Torreya taxifolia

Smilax laurifolia

Smilax rotundifolia

PLATE 5

Smilax walteri   BARBERS

Smilax pumila

Smilax glauca

Yucca aloifolia

PLATE 6

Yucca filamentosa

Salix humilis

Myrica cerifera

Myrica pensylvanica HAUGHTON

PLATE 7

Corylus americana

Quercus pumila   MILLER

Celtis tenuifolia

Myrica inodora   HAUGHTON

PLATE 8

Ceanothus americanus – New Jersey Tea – white
Ceanothus herbaceus – Red Root – white
Ceanothus microphyllus – Little Leaf Red Root – white
Cercis canadensis – Redbud – rose-pink
Chionanthus virginicus – Grandsir-Graybeard – white
Cliftonia monophylla – Buckwheat-tree – white-pink
Cornus canadensis – Bunchberry – white
Cornus florida – Flowering Dogwood – white
Cotinus obovatus – Smoketree – greenish-yellow
Crataegus marshallii – Parsley Hawthorn – white
Fothergilla gardenii – Dwarf Witch Alder – white
Fothergilla major – Witch Alder – white
Halesia carolina – Silverbell – white
Halesia diptera – Snowdrop Tree – white
Halesia parviflora – Silverbell – white
Hydrangea quercifolia – Oak Leaf Hydrangea – white
Kalmia angustifolia – Lambkill – pink-purple
Kalmia latifolia – Mountain Laurel – pink
Malus angustifolia – Southern Crab-apple – pink
Malus coronaria – Wild Crab-apple – pink
Neviusia alabamensis – Neviusia – greenish-white
Philadelphus hirsutus – Mock Orange – white
Philadelphus inodorus – Philadelphus – white
Philadelphus pubescens – Hairy Mock-orange – white
Physocarpus opulifolius – Ninebark – pink-white
Rhododendron alabamense – Alabama Azalea – white
Rhododendron arborescens – Sweet Azalea – white-pink
Rhododendron atlanticum – Dwarf Azalea – white-pink
Rhododendron austrinum – Florida Azalea – yellow
Rhododendron bakeri – Baker's Azalea – yellow-orange
Rhododendron calendulaceum – Flame Azalea – red-yellow-orange
Rhododendron canescens – Piedmont Azalea – white-pink
Rhododendron flammeum – Oconee Azalea – salmon-yellow
Rhododendron minus – Dwarf Rhododendron – rose
Rhododendron minus var. *chapmanii* – Chapman's Rhododendron – magenta
Rhododendron periclymenoides – Pinxter Bloom – white-pink-violet
Rhododendron roseum – Roseshell Azalea – pink
Rhododendron serrulatum – Hammock Sweet Azalea – white
Rhododendron vaseyi – Pinkshell Azalea – rose-pink
Rhododendron viscosum – Swamp Azalea – white-pink
Robinia hispida – Bristly Locust – pink
Robinia viscosa – Clammy Locust – rose-white
Stewartia malacodendron – Silky Camellia – white
Stewartia ovata – Mountain Camellia – white
Styrax americana – Snowbell – white
Styrax grandifolia – Storax – white
Symplocos tinctoria – Common Sweetleaf – yellow
Vaccinium stamineum – Deerberry – white
Viburnum – Viburnum – white
Zenobia pulverulenta – Zenobia – white

SUMMER-FLOWERING SHRUBS

Aesculus parviflora – Bottle-Brush Buckeye – white
Aralia spinosa – Hercules' Club – white
Aster carolinianus – Climbing Aster – purple
Callicarpa americana – Beauty Berry – pink
Clethra acuminata – Mountain Pepperbush – white
Clethra alnifolia – Sweet Pepperbush – white
Cyrilla racemiflora – Titi – whitish
Daubentonia longifolia – Rattle-Bush – yellow
Daubentonia punicea – Purple-Sesban – purple-red
Decodon verticillatus – Water Willow – purple-pink
Diervilla lonicera – Bush Honeysuckle – yellow
Elliottia racemosa – Georgia Plume – white
Franklinia alatamaha – Lost Gordonia – white
Gordonia lasianthus – Loblolly Bay – white
Hydrangea arborescens – Wild Hydrangea – white
Hypericum buckleyi – Mountain St. John's Wort – yellow
Hypericum frondosum – Golden St. John's Wort – yellow
Hypericum prolificum – Shrubby St. John's Wort – yellow
Itea virginica – Virginia Willow – white
Oxydendrum arboreum – Sourwood – white
Pinckneya bracteata – Fever Tree – pink
Rhododendron arborescens – Sweet Azalea – white-pinkish
Rhododendron catawbiense – Mountain Rose Bay – lilac-purple
Rhododendron maximum – Rose Bay – white-pinkish
Rhododendron prunifolium – Plumleaf Azalea – scarlet-red
Spirea tomentosa – Hardhack – pinkish

TALL SHRUBS OR SHRUBLIKE TREES (D=Deciduous, E=Evergreen)

Acer leucoderme – D – Chalk Maple
Agarista populifolia – E – Fetterbush
Amelanchier arborea – D – Serviceberry
Cercis canadensis – D – Redbud
Chionanthus virginicus – D – Grandsir-Graybeard
Clethra acuminata – D – Mountain Pepperbush
Cliftonia monophylla – E – Buckwheat-tree
Cornus florida – D – Flowering Dogwood
Crataegus phaenopyrum – D – Washington Hawthorn
Cyrilla racemiflora – E/D – Titi
Elliottia racemosa – D – Georgia Plume
Gordonia lasianthus – E – Loblolly Bay
Halesia carolina – D – Silverbell
Halesia diptera – D – Snowdrop Tree
Halesia parviflora – D – Silverbell
Hamamelis virginiana – D – Witch Hazel
Ilex decidua – D – Possum Haw
Ilex opaca – E – American Holly
Ilex verticillata – D – Winterberry
Magnolia virginiana – E/D – Sweet Bay

Malus angustifolia – D – Southern Crab-apple
Malus coronaria – D – Wild Crab-apple
Myrica cerifera – E – Wax Myrtle
Osmanthus americana – E – Wild Olive
Prunus caroliniana – E – Carolina Cherry Laurel
Rhododendron maximum – E – Rose Bay
Rhus copallina – D – Winged Sumac
Rhus glabra – D – Common Sumac
Rhus typhina – D – Staghorn Sumac
Robinia viscosa – D – Clammy Locust
Rosa palustris – D – Swamp Rose
Stewartia ovata – D – Mountain Camellia
Torreya taxifolia – E – Stinking Cedar
Vaccinium arboreum – D – Sparkleberry

LOW-GROWING SHRUBS (D=Deciduous, E=Evergreen)

Ceanothus americanus – D – New Jersey Tea
Cornus canadensis – D – Bunchberry
Fothergilla gardenii – D – Dwarf Witch Alder
Gaylussacia brachycera – E – Box Huckleberry
Hypericum buckleyi – D – Mountain St. John's Wort
Hypericum frondosum – D – Golden St. John's Wort
Ilex glabra -- E – InkBerry
Pachysandra procumbens – E – Alleghany Spurge
Paxistima canbyi – E – Mountain-Lover
Rhus aromatica – D – Fragrant Sumac
Rhus michauxii – D – Michaux's Sumac
Rosa carolina – D – Carolina Rose
Vaccinium vacillans – D – Lowbush Blueberry
Xanthorhiza simplicissima – D – Yellow-root

Landscaping for Wildlife

There are many ways to enjoy the beauties of nature. Foremost among these is the delight in watching a family of nesting birds, a chipmunk filling its cheek pouches with seeds, or a blue-tailed skink patiently stalking insects.

Wildlife is a product of the land, its soil, water, and most importantly, its vegetation. We commonly think of the birds and mammals associated with specific kinds of vegetation, but also associated are many interesting and unusual forms of lesser wildlife, such as butterflies and moths. The arrangement of plants in the landscape and the species composition of the vegetation largely determine the abundance and variety of wildlife living in any area. Endemic shrubs are a major component of most natural vegetative complexes in the southeastern United States. The density of shrubs and their variety and positions in relation to trees and annual herbaceous plantings will influence the kinds and numbers of birds, mammals, and other forms of wildlife that will inhabit or visit the site.

Most wildlife, at least at some period of the year, establish home-range territories containing food, cover, and habitat essential for reproduction and life. How the shrubs, trees, and annual plants are juxtaposed is significant since wildlife numbers and kinds increase with greater diversity, interspersion, and more "edge" between and among the vegetative types. For example, the numbers and kinds of breeding birds present in any area are a function of the number of acceptable home ranges; flying squirrels, grey and fox squirrels, and rabbits also exhibit this territorial behavior. The home range may be less than two acres for some small songbirds like titmice, chickadees, house wrens, and sparrows, while pileated woodpeckers may range over several hundred acres. Using native shrubs in landscaping can produce a whole new home range for songbird occupancy, or increase the use of an area by more far-reaching species of birds from occasional to regular visitation.

Homeowners interested in birds or small mammals can develop a landscape around their home to encourage wildlife. By the selection of proper shrub species, it is possible to increase both the visits of migrating birds and to attract year-round avian residents. Indigenous shrubs should be selected for the landscape that provide not only seasonal diversity in fruit, but also loafing and escape cover. Some native shrubs yield edible buds, others attractive flowers pollinated by butterflies, and other insects such as hawk moths. The exciting part is that such a landscape, if carefully planned, can be most attractive. On a larger scale, farmers can plant or encourage shrubs that will enhance the environment not just for songbirds and small mammals, but also for deer and game birds like turkey and bob-white quail. Planting fire-protection lanes with bicolor lespedeza (*Lespedeza bicolor*) and field borders and fencerows with multiflora rose (*Rosa multiflora*), introduced shrubs which have become naturalized in the Southeast, have become standard measures for bob-white quail habitat management.

Migratory birds respond to naturally or artificially supplied food and cover, and may appear as individuals or in flocks of 100 or more. The white-throated sparrow, for instance, is attracted to feeding stations, but the number of sparrows wintering nearby may be increased if a brush pile is provided for roosting and escape from predators. Other more northern breeding birds such as cedar waxwings, robins, and evening grosbeaks that winter or migrate through the southeastern region feed regularly on the fruits of hollies (*Ilex*), the wild olives (*Osmanthus*), the sparkleberry (*Vaccinium*), Japanese honeysuckle (*Lonicera*), the viburnums (*Viburnum*), and many other shrubs, and on fruits and seeds of woody vines like the fox grape (*Vitis*).

Resident breeding birds are frequent users of the fruits of shrubs, some unexpectedly so—the pileated woodpecker often feeds on sparkleberries (*Vaccinium arboreum*) in the late winter when they are the last fruits of the season available.

Native shrubs are most valuable as nesting and escape or shelter cover. That tormentor of morning sound, the yellow-breasted chat, performs his aerial evolutions over thickets of wild apple (*Malus*), blackberries (*Rubus*), alder (*Alnus*), elderberry (*Sambucus*), and blueberry (*Yaccinium*). And the brown thrasher, from whose throat come many of the musical extravaganzas attributed to the mockingbird, nests in these shrubs and in roses (*Rosa*), wax myrtles (*Myrica*), sumacs (*Rhus*), hawthorns (*Crataegus*), and many others (Plate 4).

Indigo buntings nest in borders of shrubs or in thick stands of young alders (*Alnus*), or among the wild plums (*Prunus*), while some warblers, like the Kentucky and hooded warblers, may prefer new growth of one of the laurels (*Kalmia*). Usually nests are in shrubs close to small field openings, and the acadian flycatchers almost always choose a branch, frequently of a rhododendron (*Rhododendron*), extending out over an open grassland, stream, or body of water. The plaintive songs of the wood thrush echo from a territory composed of some open grassland, some submature stands of pine and hardwoods, and understory shrubs. The nest often is built at eye level in a shrub like the plum-leaved viburnum (*Viburnum prunifolia*), disguised by the leaves and rootlets used to construct it.

Fledglings of most birds frequently require cover different from that used for nesting. Birds that build nests in trees usually seek out the thicker cover of shrubs to brood their developing biddies. Young wood ducks, born in a nesting box at the edge of a pond, usually leave the area and move to a swale, swamp, or marsh where buttonbush (*Cephalanthus*) or water willow (*Decodon*) are shrub components amid annual grasses, sedges, and rushes.

Shrubs make good feeding areas for birds because they abound with insect life high in protein necessary for nestlings during their initial life stages. Insect larvae also may be found in the fruit: songbirds seek out larvae found in the small, round, red fruits of the sumac (*Rhus*). Game birds—the ruffed grouse, bob-white quail and the introduced ring-necked pheasant—eat the seed and fleshy fruits of shrubs such as the hawthorn (*Crataegus*), and lespedeza (*Lespedeza*), and the grouse consumes many kinds of buds when the fruit and seed foods are scarce in the early spring. Squirrels feed on dogwoods (*Cornus*) almost throughout the year, sampling the leaf and flower buds, eating the drupe, and searching the floor of the forest edge for seeds in the winter. The beautyberry (*Callicarpa*), a shrub true to its common name, is a favorite food of the catbird, orioles, and thrasher. Other examples of use of shrubs and woody vines by resident and migrating birds are given in the table.

Choose the site and the arrangement of shrubs for wildlife to satisfy the cultural requirements for each species of shrub selected. Many are shade tolerant, and will grow in a forest edge understory, while others require full sun. Even the shade-tolerant kinds often will fruit more abundantly if the forest overstory of pine, oak, beech, or maple is pruned to open the stand to admit more sunlight.

This page is a large cross-reference matrix. Birds are listed as rows (labels rotated at the top/left margin) and food plants are listed as columns (labels at the bottom). An "×" marks that a bird feeds on a given plant.

Bird \ Plant	JUNIPER	PALMETTO	GREEN BRIER	BAYBERRY, WAX MYRTLE	WILLOW	ALDER	HACKBERRY	MULBERRY	BARBERRY	SASSAFRAS	SPICEBUSH	GOOSEBERRY	HAWTHORN	MT. ASH	SERVICEBERRY	BLACKBERRY	ROSE	CHERRY, PLUM	SUMAC	POISON IVY, OAK	HOLLY	BITTERSWEET	BUCKTHORN	GRAPE	VIRGINIA CREEPER	RUSSIAN OLIVE	DOGWOOD	HUCKLEBERRY	BLUEBERRY	PERSIMMON	BEAUTY BERRY	BUTTONBUSH	ELDERBERRY	VIBURNUM	SNOWBERRY	HONEYSUCKLE
HUMMINGBIRD																																			×	×
KINGLET																																				×
CRANES																																	×			×
NUTHATCH																																		×		
MOURNING DOVE													×																						×	×
JUNCO													×							×	×														×	×
INDIGO BUNTING															×	×					×				×									×		
DOWNY, HAIRY WOODPECKER													×	×		×	×				×	×					×			×				×		×
JAY													×	×		×	×				×			×		×				×	×			×		
ORIOLE			×						×						×	×					×	×	×			×	×	×						×		
KINGBIRD											×	×				×											×	×						×		
GOLDFINCH							×	×								×	×	×																		
GROSBEAK			×			×	×	×							×	×	×			×	×				×	×	×						×		×	×
WREN			×														×	×																		
VIREO		×									×	×			×	×	×	×		×	×				×								×		×	
TOWHEE		×				×	×				×	×			×	×	×			×	×		×		×								×			
TITMOUSE		×				×	×				×				×	×		×		×								×					×			
TANAGER		×				×	×								×	×		×		×							×						×			
MEADOWLARK		×									×		×		×	×											×	×	×				×			
CHICKADEE		×							×		×				×	×		×		×					×				×						×	×
QUAIL		×				×	×				×			×	×			×		×		×			×									×		
RAIL		×														×														×			×			
COMMON CROW		×				×	×				×	×			×	×		×		×					×		×						×			×
GROUSE		×			×	×		×		×		×	×		×	×	×	×	×	×		×	×		×	×				×			×		×	×
CEDAR WAXWING		×				×	×	×			×	×	×		×	×		×		×	×			×	×	×				×			×	×	×	×
SPARROW		×	×			×	×	×			×	×			×	×		×		×	×			×	×				×				×		×	×
CARDINAL		×				×	×	×			×	×			×	×		×		×	×			×	×		×		×				×		×	×
TURKEY		×	×				×	×			×	×			×	×		×		×	×			×	×	×		×		×			×		×	×
RED-BELLIED WOODPECKER	×							×				×								×				×			×						×	×		×
PILEATED WOODPECKER		×	×					×											×								×							×		×
FISH CROW		×	×	×			×							×		×		×		×	×	×		×	×		×						×	×		
WARBLER		×	×	×			×									×	×	×	×	×	×		×	×	×		×	×	×	×			×	×		
THRUSH		×	×				×				×				×	×	×	×	×	×	×		×	×	×		×			×	×		×	×	×	
BROWN THRASHER		×		×			×				×	×		×	×	×	×	×	×	×	×		×	×	×		×		×	×			×	×	×	
STARLING, GRACKLE	×		×	×			×	×	×				×			×	×			×	×			×	×		×			×			×	×		×
FLICKER	×		×	×			×	×				×				×	×			×	×			×	×		×			×	×		×	×		
SAPSUCKER	×	×	×				×				×	×				×	×			×	×			×	×		×			×			×	×		
ROBIN	×		×	×			×	×			×	×				×	×			×	×			×	×		×	×	×	×	×		×	×		×
MOCKINGBIRD	×	×	×	×			×	×		×		×	×			×	×	×		×	×	×		×	×		×	×	×	×	×		×	×	×	×
PURPLE FINCH	×		×	×		×	×	×			×	×	×	×	×	×	×		×	×	×				×									×		
CATBIRD	×		×	×			×	×			×	×	×			×	×	×		×	×			×	×		×	×	×	×	×		×	×	×	
BLUEBIRD	×		×	×			×		×		×	×		×	×	×	×	×		×	×			×	×		×	×	×	×	×	×	×	×	×	
WATERFOWL	×	×			×	×									×					×					×		×				×	×			×	
CHAT		×						×							×	×		×		×	×			×			×	×		×			×		×	×

38

Many shrubs and woody vines prefer moist sites: the climbing hydrangea (*Decumaria*) and the delicate and rare schisandra (*Schisandra*) climb on tulip popular, ash, sycamore, and many other forest trees, the leaves and vines furnishing cover to August-born young gray squirrels subject to broad-winged hawk predation. Another consideration is the time of fruiting and the length of time seed, drupe, or fruit will be available. Here again, variety is the keynote if one seeks to provide year-round use by wildlife: foods lasting through the winter are especially valuable.

The preceding discussion includes only a few illustrations of the use of shrubs and woody vines in home landscaping for wildlife. Most State Fish and Game or Natural Resource agencies will provide free information and on-site technical assistance through programs to landowners and homeowners interested in both hunted and non-hunted wildlife. Plants are usually available from these or State Forestry agencies at nominal cost. Other sources of information are The National Audubon Society, The National Wildlife Federation, The Wildlife Management Institute, and the Wildlife Extension Agent and Department of Wildlife Management of the State Land Grant College or University. Martin, Zim and Nelson, 1951; Johnson and Grahl, No Date; U.S.D.A. Forest Service, 1971.

Native shrubs and woody vines used by birds in the south-eastern states. Modified from Martin, Zim and Nelson, 1951.

Derivation and Ecology of the Flora

The southeastern states are ecologically diverse because each physiographic province—Coastal Plain, Piedmont, Appalachian Highland, Blue Ridge Mountains, Ridge and Valley, Cumberland Plateau, Highland Rim, and Interior Low Plateau—exhibits distinctive topographic, geological, climatological, and edaphic characteristics. Interspersion of these features has produced a complex mosaic of subalpine to subtropic vegetative habitats. The Southeast is a composite consisting of coastal sediments 4000 or more feet deep; of stacked crystalline rocks, some of African affinity; of karst-forming carbonates deposited in paleozoic seas; of a chaotic jumble of geo-hydroclimatic conditions: in short, a region with a myriad of optimal habitats for many varieties of plant life. Over 550 different woody vines and shrubs find life necessities here. Their relatives can be found in asian, tropical, prairie, arctic, and circumpolar or other exotic foreign lands. Other woody vines and shrubs apparently have evolved here, endemically suited to southeastern climate, soils, topography, and contemporary biota.

The southern Appalachian Mountains are among the oldest in North America. Characterized by abundant rainfall, cool climate, steep slopes, and snow cover at varying times during most winters, the region nurtures a flora and fauna attuned to transitional climates found more extensively to the north. Here one finds relicts abandoned with the retreat of the Wisconsin glaciation some 10,000 years ago, existing as disjunct colonies now separate from the parent home range. Other individual shrubs are southernmost fringe representatives of kinds found in habitats further north. Typical species are the mountain holly, *Nemopanthus mucronata;* the snowberry, *Symphoricorpos alba;* andromeda, *Andromeda glaucophylla;* heath, *Erica tetralix;* the American yew, *Taxus canadensis;* the sweet fern, *Comptonia peregrina;* the American hazelnut, *Corylus americana;* and the mountain alder, *Alnus crispa.* There are many others. At work here is the fundamental climatic-biologic relation quantified as Hopkins Bioclimatic Law: periodic events regularly occur 5 days later in the spring and earlier in the fall for each 400 feet of altitude and degree of latitude: life conditions at high altitudes in the South are similar to those at lower altitudes in the North. Shrubs on Carolina Appalachian mountaintops may be the same ones growing in the lowlands of New England or Canada. The andromeda, found at one high-elevation station at Cranberry Glades, West Virginia, is commonly found in peaty bogs from Greenland to Manitoba.

Many plants in the southeastern states are endemic here although relatives exist in Mexico, Asia, South America, or elsewhere on the planet. These are such shrubs as the Fetter-bush, *Pieris floribunda;* the rare Nevuisia, *Nevuisia alabamensis,* with an Asian relative; the Bayberry, *Myrica inodora;* and that most handsome vine, the Star-vine, *Schisandra coccinea,* restricted to rich, undisturbed woodlands. For many other shrubs, the Southeast is the population center where conditions are most favorable for a species to expand in vast numbers in optimum habitats. Azaleas have proliferated in kinds and numbers in most southeastern habitats; azaleas are fire resistant and live to old age, surviving amid mature hardwoods. There are shrubs peculiar to the Southeast in most of the regions' distinctive habitats: the witch-alder, *Fothergilla major;* the sandhill rosemary, *Ceratiola ericoides;* the buffalo-nut, *Pyrolaria pubera,* each attuned to its special habitat.

Shrub and vine habitats of the Coastal Plain are among the most variable in America: arid sandhills, beach dunes, and dry pinelands are interspersed with bogs, swamps, oxbows, pine flatwoods, pocosins, and savannahs. So this part of the Southeast supports an assortment of diverse plants, many of subtropical affinity. Here the cane, *Arundinaria,* and the palmetto, *Sabal minor,* occupy many river bottomland and pine forest understories while the beach front and brackish marsh edges are host to colonies of the marsh elder, *Iva imbricata;* false willow, *Baccharis angustifolia;* and sea ox-eye, *Borrichia frutescens.* Elsewhere in the Coastal Plain flourish the Alabama croton, *Croton alabamensis;* the anise-stinkbush, *Illicium floridanum;* the pond-spice, *Litsea aestivalis;* and the swamp red bay, *Persea borbonia,* all with more tropical antecedents. Here, too, the members of the genus *Ilex*—the yaupons, inkberries, dahoons, and winterberries—are shrubs dominating cypress ponds, bays, pocosins, pine woods. Into the Southeast have come shrubs and vines with western prairie relations more abundant along the prairie-woodland ecotone near the 100th meridian: the dwarf pussy willow, *Salix humilis;* the leadplant, *Amorpha canescens;* the meadowsweet, *Spirea alba;* and the rare spurge, *Andrachne phyllanthoides,* are examples.

Some more verdant habitats are those with basic or neutral soils in the Coastal Plain, the Ridge and Valley, and Cumberland Plateau Provinces. On taluses below chalky limestone and marble bluffs one may find the spicebush, *Lindera benzoin;* leatherwood, *Dirca palustris;* the mountain lover, *Paxistima canybi;* bittersweet, *Celastrus scandens;* Michaux's ivy, *Rhus michauxii;* or a basil, *Satureja arkansana.* On shell mounds grow the buckhorn, *Sageretia minutiflora,* and the bays and sag ponds in areas underlain by limestone lithologies are a habitat mimicking a coastal plain swamp with its dark acidic waters and deep decaying detritis, a habitat where one may find an out-of-range shrub or vine, or perhaps an unusual azalea hybrid.

Another distinctive habitat is the granitic pluton that botanists call flatrocks, a familiar landscape in the central Piedmont. This is a xeric and thin-soiled habitat where the stages of plant succession unfold in classic simplicity: lichens to mosses to herbs to perennials to shrubs to trees. Here grows the beautiful, fragrant, and romanticised yellow jasmine, *Gelsemium sempervirens,* aiding in the migmatite's destruction in the evolution of rock to soil.

Newcomers to the southeastern flora were brought here with the earliest human immigrants: from the northern states came both native shrubs and shrubs originating in Europe and Asia. The list is long of cultivated shrubs that have escaped, become acclimated, and now remain around deserted house places as vestigial outposts of failed colonization. Best known, perhaps, are the scotch broom, *Cytisus scoparius,* and the fire-thorn, *Cotoneaster pyracantha,* from Europe, or the rose-of-sharon, *Hybiscus syriacus,* which may have originated in the Mediterranean region with the fig, *Fiscus carica.* And introduced from the Argentine, the golden shower, *Cassia corymbosa,* has escaped to become established along southeastern woods edges and fencerows.

Japan and Southeast Asia have supplied most of the exotic shrubs and vines that have become acclimated. Many introduced for landscaping or erosion control have become pests difficult to control or eradicate. Among the introductions are *Spiraea japonica, Lonicera japonica, Kerria japonica, Berberis thunbergii, Ligustrum sinensis, Ailianthus altissima, Lespedeza bicolor, Rosa multiflora,* and that bane of those who maintain forests and utility lines, the kudzu, *Pueraria lobata.*

The diversity of habitats, climatic types, post-phytogeographic history, and the introduction of newcomers all combine to make the shrub and woody vines of the southeastern United States exciting and stimulating plant material.

Conservation of Endangered and Disjunct Species

The Endangered Species Act of 1973 (U.S. Public Law 93-205) directed the Smithsonian Institution to prepare a list of endangered (E) and threatened (T) plant species, to review methods for conserving those species and make recommendations to Congress. The Act also instructed the Secretary of The Department of Interior to examine the lists and determine whether or not any species is truly threatened or endangered. The Fish and Wildlife Service (1975, updated December 2, 1985) published a tentative list for review of status prior to the Secretary's making a final determination. This list includes the following southeastern shrubs and vines: Chapman's rhododendron (E); Florida torreya (E); fragrant prickly-apple (E); miccosukee gooseberry (T); mountain golden heather (T). Other species on the Smithsonian list included the Allegheny plum (T); kelsey locust; bottlebrush buckeye; elliottia (E); sarvis holly (T); corkwood (T); pinckneya (T).

After the passage of the Federal Endangered Species Act similar legislation was enacted in most of the southeastern states. Usually the state acts required initiation of a list of native species of plants that were considered endangered, threatened, rare, or unusual within the borders of the state, and these species were designated "protected species." Although the criteria for each classification varied somewhat from state to state, the lists generally reflected species that were rare throughout, or disjunct; that is, confined to only a few occurrances within the state, disconnected from the plant's major range. Others were species that were rare peripherals, consisting of plants on the edge of their normal range, and lastly, species being exploited, or those subject to rapid habitat loss.

In this volume, species that are noted to be rare or endangered are those so designated by the appropriate state agency. The terms "local" and "uncommon" used in this volume are general subjective evaluations of abundance on the basis of field experience, comments of other specialists, and analyses of studies or specimens in herbaria.

If an endangered species is found in a location suspected to be new, it should be reported to the appropriate state agency and the state university herbarium for confirmation so it can be included in the state listing. A similar report should be made if a known colony of an endangered species is extirpated or about to be destroyed.

Studies are in progress to determine management measures to preserve endangered species. Mere protection from picking, digging, transplanting, grazing, or logging often is not sufficient to insure plant perpetuation. Some species are climax-forest species, while others survive only in habitats in the early or middle-forest successional stages. Many shrubs respond to increased sunlight which may be provided by carefully thinning the forest canopy. Others are dependent upon wetlands, or conversely, habitat drainage. Some require intermittent or regular burning to maintain optimum habitat conditions.

Propagation of Native Shrubs and Woody Vines

Southern gardeners are taking an interest in growing increasing numbers of our native shrubs and woody vines. Clearly adapted to our area, many of these plants can be used to advantage in the natural landscape and others make splendid ornamentals. Low-maintenance, naturalistic landscaping and the back-to-nature movement have caused an increased availability of propagated native woody plants. Gardeners should encourage local garden centers to obtain native shrubs and woody vines from wholesale nurseries in the Southeast that are growing more and more of our excellent indigenous plant material. If desired plants are unavailable in nurseries but can be located in the wild, most can be easily propagated rather than collected, thus aiding in their conservation.

For the gardener, propagation of indigenous plant material provides an interesting and rewarding challenge. Developing an awareness of propagation methods and cultural requirements of native plants is the first step. Collecting small quantities of seed and other propagation parts from an established colony will have little or no effect on the reproductive potential of the population. The establishment in nature of woody plants from seed often is a rare event.

PROPAGATION FROM SEED

Late summer and fall are optimum times for collecting fruits and seeds of many species, but some must or can be collected at other times of the year. For a few, the collection period between fruit and seed maturation and natural dispersal is short; for others, relatively long. The successful collector starts gathering seeds only when they are mature. Fortunately, this stage frequently is reached a week or more before fleshy fruits drop, or dry fruits, such as capsules, open and dehisce to release their seeds. Clearly label each container of seed or fruit with waterproof labels and make notes in a field notebook indicating the name of the seed, location where collected, the habitat, and any distinctive features of the plants.

Once collected, place dry fruits, such as capsules, in a paper sack or envelope and allow to dry at room temperature. Capsules will normally split and release seeds in a few days to several weeks. Some dry fruits may need to be shaken or macerated to separate seeds from the fruit. Fleshy fruits, including berries, drupes, and pomes, must be processed to extract seeds for storage, treatment and planting. Processing should begin promptly after collection to avoid damage by fermentation. If storage is necessary, spread fleshy fruits in thin layers on the floor of a dry, cool room to help avoid fermentation. Soaking overnight in water often facilitates removal of the fleshy pulp. Following this, macerate small lots of fruit by hand squeezing or by some mechanical means such as a rolling pin. After maceration, wash away the flesh with large amounts of water and air dry the seed on newspaper.

Delayed germination of seed can be a serious problem but may be overcome by one of several methods. Scarify those seed with impermeable seed coats by soaking in 95% sulfuric acid which usually can be obtained at a local pharmacy. Other treatments, including stratification at low but not freezing temperatures in moist sand, peat moss, or sphagnum moss, are designed primarily to counter the effects of internal physiological dormancy. Effective pregermination treatments for the seeds of many woody genera are given in *Seeds of Woody Plants in the United*

States. (U.S.D.A. Forest Service, 1974). This reference should be consulted for special techniques to enhance germination.

Some seeds may be sown directly in prepared outdoor nursery beds while others may require greenhouses, cold frames, or hotbeds. Outdoor sowing offers the great advantage of requiring less time and attention to maintain the seedlings. *Growing and Propagating Wild Flowers* (Phillips, 1985) should be consulted for techniques for preparing soil, sowing seed, transplanting, and maintaining seedlings. *Native and Some Introduced Azaleas for Southern Gardens* (Galle, no date) is recommended for details on propagating native azaleas by both seed and asexual means.

ASEXUAL PROPAGATION

Many native shrubs and woody vines can be propagated by layering or by cuttings. Layering often can be satisfactory but is rather slow and cumbersome. In layering, a low branch is bent; the stem is slightly wounded on one side with a long, narrow cut; and the stem is placed in a shallow trench, covered with soil, and weighted down with a rock. It may be a year or two later when the branch has rooted and is strong enough to be cut from the parent plant and transplanted. Other plants may be air layered with soil or other growing medium held in place around a wounded branch by a plastic or cloth wrap until roots have formed.

Certain of our indigenous shrubs and woody vines can be propagated by stem or root cuttings placed in a rooting medium. For the home gardener, the practice of sticking soft-wood cuttings in a styrafoam cooler merits attention. Three to five inches of an equal mixture of peat moss and perlite (or peat moss and sand) is placed in the bottom of the cooler. Soft-wood cuttings of the current season's growth are taken, usually in late June, when the growth has hardened. These are stuck in the rooting medium, immediately watered, and the top of the cooler covered with clear plastic film. The cooler must be placed in the shade and the contents checked from time to time. Dipping the ends of the cuttings in a hormone rooting powder may speed the development of roots. When the cuttings have rooted, it is advisable to gradually remove the plastic covering prior to transplanting the rooted cuttings into nursery beds or pots. If pots are used, they should be sunk into the ground for winter protection. After several years here, the young plants can be moved to a permanent location. Some native shrubs, such as *Aralia spinosa,* can be propagated by root cuttings handled in much the same way as stem cuttings.

By propagating and growing native shrubs and woody vines, you will not only enjoy their beauty but also gain the satisfaction that comes from observing native plants throughout the year in your own garden. In this way you can participate in the conservation of many of our delightful southeastern species of native shrubs and woody vines.

Photographing Shrubs and Vines

Photographs of native shrubs and vines can aid identification. Inexpensive 35 mm cameras that allow viewing through the lens produce artistic images suitable for projection or display. Professional botanists usually can identify an unknown shrub or vine from a color transparency examined through a binocular microscope if the photograph has been properly made. Photographs also provide a means of documenting the presence of a rare or endangered shrub or vine without its destruction. Companion photographs, made at the site, of local habitat features are useful in searching for similar areas where the plant may be found. Either cameras or portable television recorders may be used. If shrubs are infested by insects or damaged by disease, photographs may enable the local agriculture extension service representative to identify the causative agent.

Modern 35 mm cameras with through-the-lens viewing are ideal instruments to photograph wild things of all kinds. They are portable and most of the popular brands have a myriad of interchangeble lenses and attachments available. A cardinal rule is to frame the subject in as close as possible; supplementary close-up lenses that attach in front of the normal camera lens, or extension tubes that fit between camera and lens will provide an enlarged view of the subject. Other lenses, designed especially for close-up photographs, are called "macro" lenses. They show intimate flower details not readily seen without magnification, such as vestigial or minute sepals, anthers, filaments, or seeds, and form a permanent record of color and form lost even when the plant has been properly preserved. Macro lenses in several focal lengths are available for most through-the-lens viewing cameras. Although the cost is greater, many nature photographers employ them.

Photographs appearing in this volume were taken with a variety of techniques essentially the same as those used by a portrait photographer. Control of light and shadow is advisable although less exacting than that employed under indoor conditions. The motion of wind-blown leafy shrubs can be stopped with a high-speed strobe light, but often there are still moments that allow photographing with natural light. Natural light is preferred, and it may be reflected, using homemade aluminum-foil-covered cardboard, or mirrors to bounce sunlight where it is needed. A white umbrella will reflect diffused light and tends to concentrate this as from a parabolic surface, yet the resulting lighting is quite flat. Overcast days reduce the risk of excessive highlights and reflected glare from leaf and flower surfaces. Where natural light is ample, back—or sidelighting may be used with some light reflected to fall on the front of the subject. Backlighting produces a pleasing "sunburst" effect, and sidelighting is essential to bring out surface texture; either will show cilia along a margin or scurfiness of a leaf surface that would not be obvious with frontlighting.

Subjects that are dainty and seem to melt into the background may be highlighted by reflection or, with the camera on a tripod and the shutter set for a long exposure, the subject may be lighted by bulb or strobe flash. The overall habitat is thus preserved in the photograph while the subject is emphasized. Conversely, by shooting with a fast shutter speed and a "wide-open" lens, the depth of focus can be reduced so the subject is sharply outlined against a diffuse background.

Collecting and Preserving Specimens for Herbaria

Collections of plant specimens are essential to understand plant relations. They circumscribe species and document species variation and are the prime sources for establishing floristic records of geographic range and types of preferred habitats. Collections of plants for these purposes are maintained in herbaria at most colleges and universities, at many major botanical gardens, and at floristic research centers. Since herbarium specimens may become a permanent record for later investigators to examine, specimens must be carefully selected, prepared, documented, and preserved (Jones and Luchsinger, 1986).

In the herbarium (plural herbaria), the plant often is filed according to its relationship to all other plants. Unless the plant specimen is unusually rare it will be grouped with one of several-to-many of the same species collected by other collectors from different parts of its range and at different times of the year. Some modern herbaria may contain millions of specimens documenting the flora of a continent. Study of these specimens tells one where the plant grows, its habitat, how variable its characteristics are, and how it differs and resembles its close relatives. Herbarium specimens form the basis of the records used to compile lists of threatened and endangered species. Herbaria are the repository of "original documents"—that is, the specimens upon which all our knowledge of the relations, evolution, and distribution of our flora rests. Manuals, monographs, and books such as this guide eventually stem from herbarium resources.

More and more environmentally aware individuals are contributing to herbaria and experiencing the satisfaction of extending our floristic knowledge. The best specimens for identification and documentation are intact and complete plants. Attempts to identify a specimen from a single leaf, leaflet, or flower usually fail. But while it is possible to collect entire plants of small annuals and some herbaceous perennials, one would not attempt to preserve an entire shrub or vine. For woody plants representative leaves, stems, and reproductive structures are essential. The flowers, fruits, and seed of shrubs and woody vines are especially important because these are often the most definitive of species characteristics. Select specimens that are representative of all phases of the natural population. Avoid insect-damaged or diseased material. When pressed and dried, the specimen should yield the maximum amount of information about the living plant species and be representative of the population.

A simple press is needed to press and dry plant specimens. It may be inexpensively constructed from two pieces of ⅜-inch plywood measuring 12x18 inches to constitute the two ends of the press. Use straps of webbing with claw buckles or ropes made of sash cord approximately 5-feet long to tighten the press. Have available blotters to absorb moisture from the plant specimen, and corrugated cardboards to separate and ventilate the pressed material. Fold half sheets of newspaper and place the plant specimen between the folds. Follow the sequence of plywood press, corrugate, blotter, newspaper with specimen, blotter, and corrugate until all specimens have been placed in the press. Then compress the press by tightening the webbing or ropes.

The arrangement of plant material in the newspaper folds will determine the final appearance of the specimen when it is mounted on paper. Place the specimen so as to look more or less natural and show essential botanical structures. Overlapping of leaves slows drying. Arrange at least one leaf with the lower side uppermost so this surface can be studied after mounting. Avoid crowding.

For best results, dry the specimens as rapidly as possible. Artificial heat such as that supplied by several 60-watt light bulbs arranged so the heat from them will flow through the corrugate tubes of the paperboard usually will dry a press in 12 hours. There are many other means of applying air circulation for drying.

A field notebook is an indispensible item for the collector. Record data on each plant in the field. Include specific locality, elevation, habitat, associated plants, soils, aspect and topography, state, county, date of collection, and, if known, the plant's scientific name. A data slip containing this information sometimes is pressed with the plant and remains with it until the plant is mounted and formally labeled in the herbarium. A preferred method for the dedicated collector is to mark the newspaper with a collection number referring to the field notebook.

Comments on Texts

The text for each major species gives its common and scientific names, key recognition characteristics, flowering to fruiting time, geographical distribution, origin if introduced, preferred habitats, abundance if rare or uncommon, and status in regard to endangeredness. If the shrub or vine has economic or medicinal value, or is poisonous, or if it is of special value to man or wildlife, this is noted, as are items regarding its discovery or propagation. Often a reference is given for additional information.

PLANT NAMES

Plants are arranged by plant families: the name of the family to which the plant belongs appears in CAPITAL LETTERS at the top of the page or on the page above the plant name. Almost every species discussed has a common name—some have several—and all have a scientific name. Although several different plants may occasionally have the same common name or be called by the same common name in different places, each plant has only one correct scientific name. The latter are thus more exact and reliable; they also are internationally constant, everywhere recognized to apply to that plant and only that plant, regardless of national language. They make possible the understanding of relations of species belonging to the same genus. The keys for identifying shrubs and woody vines in this volume consist of a key to plant families and separate keys to species in each genus comprising 3 or more species.

Scientific names assure the orderly arrangement of plants according to their generic relationships, and the names frequently use descriptive or diagnostic terms which aid in identification. Thus a plant called *hirsuta* is probably hairy, while one called *rosae* is pink-colored. Other names may be locality specific such as *alabamiensis*, denoting where the plant is found or where it was first found. Still other plants are named to commemorate an individual, *michauxii* for example, named for the botanist Andre Michaux who traveled in the southeastern area in the late 18th century.

The scientific name is followed by the name, sometimes abbreviated, of the individual or individuals who first described the plant. If the generic name later was changed, the original author's name is placed in parentheses and the name of the person making the change is added. These authors names are useful in locating the proper species in a manual. Occasionally through error or lack of information, a plant may receive two scientific names; if this occurs, the *International Code of Botanical Nomenclature* mandates that the older name normally is the legitimate one.

There is no list of preferred common names. In this volume the common names given are those in common usage and likely to be recognized within the known range of the plant. Thus *Rhododendron maximum* L., which is known as the rose bay, great laurel, or white laurel, depending upon its location, is called rose bay in this volume.

PLANT CHARACTERISTICS

The text description provides recognition characters in some detail for the most common shrubs and woody vines, and short remarks of key distinguishing characters of the less common, less widely distributed, related species. Illustra-

48

Aristolochia macrophylla

Buckleya distichophylla

Castanea pumila

Aristolochia tomentosa

PLATE 9

Pyrularia pubera

Pyrularia pubera

Xanthorhiza simplicissima

Cocculus carolinus

PLATE 10

Illicium parviflorum

Illicium floridanum

Magnolia virginiana

Asimina parviflora

PLATE 11

Asimina triloba MILLER

Asimina triloba MILLER

Schisandra coccinea

Calycanthus floridus

PLATE 12

Persea borbonia

Sassafras albidum

Itea virginica

Lindera benzoin

PLATE 13

Decumaria barbara

Philadelphus hirsutus

Philadelphus inodorus

Hydrangea arborescens

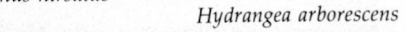

PLATE 14

Hydrangea quercifolia

Ribes cynosbati

Ribes rotundifolia

Hamamelis virginiana

PLATE 15

Rubus odoratus

Rubus argutus

Fothergilla major

Rubus flagellaris

PLATE 16

tions are provided for many of the common species, so a correct identification usually results from comparing the descriptive text with the photograph. A glossary is provided which defines technical terms used in the descriptions, and the line drawings of vegetation and fruit illustrate many of these terms. Most also are defined in a good dictionary, and after a bit of practice and use, the terms will become readily familiar and easily understood.

MEASUREMENTS

The metric system is used in this book because it permits the ready comparison of sizes from the smallest to the largest encountered among our shrubs and woody vines. The centimeter (cm) scale and the table may be used for reference.

1mm=.04in.	10mm=1cm
1cm=.4in.	10cm=1dm
1dm=4.0in.	100cm=1m
1m=39.4in.	

Millimeters, centimeters, decimeters, and meters are the only measurement units used in this book. For most characters, a range of sizes is given; drupes from a particular plant, for example, may be described to vary from 5–9 mm in diameter.

FLOWER TO FRUITING PERIOD

The period from the beginning of flowering to the maturation of fruit is given for each shrub and vine over the entire distribution in the Southeast and denoted by months. "Apr.–Oct." means that flowers are formed beginning in April, and fruits are mature by October.

DISTRIBUTION

The occurrence of a species may be considered in relation to its habitat and its geographical distribution, sometimes referred to as its range. Knowing what type of habitat a plant usually is found in is an aid in identification or an aid to locating plants of certain species. Geographical distributions are similarly useful, so the kinds of habitats and ranges are given for most of the species in this volume. In spite of much collecting and volumes of records of the known localities in which specific plants may be found, new range extensions frequently occur as additional habitats are botanized more intensively. Conversely, habitat destruction from changing land uses may decrease the range of many species. Disjunct distributions represent colonies of a species widely seperated from its main range. In the Southeast disjunct colonies occur of shrubs whose major range is to the west and others whose range is to the north.

Both the state and the physiographic province in which the plant is found are given. The latter are the Coastal Plain, Piedmont, and Mountains, which includes the Appalachian, Blue Ridge, Ridge and Valley, and Cumberland Plateau physiographic provinces.

SPECIAL VALUES AND ITEMS

Shrubs and woody vines are important in their relations to other forms of life, both domestic and wild. Some may be successional intermediates, a stage in the maturation of land toward a climax forest; others are essential understory components of that forest. Man has put some to use as living fences, others to seal soil-erosional areas. Many are used to beautify the landscape or as progenitors of selected or hybrid varieties for food and fiber. Some are planted especially for wildlife to use and many have medicinal values and qualities, including some that have figured prominently in American history. Others are poisonous to man or domestic stock.

ABUNDANCE

A general subjective evaluation of the abundance of woody shrubs and vines can be made on the basis of field experience, comments of other ecologists or members of organized botanical societies, and numbers of specimens found in university herbaria. In this volume species may be recorded as uncommon or rare. Often those considered to be rare will be listed as of special significance, threatened, or endangered on lists prepared by state university or natural resources agencies. A summary of these designations by states is included in an Appendix, and statements are included in the text for plants of limited abundance. The status of these plants may change as more information becomes available.

Plant Descriptions

TAXACEAE

FLORIDA YEW   *Taxus floridana* Nutt.
A bushy shrub to small tree to 6 m tall with leathery leaves, only slightly aromatic when bruised. Leaf blades narrowly linear, 1–2.5 cm long, the tips pointed, but not piercing to the touch. Aril light red. Coast Pl. River bluffs and ravines. Gadsden and Liberty Counties, Fla. (Plate 5).

The AMERICAN YEW, *Taxus canadensis* Marshall, is similar, with leaves yellow-green beneath. Nfld. to Man. s to Va., Ky., Ill.

American yew is effective when used to form a beautiful, low, evergreen clump in shaded situations where the soil is rich with humus and is moist and cool. It is easy to grow when provided with a congenial location.

The evergreen FLORIDA YEW may be confused with *Torreya taxifolia* Arn., the STINKING CEDAR, endemic to the same area. The latter has a pungent odor and sharp, stiff-pointed, piercing leaf tips. It is a handsome large shrub or tree. Endangered in its native habitat, probably by changing land-use patterns, its survival likely will depend upon cultivation in gardens.

CUPRESSACEAE

JUNIPER   *Juniperus communis* L. var. *depressa* Pursh. Evergreen, decumbent shrub-forming mats a meter or so in diameter. Leaves stout, 5–18 mm long, flat, subulate, sharply pointed with a white stripe above. Ripe female cones black or blue, fruits 6–10 mm in diameter. Mts. and Pied. Sandy and rocky soils. Can. to Minn. s to Ga. Uncommon.

The grayish blue plumes are pleasing in appearance; the shrub is effective when used as a cover for barren spots on slopes and ridges where few other plants will grow.

POACEAE or GRAMINAE

GIANT CANE   *Arundinaria gigantea* (Walt.) Muhl.
Woody perennial from hard, tough rhizomes, forming open to dense brakes; stems 1–8 m tall, 0.2–2 cm thick, at first unbranched, later branching and forming fanlike clusters. Leaves of two types: leaves of basal shoots and primary branches are short, narrow, and without petioles; upper leaves have petiolate blades 10–30 cm long, with ciliate sheaths. Spikelets solitary, racemose, or paniculate, 8–12 flowered on long, slender stalks, flowering at infrequent intervals, the flowering stems dying after the seeds mature. April–July. Coast. Pl., Pied., Mts. Bogs, savannas, riverbanks and dry woods. Leaves furnish cattle browse, the canes fishing poles, and mats and baskets are made from the foliage. Once abundant, this CANE declined rapidly with European settlement.

The SWITCH CANE, previously named *Arundinaria tecta* (Walt.) Muhl. is now considered to be a subspecies of *A. gigantea;* the two taxa can be distinguished only by technical characteristics.

Several species of the BAMBOO Genus *Phyllostachys* may be encountered as possible escapes or residuals from cultivation in the warmer parts of the Southeast, e.g., *P. bambusoides* Sieb. and Zucc. and *P. aurea* Riv. were formerly planted for fishing poles or as ornamentals.

ARECACEAE or PALMAE

DWARF PALMETTO
Sabal minor (Jacq.) Persoon.

Small shrub, its caudex-stem not visible above ground. Leaf blades without midrib. Drupes globose, 6–8 mm in diameter. The common fan-shaped palm with filaments. May–Oct. Coast. Pl. Low woods. N.C. to Fla., Tex. and Ark. The SAW PALMETTO, *Serenoa repens* (Bartr.) Small, has petioles armed with recurved spines. Stems above ground, much branched horizontally. Drupe ellipsoid or sub-globose, 15–20 mm in diameter. Coast. Pl. Barrier Islands, pinelands, hammocks. S.C. to La. The flowers are a source of honey, and the fruits were used by aborigines for food. It is an excellent choice for naturalistic landscaping of homes located on coastal barrier islands (Plate 5).

NEEDLE PALM
Rhapidophyllum hystrix (Pursh.) Wendl.

Armed shrub with erect or spreading stems. Leaf sheaths fibrous with long needlelike stiff and sharp spines, 1–4 dm long. Drupe red, ovoid or globular. Coast. Pl. Swamps, hammocks, dry rocks. Central Ga. s to Fla., Ala., Miss.

This is a handsome ornamental plant giving a tropical or exotic effect in the landscape. Native palms should be used in landscape habitats similar to where they are found in nature. Palms would be considered out-of-place if utilized in the Piedmont but effective in parts of the Coastal Plain.

SMILACACEAE

BAMBOO-VINE
Smilax laurifolia L.

Stout, tough, climbing vines, with thick, oblong to oblong-lanceolate ever-green leaves. Stems vigorous with stout prickles. The leathery leaves tend to stand erect: they are dark green above with a prominant midvein beneath. The green, scented flowers are in umbels from the leaf axils: berry black to dark blue, bearing a single seed and requiring nearly 2 years to mature. Coastal Pl. and lower Pied. Bays, pocosins, stream banks in dense thickets. W. Va. s to Tex. (Plate 5).

The evergreen DWARF SMILAX, *Smilax pumila* Walt., is a trailing plant with densely pubescent stems, red berries, and leaves that are hairy beneath. It is less common along the coast from S.C. to La. (Plate 6).

The SAWBRIER, *Smilax glauca* Walt., a much shorter and less climbing vine is common throughout the Southeast and has leaves that are partially deciduous, ovate, and whitish on the underside. The bluish black berry is persistent. Flowers yellowish brown. May–Oct. Wet to dry habitats. N.J. s to Fla. and Tex. (Plate 6).

BULLBRIER
Smilax bona-nox L.

Climbing vine, with somewhat 4-angled stems and branches and leaf blades varying from deltoid to fiddleform, with a thick marginal band often spiny and bristle tipped. Berries black, small, usually with a bloom, having a single seed. May–Nov. Coast. Pl. and Pied. Less common in the Mts. Md. to Ill. s to Fla. and Mex. The Bullbrier is reputed to have medicinal properties.

The Bullbrier is armed with hard and ridged prickles while the CHINA-ROOT, *Smilax hispida* Muhl. has round prickles, pliant and bristlelike; the plant is high-climbing and bears bronze to green flowers, black fruit with a single red-brown seed. Conn. s to Fla. and Tex.

GREENBRIER   *Smilax rotundifolia* L.
Tough, woody vine with stems terete to quadrangular, bearing stout, flattened prickles. This thickety, high-climbing plant is deciduous to partly evergreen, with thin, submembranceous, broadly ovate, glabrous leaf blades. Spines
confined to the stem, up to 8 mm long, usually with a reddish or brownish point.
Flowers in umbels of 6–25, bronze to greenish. Berries blue to black with bloom,
almost always 2-seeded. Coast. Pl., Mts., Pied. N.S. to Ont. s to Fla. and Tex. The
berries are an important food of the Ruffed Grouse throughout its range and are
also eaten by black bears (Plate 5).
Smilax auriculata Walt. the WILD-BAMBOO, occurs only in the Coastal Plain,
and bears evergreen arrowhead-shaped leaves rounded to a short acuminate
apex. Flowers green, in umbels, those in the first 3–8 leaf axils usually few
flowered. June–Oct. Berry black. Sand dunes, and river bars. N.C. to La. and Ark.

CORAL GREENBRIER   *Smilax walteri* Pursh.
The Coral Greenbrier has bright red fruits, and, except for a few prickles close
to the base, is unarmed. It is slender, with leaves that are smooth, thin, leathery, and
bright green above and below and ovate to ovate-oblong in shape. Leaves are
almost always deciduous, but the berries are persistent. The stems are yellow to
brown. Chiefly Coast. Pl., rare in the Pied. Swamps and marshes and along other
wetlands. Del. to Fla., La., Ark. (Plate 6).
Another mostly unarmed Smilax is the SWEET-SCENTED SMILAX, *Smilax
smallii* Morong., a high-climbing vine with evergreen, thin leaves. Umbels occur in
all the leaf axils to the end of the branch. Leaves of this brier are said to retain their
shape and color long after cutting, so large quantities have been shipped to the
florist trade. Coast. Pl., rare in the Pied. Various habitats, more often in sandy
woodlands. Del. to Fla., Tex. and Ark. This is an excellent vine for a trellis or for
accenting railings, stairs, and entranceways.
A difficult genus; see Godfrey and Wooten, 1979.

AGAVACEAE

SPANISH DAGGER   *Yucca aloifolia* L.
Woody shrub with a thick stocky trunk to 3 m tall, with thick, evergreen leaves
to 6 dm long, with spinulose margins, without frayed filamentous fibers. Fruit pendant, berry 7–9 cm long. June–Dec. Coast. Pl. Sand dunes, marshes. N.C. s to Fla.
and Tex. (Plate 6).
Yucca gloriosa L., SPANISH BAYONET, is similar, but has entire or scaberulous
leaf margins. Oct.–Dec. Sand dunes, brackish marsh edges. Coast. Pl. N.C. to Fla.
and Miss.

BEAR-GRASS   *Yucca filamentosa* L.
Shrub with a short trunk, or trunk absent, leaf margins fraying into filamentous threads; leaves from a rosette, firm, to 6 dm long, with a long, slender, terminal spine. Flower spike to 5 m tall, fruit erect. Apr.–Oct. Coast. Pl., Pied., Mts.
Dry, open habitats. Va. s to Fla. and Miss. Pollinated only by the Pronuba Moth,
Tegeticula alba, which deposits its eggs in the flower's ovary where the larvae hatch
and feed on the yucca seeds (Plate 7).
SPANISH DAGGER and BAYONET can withstand salt spray and are excel-

lent evergreeen choices for naturalistic landscaping of coastal properties. All three species of *Yucca* give an impression of Spanish or desert influence and accent southwestern architecture. Used improperly, they quicky can become an eyesore. *Y. filamentosa* tends to be less formal in appearance than the other two species. Variegated cultivars of *Yucca* are available in the nursery trade, including 'Golden Sword' with a green margin and yellow center, and 'Bright Edge' with the reversed color pattern.

SALICACEAE

DWARF PUSSY WILLOW
Salix humilis Marsh.

Shrub with entire leaves, erect branches, yellowish to brownish twigs; leaves dark green above, whitish beneath, the plant forming thickets. The fruiting catkins 1.5–3 cm in length. Apr. Mts., Pied., Coast. Pl. On rocky slopes and balds and in moist thickets. Nfld. to N.D., s to N.C., Fla., and Tex. (Plate 7).

The PUSSY WILLOW, *Salix discolor* Muhl. has leaves that are glaucous beneath, and twigs and bud scales that are glabrous. Apr. Swamps and meadows. N.S. and Man. s to N.C. and Mo.

The CAROLINA WILLOW, *Salix caroliniana* Michx. Has reddish twigs; long, narrow, pointed leaves whitened beneath. Md. to Ohio, Fla., Tex.

The SILKY WILLOW, *Salix sericea* Marsh., has leaves that are silvery silky beneath, lanceolate or elliptic and glabrous above. The twigs are purplish brown. N.S. to Mich. s to Ga., Mo. This species is largely insect pollinated, as are most willows, and freely hybridizing. The SILKY WILLOW and the previous species are important foods of the cottontail rabbit.

The GRAY WILLOW, *Salix cinerea* L. bears large, showy catkins in April. The branches are not pendulous but the branchlets are black and tomentose. Escape from cultivation. N.S. s to N.C., Ky.

Other shrubby willows include *Salix lucida* Muhlenberg, *S. exigua* Nutt., *S. bebbiana* Sargent, *S. purpurea* L., and *S. eriocephala* Michaux. Because of their tendency to hybridize, and willow migration during the Full Glacial period, they are a complex group, difficult to identify. See Argus, 1986. All of our willows are deciduous.

MYRICACEAE

SWEET FERN
Myrica asplenifolia L.

A colonial pubescent shrub to 1.5 m tall with brownish gray twigs. Leaves pinnate-divided, linear-elliptic to lanceolate, dark green above, pale beneath, resinous, deciduous with a pleasant fragrance. Flowers in staminate and pistillate catkins. Fruit a nutlet, lustrous, brown, not waxy. Mts. and Pied. Occurs in dense colonies on poor soils in dry woods and on balds. N.S. to Minn. s to Ky., Ga. Once known as *Comptonia peregrina*.

The WAX MYRTLE, *Myrica cerifera* L. is a common aromatic shrub with elliptic to oblanceolate toothed, scurfy leaves borne on young, waxy branchlets. The evergreen leaves are coated with waxy granules above and beneath.The fruit is a waxy berry; the root bark has medicinal properties. Coast. Pl. and Pied. N.J. to Fla. Tex., Ark. (Plate 7).

The BAYBERRIES, *Myrica pensylvanica* Loisel. and *Myrica heterophylla* Raf., have larger evergreen leaves, orange waxy glands on the lower leaf surfaces. N.S. s to Fla. and Tex. Candles were made from the wax (Plate 7).

Myrica inodora Bartr., is odorless with entire, smooth, evergreen leaf blades. Coast. Pl. Savannas, Fla. to La. (Plate 8).

The SWEET GALE, *Myrica gale* L., is deciduous and very rare. Mts. Tenn., N.C.

Myrica cerifera is an excellent plant for informal screening in full sunlight or light shade. When used in the Middle to Upper South, seed should be gathered from more northern populations. Wax Myrtle seems to benefit from being cut back to the ground every 8–10 years. *Myrica pensylvanica* and *Myrica heterophylla* have large berries which are deeper green in color. *Myrica inodora* can be an excellent ornamental choice. Myricas will tolerate infertile soils but respond to good growing conditions. Ice and snow load frequently will bend or split plants of *M. cerifera*. *Myrica gale* responds readily to cultivation.

LEITNERIACEAE

CORKWOOD   *Leitneria floridana* Chapm.
Wandlike to treelike deciduous shrub with reddish brown bark and soft wood which is lighter than cork. Swamps, sawgrass, or palmetto marshes. Ga. to Tex., Uncommon.

BETULACEAE

TAG ALDER   *Alnus serrulata* (Ait.) Willd.
A tall deciduous shrub to 5 m in height with smooth bark, leaves green and slightly downy beneath, especially along the veins, sharply serrulate margins. Flowers developed in the fall or in the early spring, nutlets wingless; woody pistillate catkins 0.5–1.9 cm long, persistent year around. Bark astringent. Food of deer and mourning doves; used by beavers for food and lodge construction. Coast. Pl., Mts., Pied. Wet soils along streams and ponds. N.S. to Ill. s to Fla. and Tex.

The rare GREEN or MOUNTAIN ALDER, *Alnus crispa* (Ait.) Pursh, has winged nutlets and flowers appearing with the leaves. Mts. Lab. and Man. s to N.C. and Tenn. See also Clarkson, 1960. Alders have nitrogen-fixing nodules on their roots.

HAZEL-NUT   *Corylus americana* Walt.
A colonial shrub 1–3.5 m. tall, pubescent with glandular-pubescent twigs and petioles. Pistillate flowers in a short head, 2 to each bract; staminate flowers in pendulous aments; nuts acornlike. Leaves thickish, oval or suborbicular to 15 cm long. Fruits enclosed in thin, flattened, hairy, ragged-edged husks. Feb.–Sept. Mts., Pied., rare in Coast. Pl. Woods and thickets. Me. to Sask. s to Ga. and Okla. (Plate 8).

The BEAKED HAZEL-NUT, *Corylus cornuta* Marsh., is similar but has fruit enclosed in bristly husks which are prolonged to form a beak; glandular pubescence lacking. Mts. and Pied. Prefers acid soils. N.S. to Sask. s to Ga. and Kans.

Nuts and browse are used by many kinds of wildlife. The Hazel Nuts lend themselves to naturalizing along roadsides or at the edge of woodland landscape settings.

FAGACEAE

ALLEGHENY CHINQUAPIN   *Castanea pumila* (L.) Mill.
A large deciduous shrub or small tree with slender, spreading branches and

light brown bark sometimes tinged with red. Leaves are oblong and acute, serrate with sharp bristles at the tips, whitish-downy beneath, bright yellow-green above, alternate. Flowers: the staminate in catkins 10–15 cm long; the pistillate scattered and small, often in spikes. Fruit a prickly bur with dense spines bearing a single plump nut used by many species of wildlife. The sweet nuts are sometimes infested with the nut-weevil, *Balaninus proboscideus*. July–Oct. Mts., Pied., Coast. Pl. N.J. s to Fla., Tex. and Ark. (Plate 9).

The RUNNING CHINQUAPIN, *Castanea alnifolia* Nutt., is similar, but its leaf blades are essentially glabrous and greenish beneath. Coast. Pl. N.C. to Fla. and La. This is a low colonial shrub while var. *ozarkensis* (Ashe) Tucker is a large shrub or small tree. Ark., Mo. Chinquapins are only moderately susceptible to the Chestnut Blight, *Endothica parasitica*, and will occasionally hybridize with the American Chestnut tree, *Castanea dentata*. The rare hybrid has been named *Castanea × neglecta* Dode.

RUNNING OAK, *Quercus pumila* Walt. is a clonal, stoloniferous shrub, suckering from roots, with bristle-tipped unlobed evergreen leaves whitish beneath. Mar.–Sept. Coast. Pl. Sandy soils, pinelands. N.C. s to Fla. and La. (Plate 8).

ULMACEAE

HACKBERRY   *Celtis tenuifolia* Nutt.
Shrubs with leaves with oblique bases, three main veins and with greenish axillary flowers, appearing with the leaves. The flowers are usually single, and the fruit is an orange to brown drupe 5–8 mm long. The leaves are deciduous. Pied., Coast. Pl. Dry habitats. Md. to Mo. s to Tex. and Ark. Used by 25 species of birds. Subject to a witches'-broom caused by the mite *Eriophyes* (Plate 8).

PLANER-TREE   *Planera aquatica* Walt. ex. J. F. Gmel.
A small tree, often with flaky bark. Leaves glabrous beneath, deltoid-ovate, serrate, deciduous. Fruit a burlike nutlet. Coast. Pl. Alluvial flood plains. N.C. to Ky. s to Fla., Tex. and Okla.

MORACEAE

PAPER MULBERRY   *Broussonetia papyrifera* (L.) Vent.
Stoloniferous shrub to small tree up to 10 m tall with a spreading crown. Young bark mottled greenish gray, older bark smooth, tan. Leaves textured, mostly alternate, or opposite or whorled, irregularly lobed, sandpapery above, velvety beneath, deciduous. Hirsute twigs with large white pith. Male flowers in catkins, female in globose heads. Fruit, red drupes in multiples, scarcely edible. Apr.–Sept. Coast. Pl., Pied., Mts. N.Y. to Mo. s to Fla., Tex. Intro. from Asia, escape from cult. Fruit used by song and game birds and woodland rodents.

TEXAN MULBERRY   *Morus microphylla* Buckl.
A large deciduous shrub to small tree, thicket forming, usually dioecious, the fruit a compound drupe. Mar.–June. Coast. Pl. Dry, well-drained sites. E. Tex.

OSAGE ORANGE   *Maclura pomifera* (Raf.) Schneid.
At first appearing as a spiny shrub growning in dense, impenetrable thickets, matures to a small tree to 20 m tall. Twigs with axillary thorns, sap milky. Leaves simple, alternate, deciduous. Fruit large, wrinkled, globular, orangelike in shape,

yellow-green in color, 7–12 cm in diameter. Apr.–Oct. Coast. Pl., Pied., Mts. Spread from cult. to roadsides and fencerows, clearings. New Engl. to Ia. s to Fla., Ark. and Tex.

FIG   *Ficus carica* L.
A shrub, residual from cultivation, 4 m tall with palmately 3–5 lobed leaves rough above, coarsely pubescent beneath and deciduous. The connate stipules enclose the terminal buds and the minute flowers are enclosed in a pear-shaped receptacle. The fleshy receptacle is the fig of commerce. Apr.–Oct. Intro. from Asia and now remaining after cultivation in waste places and cleared lands, expecially to the south. Va. s to Fla. and Tex.

LORANTHACEAE

AMERICAN MISTLETOE   *Phoradendron flavescens* (Pursh.) Nutt.
Yellow-green, fleshy, woody half-parasite growing on trunks and limbs of hardwood trees. The fruits are one-seeded, white, pulpy, very sticky drupes spread largely by birds on feet, bills, and plumage. Once used as a sticky trap for small birds, mistletoe was of religious significance to the Druids of England: now used during the celebration of Christmas. Nov.–Dec. Coast. Pl., Pied., less common in the Mts. N.J. to Ill. s to Fla. and Tex. cf. Allard, 1943.

ARISTOLOCHIACEAE

DUTCHMANS PIPE   *Aristolochia macrophylla* Lam.
A deciduous woody vine climbing to 10 m with cordate, alternate, abruptly pointed leaves appearing opposite on spur shoots associated with flowers. Calyx tube strongly bent, limb dark purple; capsule ribbed, 5–8 cm long; peduncles with a leafy bract. May–Sept. Rich woods, usually on calcareous soils. Pa. and W. Va. s to Ga. and Ala. (Plate 9).
Formerly known as *A. durior,* The WOOLLY PIPE VINE, *Aristolochia tomentosa* Sims, has tomentose leaves, rounded at the apex, bractless peduncles, white-pubescent branches, a yellowish to greenish calyx, and a capsule 4–6 cm long. May–Sept. Rich woods, calcareous soils. Ind. and Ill. s to Fla. Tex. (Plate 9).
Both species of *Aristolochia* have value in the landscape as woody vines on trellises. Their unique flowers are great conversation pieces. *A. macrophylla* is relatively fast growing and is useful for providing sun screens for porches. It should be used in the Upper South.

SANTALACEAE

NESTRONIA   *Nestronia umbellula* Raf.
Colonial shrub 0.5–1.5 m tall, parasitic on the roots of trees. Greenish axillary flowers. Leaves opposite, broad bladed, 3–6 cm long, acute or acuminate. Anthers connected to sepals by a tuft of hairs. Fruit a globose drupe, about 1.3 cm long, rarely seen. Apr.–July. Mts. and Pied. Woodlands. Va. s to Ga. and Ala. Uncommon, endangered species.

BUCKLEYA   *Buckleya distichophylla* (Nutt.) Torr.
A deciduous shrub to 3 m tall growing parasitically on roots of *Tsuga* and *Pinus.* Twigs slightly hairy, branchlets pale brown. Leaves opposite, lanceolate, subsessile, 3–7 cm long. Leaf scars with one bundle scar. Flowers greenish; stami-

nate in 3–7 flowered umbels; pistillate solitary, terminal. Fruit an ellipsoidal drupe 1.8 cm long. Mts. Va., N.C., Tenn.

Rare, listed as threatened. The peduncle of the staminate umbel is very short stocked; in *Nestronia* the peduncle is elongate (Plate 9).

BUFFALO-NUT   *Pyrularia pubera* Michx.

Shrub 2–3 m high, parasitic on roots of hardwood trees and shrubs. Leaves alternate, elliptic, widest above the middle, to 15 cm long, apple green, thin, pubescent beneath. Leaf fall late, fallen ones remaining green for some time. Inflorescence a spike, flowers greenish, unisexual; calyx 5-lobed; petals absent; style short and thick. Fruit a fleshy drupe, pear shaped, 2–2.5 cm long, with a very acrid poisonous oil. Apr.–Oct. Mts. and Pied. In hardwoods and along stream banks. Pa. s to Ga. and Ala. (Plate 10).

POLYGONACEAE

LADIES EARDROPS   *Brunnichia cirrhosa* Gaertn.

A deciduous woody vine with a grooved stem, climbing by axillary and terminal tendrils. Leaves simple, alternate, ovate: base truncate to slightly cordate. Greenish flowers 2–5 in a fascicle, in axillary and terminal paniculate racemes. Fruiting calyx to 2–3 cm long, winged, pink and showy, persistent. Fruit an achene, enclosed in an hypanthium, obscurely 3-angled. Coast. Pl. Riverbanks, swamps. Ky., S.C. and Mo. s to Fla. and Tex. Rare. The persistent pendant fruiting structures make this plant an interesting possibility for use as an ornamental vine on an arbor or trellis.

Two JOINTWEEDS, *Polygonella americana* (F. and M.) Small, and *P. polygama* (Vent.) Englem. and Gray, are suffrutescent perennials with branches appearing internodal and alternate leaves arising from ocreae. Coast. Pl. and Pied. Sandy soil. Va. s to Fla., Miss., and Mo.

RANUNCULACEAE

YELLOW-ROOT   *Xanthorhiza simplicissima* Marsh.

Small, colonial, low-growing, erect shrub to 7.5 dm tall, with alternate, pinnate, deciduous leaves. Leaflets mostly 5; blades ovate to ovate-lanceolate, incised, toothed. Flowers brown-purple, 4 mm wide, in compound racemes 5–15 cm long, appearing with the leaves. Sepals 5, petals absent. Fruit a one-seeded follicle. Bark and roots bitter, bright yellow, yielding a yellow dye. Apr.–June. Mts., Pied., Coast. Pl. Moist soils along shaded stream banks, on wet rocky ledges. N.Y. s to Ga. and Miss. (Plate 10).

This low-growing plant is an excellent choice for naturalizing in the boggy soil of springheads or along moist stream banks. Seldom seen in the landscape, it has been overlooked by gardeners.

BERBERIDACEAE

AMERICAN BARBERRY   *Berberis canadensis* Mill.

A smooth deciduous shrub 2–20 dm tall with alternate leaves often subtended by 3-spined thorns. Leaves sharply and widely toothed; leaflets 3–6 cm long, the blades spatulate, spiny serrate. Twigs brown and rough-warty; inner bark and wood yellow; Flowers yellow in few-flowered racemes; petals 2.5–3.5 mm long. Fruit a juicy red berry 5–7 mm long. Apr.–Oct. Mts. and Pied. W.Va. s to Ga. and Mo. Birds use berries sparingly if other more preferred foods are unavailable.

The related JAPANESE BARBERRY, *Berberis thunbergii* D.C., is smaller with single thorns and entire leaves; flowers solitary or in small umbels: berries red, dry, and persistent. Apr.–May. Introduced, escaped to wooded slopes, hedgerows and thickets. N.S. to Mich. s to Ga. and Mo.

Berberis vulgaris L., the COMMON BARBERRY, has ash-colored arched branchlets, leaves bristly-serrate, racemes many flowered, and scarlet ellipsoidal berries. Introduced. N.S. to Mo. and s. Susceptible to wheat stem rust, *Puccinia graminis.*

Other escapes are the NANDINA, *Nandina domestica* Thunb., an evergreen shrub with pinnately decompound deltoid leaves and red berries 6–9 mm in diameter, and *Mahonia bealei* (Fortune) Carr., with yellow wood, spinulose evergreen leaves, axillary racemes of bright yellow flowers. Berries dark blue, glaucous, favored by birds.

LARDIZABALACEAE

AKEBIA   *Akebia quinata* (Houtt.) Dcne.
An Asiatic deciduous to semi-evergreen woody vine with 5-foliate leaves and flowers with 3 purple sepals. Flowers fragrant. Follicle fleshy, purple or violet. Rare escape. Md., N.C., Ga.

MENISPERMACEAE

CORALBEADS   *Cocculus carolinus* (L.) D.C.
Prostrate or twining vine with minutely pubescent stems, hastate leaves that are glabrous above, pubescent beneath but not peltate. The yellow-green flowers are in panicles, and have 6 petals and 6 sepals. Fruit is a globose red drupe, the size of a small pea, 1-seeded, the seed crescent shaped. June–Aug. Coast. Pl. and Pied. In woods and thickets, frequently on sandy soils. Va. to Ill. s to Fla., Kans. and Tex. (Plate 10).

MOONSEED   *Menispermum canadense* L.
A stout, twining, woody vine with 3–7 lobed leaves 10–15 cm wide and long, pale beneath; base peltate and cordate. Panicles axillary, to 15 cm long, loose; flowers white, 4 mm wide; stamens 12–24, petals 4–8. Fruit a blue to bluish black, usually glaucous drupe, 6–15 mm in diameter and wrinkled. The grooved stone is moon shaped and flat. June–Sept. Coast. Pl. and Pied. Rich woods and thickets. Que. and Man. s to Ga., Ala. and Okla. The root is used as a diuretic and stomachic for arthritis and blood disorders.

CUPSEED   *Calycocarpum lyonii* (Pursh) Gray.
A twining woody vine with simple, alternate, palmately veined leaves with 3–7 lobes and a cordate base. The apetalous flowers numerous, green, with 6 sepals, 12 stamens. Fruit a globular drupe 2.5 cm long, black, with a marginally ridged slightly cup-shaped stone. Rich woods, river bottoms and banks. Coast. Pl. Ind. and Kans. s to Fla. and La. Named for John Lyon, English botanist who explored North America in the early 19th century.

ILLICIACEAE

ANISE-STINKBUSH   *Illicium floridanum* Ell.

A strongly scented aromatic shrub 2–3 m tall. Leaves evergreen, elliptic, acuminate, entire; blades 6–15 cm long. Flowers nodding, petals 20–30, linear or nearly so, dark red; sepals more than 10 mm long. Fruit 2.5–3.0 cm wide. Coast. Pl. Swamps and low hammocks. Ga. s to Fla. and La. (Plate 11).

A related species, *Illicium parviflorum* Michx., has ovate or suborbicular yellow petals; sepals less than 10 mm long; fruit about 2 cm wide. Coast. Pl. Sandy swamp edges. Fla. Uncommon (Plate 11).

Both species are ideal as ornamentals and are cold tolerant. Our two native species of *Illicium* are rapidly gaining favor as ornamental shrubs as more and more nurserymen and landscapers learn of the desirable characteristics of these two broadleaf evergreens. They blend nicely into the gardens: a white flowered form of *I. floridanum* is available.

MAGNOLIACEAE

SWEETBAY   *Magnolia virginiana* L.

Shrub or tree to 25 m tall. Leaves evergreen in the South, deciduous north, the blades 6–15 cm long, elliptic, oval or oblong, glabrous above, silvery beneath. Flowers fragrant, creamy white, petals 9–12, usually less than 5 cm long. Fruit a glabrous cone, 2.5–5 cm long. Coast. Pl. and Pied. Low wet woods, titi bogs and swamps, pocosins, savannas, Mass. s to Fla. and Tex. (Plate 11).

Numerous selections have been made for cultivars. The attractive flowers and fine texture of the foliage and stems make SWEETBAY an ideal choice for many landscape situations. Under cultivation, SWEETBAY usually grows in a bushy, treelike form. The silvery lower leaf surfaces are especially attractive, and some clones retain most of their leaves in winter. This species often is available in garden centers.

Magnolia ashei Weatherby is a large, coarse deciduous shrub with a distribution centered in Walton County, Fla. Similar in appearance to *M. macrophylla*, it is distinguished by its shrublike habit and its rather narrow infrutescence. Having a distinctive shrubby habit, *M. ashei* often will flower when relatively young. This characteristic in combination with its rather large leaves make this shrub an ideal choice for a bold contrast plant in a landscape setting. It also is a marvelous conversation plant.

ANNONACEAE

DWARF PAWPAW   *Asimina parviflora* (Michx.) Dunal.

A shrub to 2 m tall with rusty-pubescent twigs. Leaves membranous, glabrous above, rusty-pubescent beneath 11–17 cm long, 4–8 cm wide. Flowers purple or purplish green, inconspicuous in axils of previous year's leaves. Corolla less than 2 cm wide, recurved at the tip. Fruit 2–6 cm long, green July–Sept. Coast. Pl. and Pied. Well-drained soils. Va. s to Fla. and Miss. An important food for many woodland animals, but particularly for fox and oppossum (Plate 11).

The PAWPAW, *Asimina triloba* (L.) Dunal, is a shrub or small tree to 12 m tall with fruits 5–13 cm long, Leaves deciduous, 15–25 cm long and 6–12 cm wide. Corolla 3–4 cm wide. Rich woods and bottoms. N.Y. and Neb. s to Fla. and Tex. (Plate 12).

Other PAWPAWS, *Asimina longifolia* Kral, *Asimina incana* (Bartr.) Exell., and *Asimina pygmaea* (Bartr.) Dunal, are low shrubs with tardily deciduous, coriaceous leaves. Flowers of the latter have a fetid aroma and appear after the leaves, while those of the FLAG PAWPAW, *A. incana,* appear with or before leaf development. Coast. Pl. Sandy pinelands, savannas, old fields and roadsides. Ga., Fla.

SCHISANDRACEAE

STAR-VINE   *Schisandra coccinea* Michx.
Aromatic, twining, climbing, woody vine. Leaves thick, glossy, alternate, acuminate, deciduous, 8–15 cm long. Flowers axillary, solitary, drooping; perianth segments 9–12, thickened at base; stamens 5. Fruit red, 6–10 mm long, berrylike, in elongate clusters; seeds 1–2. June–Aug. Coast Pl. and Pied. Undisturbed stream bottoms, rich woods, ravines and bluffs. N.C. and Tenn. s to Ga., Fla. and La.

Threatened species. Once known as *S. glabra* (Brick.) Rehd., this interesting vine is excellent for use in woodsy settings as a groundcover or as a low climber on trunks of pine trees (Plate 12).

CALYCANTHACEAE

SWEET-SHRUB   *Calycanthus floridus* L.
Shrub to 3 m tall with opposite branches. Leaves entire, opposite, without stipules, lanceolate to ovate-lanceolate, to 18 cm long, deciduous. Flowers sweet scented, terminal, the perianth of numerous, similar parts; ovules borne on a fleshy floral cup. Fruit an ovoid leathery pendant structure containing numerous brown seeds. Apr.–Sept. Pied. and Coast. Pl. Hardwood and mixed pine woods, particularly around openings. Pa. and Ohio s to Fla. and Miss. Woodland rodents cut into the pendant leathery capsule for the seeds (Plate 12).

Long admired for its sweet-scented, purple-brown flowers, SWEET SHRUB is unexcelled as a garden border shrub. Yellow-flowered cultivars are available in the nursery trade. Some clones appear to be aggressive colonizers by means of underground rootstalks and must be constrained. Fragrance also is variable from population to population. The SWEET SHRUB is easily transplanted.

LAURACEAE

SWAMP RED BAY   *Persea borbonia* (L.) Spreng.
Aromatic shrub, 2–6 m tall. Leaves deciduous, glabrate to rusty-pubescent beneath, pinnately veined, elliptic to lanceolate, 6–15 cm long, 3–6 cm wide, often marked by gall-like structures. Fruit a dark blue drupe, sometimes with a bloom. Coast. Pl. Low pine woods, maritime forests, bayheads. Del. s to Fla. and Tex. The leaves are used as bay leaves in cooking, especially for flavoring gumbo. The dense, orange-colored heartwood takes a high polish. Hardy in the Georgia Piedmont; an attractive specimen grows near the main gate to the University of Georgia campus (Plate 13).

SASSAFRAS   *Sassafras albidum* (Nutt.) Nees.
Shrub to small tree with ridged bark. Young twigs smooth, yellow-green, and aromatic. Leaves entire, mitten-shaped or 3-lobed, alternate, deciduous, 8–15 cm long. Flowers greenish yellow, appearing before the leaves; plants dioecious. Fruit is a blue-black drupe. Mar.–July. Coast. Pl., Pied., Mts. In fencerows and woods

openings, waste places. Me. to Kans. s to Fla. and Tex. Oil pressed from the plant was once used medicinally and for flavoring. Thought to contain carcinogens. Sassafras tea is made from the roots. Chewing the bark is said to aid in breaking the tobacco habit. Tender leaves are used in Louisiana in making "file" for gumbo. The abundant shrublike regeneration seen in old fields is deceiving since SASSAFRAS may grow into trees 30" in diameter (Plate 13).

POND-SPICE   *Litsea aestivalis* (L.) Fern.
Shrub to 2–5 m tall, with zigzag branches. Leaves alternate, deciduous, entire, narrowly oblong, coriaceous, to 3 cm long and about 1 cm wide. Flowers in terminal or axillary clusters of 2–4, appearing before the leaves from overwintering buds; perianth segments 6, yellow. Fruit a red, subglobose drupe. N.C. s to Fla. and La., Tenn. Endangered species. One of the rarest shrubs in the Southeast, now probably extinct from its former range in Virginia and Tennessee.

SPICE-BUSH   *Lindera benzoin* (L.) Blume
A strong-scented shrub, 1–3 m tall; young stems usually glabrous. Leaves deciduous, ovate to obovate, tapering at the base; blades 5–12 cm long, thin, usually acuminate and acute at the apex and slightly ciliate; petioles are fine and delicately slender. Honey-yellow flowers appear before the leaves, in dense clusters 6–8 mm broad; pedicels 3–5 cm long. fruit a drupe 8–9 mm long, bright, deep red, oblong and fragrant when crushed. Mar.–Sept. Mts. and Pied. Wet woods, stream banks and around springs and seeps, an indicator plant of carbonate outcrops. Ont. to Kans. s to Fla. and La. The bark is used to treat dysentery, coughs, and colds. The leaves are glabrous above and glabrous or pubescent beneath and spicy-fragrant when crushed (Plate 13).

A pleasant shrub for naturalizing in moist woods in light shade. The yellow fall leaf color and the bright scarlet, glossy fruit provide interest, and the pale yellow blossoms give a pleasing touch in the spring. It is easy to cultivate, taking kindly to any situation where the soil is moist and fertile. It grows best on neutral or alkaline soils, so the addition of dolomitic lime to acid soils may be beneficial.

JOVE'S FRUIT, *Lindera melissaefolium* (Walt.) Blume, is similar but has broadly lanceolate to narrowly ovate leaves, rounded at the base, the blades quite firm and minutely pilose to densely pubescent on both sides. The young stems are also pubescent and the crushed leaves yield a sassafraslike odor, Mar.–Sept. Coast. Pl. Swamps and pond margins. N.C. and Mo. s to Fla. and La. Extremely rare.

Another SPICE-BUSH, *Lindera subcoriacea* Wofford, has thick obovate leaves. Recently described, S. Miss., La., N.C. Rare, endangered.

SAXIFRAGACEAE

VIRGINIA WILLOW   *Itea virginica* L.
Shrub 1–3 m high with white bell-shaped flowers in dense, terminal, drooping racemes 5–15 cm long. Leaves deciduous, alternate, elliptic to obovate, 4–9 cm long, serrate or serrulate, acute or acuminate. Petals and sepals 5; pedicels 2–3.5 mm long; petals linear to linear-lanceolate, 4–6 mm long. Capsule cylindric, styles separating at maturity, pubescent, 3–7 mm long; seeds dark brown, smooth, 1.2 mm long. May–June. Coast. Pl. and Pied. Wooded swamps along streams. N.J. to Ill. s to Fla. and Tex. (Plate 13).

An attractive plant for landscaping, valued for its fragrant snowy blossoms,

62

and best situated in moist or wet areas in the garden. It is an ideal choice for naturalizing in moist, woody situations in thin shade.

HYDRANGEACEAE

CLIMBING HYDRANGEA *Decumaria barbara* L.
A high-climbing woody vine with smooth, shining ovate to elliptic leaves and aerial rootlets. Leaves opposite and deciduous, entire or toothed, 5–10 cm long, glossy above, glabrous or minutely pubescent beneath. Fragrant flowers many, in terminal, flat-topped corymbs, 4–10 cm broad; flowers small and white; petals 7–10; stamens 20–30; the thick style solitary. Fruiting capsules urn shaped, strongly but delicately ribbed, 4–5 mm long; seeds yellow, 2 mm long, terete. May–Oct. Coast. Pl., Pied., Mts. Rich woods, swamps, riverbanks on hardwoods like Tulip Poplar, *Liriodendron tulipifera* L., often where soil is very acid; on rock outcrops. Va. s to Fla. and La. (Plate 14).

One of our most handsome native woody vines, often overlooked by gardeners. *Decumaria* can be effectively used as a groundcover, a high climber on trees, or a cover for ledges or rock outcrops. It is particularly well suited to moist situations.

MOCK-ORANGE *Philadelphus hirsutus* Nutt.
Shrub to 2–3 m tall, with hirsute young branches. Bark of the previous season exfoliating; twigs brownish. Leaves deciduous, serrate, dentate, ovate to elliptic, prominetely 3-nerved, hirsute beneath, acute or acuminate, with rounded or narrowed base, opposite, 4–8 cm long; petioles 1 cm long. Flowers white, 1–3, terminal; petals 1–2 cm long, obovate; calyx lobes divergent; styles fused; peduncles and pedicels pubescent. Capsule hemispheric, to 1.5 cm long, seeds red, 2–3 mm long. Apr.–Aug. Coast. Pl., Pied., uncommon in Mts. Dry, rocky sloped, bluffs and ledges, often on calcareous or neutral soils. Ky. and N.C. s to Ga. and Ala. (Plate 14).

PHILADELPHUS *Philadelphus inodorus* L.
Shrub to 2–3 m tall. Leaves deciduous, ovate to elliptic, to 10 cm long, opposite, serrate, entire, usually glabrate above and below, 3-veined; petioles less than 1 cm long. Flowers in terminal cymules of 3 or axillary; petals 1.5–2.5 cm long; upper part of the style separate. Seeds yellow to red, smooth, 2–3 mm long. Apr.–Aug. Mts. and Pied. Rich rock slopes, stream banks, granitic outcrops, abandoned house sites. Pa. to Tenn. s to Fla. and Miss. (Plate 14).

A valuable landscaping plant, its domestic derivatives often used for home plantings. A variable species including the large-flowered SYRINGA once considered a distinct species, *Philadelphus grandiflorus* Willd.

The HAIRY MOCK-ORANGE, *Philadelphus pubescens* Loisel., has flowers in racemes rather than in cymules of 3 or solitary, leaves that are softly and densely pubescent on the lower surfaces, and bark of shoots that is grey or yellowish and not exfoliating. Sandstone or calcareous bluffs, riverbanks. Ill. s to Tenn and Ark.

Philadelphus is easily grown in full sun to light shade, preferring moist, fertile, soil. The plants are attractive in flower but are of little interest during the remainder of the year.

WILD HYDRANGEA *Hydrangea arborescens* L.
Shrub with exfoliating bark on old stems, to 2 m tall. Leaves thin, opposite, unlobed, ovate, pointed, toothed, base rounded to cuneate, glabrate or slightly

downy to densely tomentose beneath, 7–15 cm long, deciduous, petioles elongate. Flower clusters flat-topped, 5–15 cm broad. Petals 5, white; the 10 stamens exserted. Capsules ribbed, 1–2 cm long: seeds brown, longitudinally ribbed. May–June. Mts. and Pied. Ledges, cliffs, shale outcrops, wet roadsides, often on calcareous soils. N.Y. s to Ga., La. and Ark. Roots and rhizomes used medicinally. A highly variable species (Plate 14).

An interesting plant for transplanting to rock crevices in shady woods. Several cultivars are available in the nursery trade which have more sterile flowers than the wild form and hence are more showy but perhaps not as graceful.

The OAK LEAF HYDRANGEA, *Hydrangea quercifolia* Bartram, is a large shrub with exfoliating bark, and large oak-shaped, 3–7 lobed, yellow-green deciduous leaves. Flowers showy, in elongate clusters, 15–30 cm long. May–Oct. Mts., Pied. Coast. Pl. Riversides, bluffs and woods, often on taluses. Ga. and Tenn. s to Fla. and La. (Plate 15).

Discovered by William Bartram at "a large brook called Sweet Water" near Knoxville, Georgia (Harper, 1958).

Prized as an ornamental shrub with numerous named cultivars, e.g., 'Harmony', 'Roanoke', 'Snow Queen', and 'Snowflake'. A coarse shrub but used in the lightly shaded border or massed in shady locations. Its interesting foliage and large panicles of flowers enhance the value of this species in the landscape. Although often found on dry, exposed bluffs in nature, the species seems to perform best when cultivated in moist, fertile soil under light shade.

GROSSULARIACEAE

WILD GOOSEBERRY   *Ribes cynosbati* L.
Straggly deciduous shrub, sometimes spiny at the nodes, with prickly berries. Leaf blades 1–2 cm in diameter, 3–5 lobed, almost palmate, pubescent when young, glabrate in age; petioles slender. Flowers usually solitary; pedicels 6–15 mm long. Calyx lobes much shorter than the campanulate tubes; petals 1–2 mm long; styles usually solitary. Berry densely spiny, bristles not gland tipped, 8–12 mm in diameter. May–Sept. Mts. Rocky woods and hillsides, balds. Que. s to Ga., Ala. and Ark. From the Danish name for red currant, *ribs* (Plate 15).

The SMOOTH GOOSEBERRY, *Ribes rotundifolium* Michx., is similar, but has fruit without spines and leaves which are puberulent or short-hairy, above. Peduncles are short, flowers greenish purple, usually solitary; the calyx lobes exceed the tube. Berry globose, smooth, purplish, 8–12 mm in diameter. Apr.–June. Mts. Rich rocky woods and balds. W. Mass. s to N.C. and Tenn. (Plate 15).

The SKUNK-CURRENT, *Ribes glandulosum* Grauer, lacks nodal spines and the internodes are glabrous. Its leaves are usually 5–7 lobed, deeply cleft; the blades are up to 10 cm wide; margins doubly serrate. Racemes are erect and slender; pedicels 4–5 mm long, glandular, jointed beneath the ovary; flowers about 5 mm broad; calyx tube glabrous, saucer shaped, 0.5–1 mm long. The red berry is glandular-bristly, 6–8 mm in diameter. May–Sept. Mts. Restricted to high-elevation coniferous forests. Nfld. to B.C. s to N.C. and Tenn. Bruised shrub and berries have skunklike odor.

The DROOPING GOOSEBERRY, *Ribes curvatum* Small, a low-branching

Rosa setigera

Rosa multiflora

Rosa palustris

Rosa carolina

PLATE 17

Amelanchier spicata

Neviusia alabamensis

Amelanchier arborea

Spiraea japonica

PLATE 18

Kerria japonica

Malus angustifolia

Aronia arbutifolia

Aronia arbutifolia

PLATE 19

Aronia melanocarpa

Sorbus americana

Prunus angustifolia

Prunus serotina

PLATE 20

Crataegus spathulata

Prunus caroliniana

Crataegus crus-galli

Crataegus flabellata

PLATE 21

Cytisus scoparius

Crataegus marshallii

Licania michauxii

Amorpha fruticosa

PLATE 22

Daubentonia punicea FAIRCLOTH

Wisteria frutescens

Pueraria lobata

Robinia hispida

PLATE 23

Ptelea trifoliata MILLER

Poncirus trifoliata

Croton alabamensis

Sapium sebiferum MILLER

PLATE 24

shrub armed with 1–3 red spines at the nodes or internodes, has purplish branches. The bark peels off in papery sheets. Leaves 3–5 lobed, irregularly toothed. Flowers white, small. Sepals linear, 6–12 mm long; petals toothed at the apex; stamens erect, conspicuous. Berries greenish, not spiny. Pied. and Mts. Rocky woods. Tenn., Ga., Ala., La. and Ark.

The FLORIDA GOOSEBERRY, *Ribes echinellum* (Coville) Rehd., has 3-lobed small leaves not exceeding 3 cm long and wide. Flowers solitary or in clusters of two. Pedicels are densely glandular-pubescent; the berry is green, echinate, oval to globular, to 15 mm in diameter. Coast. Pl. Rich woods. S.C. and Fla. Very rare.

HAMAMELIDACEAE

WITCH-HAZEL   *Hamamelis virginiana* L.
Large shrub with pubescent to glabrate twigs. Bark thin, light brown and broken into scales; twigs zigzag with greenish yellow or tan-colored buds on stalks, terminal bud without a scale covering. Leaves suborbicular, margins crenate to undulate, 4–15 cm long, stellate pubescent above when young, glabrate at maturity, deciduous. Flowers yellow with several strap-shaped petals. Fruit a woody capsule, oblong, 1–1.5 cm long. The shining brown seeds may be ejected to distances of 40 feet. Mts., Pied., Coast. Pl. Oct.–Jan. Rich woods. N.S. and Ont. s to Fla. and Tex. An after shave is made from the oil; the bark has been used medicinally (Plate 15).

A small shrubby form with woolly twigs that flowers in the spring is the SPRINGTIME WITCH-HAZEL, *Hamamelis vernalis* Sarg. Rocky stream beds. Ark., Okla. and Mo.

WITCH-HAZELS are pollinated by winter moths, the cuculiids, which are nocturnal, able to fly at air temperatures as low as freezing, and feast on the flowers. (Heinrich, 1987). In late autumn, when the foliage of other deciduous plants is falling, the golden yellow flowers of *H. virginiana* appear. *H. vernalis* flowers in late winter. The leaves of both species turn a gorgeous yellow in autumn. They can be used in light shade for massing on the border of woodlands.

WITCH-ALDER   *Fothergilla major* (Sims) Lodd.
Small shrub to 1.5 m tall with stellate pubescent twigs. Leaves 8–12 cm long and 6–8 cm wide, lobed or coarsely toothed near the apex, or entire, base rounded to slightly cordate. Flowers white, appearing with the leaves. Fruit a capsule 11–13 mm long with a persistent beak. Apr.–Oct. Mts. and Pied. Dry woods and balds, often on sandstones. Tenn., Ga. and Ala. Rare. Endangered (Plate 16).

The DWARF WITCH-ALDER *Fothergilla gardenii* Murray, is similar but smaller, to 1 m tall. Leaves 4–8 cm long, 1.5–5 cm wide, and toothed near the apex. Flowers white, tipped with pink, appear before the leaves in dense terminal spikes; stamens numerous and club shaped. Apr.–Oct. Coast. Pl. Pocosins and savannas. N.C. s to Ga. and Ala. Endangered species. Rare.

The Fothergillas are fine choices in very light shade for the shrub border, particularly when employed in masses. They add considerable contrast in spring with their early-blooming showy white spikes; in the fall the brilliant yellow-orange to scarlet deciduous leaves are a strong color contrast against a dark pine background.

ROSACEAE

FLOWERING RASPBERRY — *Rubus odoratus* L.

An unarmed deciduous shrub with glandular twigs, and simple, palmately 3–5 lobed leaves which are cordate and pubescent beneath on the veins, 10–30 cm wide and long. Flowers in terminal corymbs, the petals deep rose to magenta, 1.5–2.5 cm broad. The fruits are red, 15–20 mm broad, dryish. June–Oct. Mts. Rich hardwood coves. Que. to Ont. s to Ga. and Tenn. (Plate 16).

The rose to magenta flowers and handsome leaves can add excitement to the naturalistic landscape in the higher elevations of our mountains. It is best used in masses on the slopes of a rocky, shady hill in a woodland garden as a background plant. The species grows luxuriantly where there is sufficient soil moisture.

The WINEBERRY, *Rubus phoenicolasius* Maxim., has a densely hispid stem, the bristles red to purple and gland tipped. The leaves are ternately compound, white tomentose beneath, the leaflets 3–9 cm long. The corolla is rose-purple; sepals erect during maturation of the fruit. The drupelets are united in an aggregate fruit. May–July. Mts. and Pied. Thickets, fencerows, old house places. W. Va. and Va. Introduced from E. Asia, cultivated for its juicy fruit.

RED RASPBERRY — *Rubus ideaus* L. var. *canadensis* Richards.

Canes erect, not tip-rooting, stems densely bristly with gland-tipped hairs. Leaves 3–5 foliolate, double toothed, prickles on veins and petioles, white tomentose beneath. Fruits red, drupelets united to an aggregate fruit. June–Aug. Mts. Borders and fencerows. Lab. to Alaska s to N.C., Ariz. Ancestor of cultivated red raspberry.

The WILD BLACK RASPBERRY, *Rubus occidentalis* L. has arching stems, rooting at the tip, with flattened, recurved prickles. Corolla white, petals erect, few flowered. Fruit glaucous, 1–1.5 cm broad, juicy, receptacle remaining on the plant. Apr.–July. Mts. and Pied. Clearings and fencerows. Que. to Minn. s to Ga., Tenn. and Ark. Cultivated black raspberry.

DEWBERRY — *Rubus flagellaris* Willd.

Stems long, flat, trailing, arching, prostrate or nearly so, often rooting at the tip, flowering and fruiting on wood of the previous year; floricanes woody, tough, reddish or purple. Leaves compound, with 3 leaflets on flowering stems, usually 5 on new canes; leaflets glabrous or finely pubescent. Usually 2 or more flowers on a branch, on pedicels up to 2.5 cm long. Petals much longer than sepals; calyx pubescent, petals white, to 1.5 cm long. Berry black, juicy, sweet and large, to 2.5 cm long. Apr.–July. Mts., Pied., Coast. Pl. Old fields, log landings, often xeric waste places. Que. s to Fla. and Ala. (Plate 16).

Canes and berries used by many kinds of wildlife. Fruit freezes well, plant easily propagated by tip layering. A variable species, one from which many domestic dewberries have been derived.

SWAMP DEWBERRY — *Rubus hispidus* L.

Slender stems trailing on ground, terete, with bristles. Leaves coriaceous, some evergreen, often purple- or bronze-tipped beneath; terminal leaflet 2.5–7 cm long, 2–5.5 cm broad. Flowers in a lax corymb, pedicels spreading or ascending, minutely pilose; calyx pubescent. Fruit a dark red to purple, tardily blackening, seedy, sour aggregate. May–July. Mts., Coast. Pl. Low woods, often on acid soils. Que. and N.S. s to N.C. and Mo.

SOUTHERN DEWBERRY
Rubus trivialis Michx.

Similar to *R. flagellaris* but with shorter pedicels and smaller petals. Primocanes with 5 leaflets. Leaves persistent, smooth, ovate to orbicular, sharp toothed, green and shiny above, dull below. Flowers usually solitary, petals white, 1.5–2.5 cm long. Drupelets globose, black, in aggregate 1.5–2 cm long; juicy. Mar.–May. Coast. Pl. and Pied. Roadsides, old fields. Va. s to Fla. and Tex.

HIMALAYA-BLACKBERRY
Rubus bifrons Vest.

A thorny shrub with long, coarse, sprawling stems, angulate. Leaves with 3 leaflets on the floricanes, 5 on the primocanes, (hence the name *bifrons*); leaflets glabrous to slightly pubescent above, white tomentulose beneath, rounded to cuneate at the base. Flowers in paniculate cymes; sepals densely white tomentose on both sides, elliptic lanceolate, 6–8 mm long; petals roseate to white, short clawed, 1.5–2 cm long. The black aggregate 2 cm long, juicy. May–July. Coast. Pl. and Pied. Roadsides, old house places. Escape from cult. Va. to Mo. s to Fla. and Tex. Susceptible to an orange-colored rust, *Gymnoconia interstitialis*.

SAND BLACKBERRY
Rubus cuneifolius Pursh.

Stem erect to arching, about 2 m high, well armed with prickles. The broad-based thorns are slightly recurved. Primocanes 3–5 foliate, with small lateral wedge-shaped leaflets that are thick, dark green, sparingly pilose above and white tomentose beneath. Petals 1–1.5 cm long, obovate to elliptic, 8–12 mm long, white; inflorescence of 3–9 flowers, prickly; sepals white, both sides woolly; calyx lobes 6–10 mm long. Fruit is a rather dry aggregate 2.5 cm long, of good flavor. Apr.–July. Coast. Pl. and Pied. Sandy borders and savannas. Conn. s to Fla. and Ala.

SOW-TEAT BLACKBERRY
Rubus alleghaniensis Porter

Stout erect and arching shrub. Stems armed with broad-based straight to curved thorns. Leaf blades green-tomentose beneath. Inflorescence axes with long-stalked glands; sepals 6–10 mm long, pubescent and stipitate-glandular; petals white, 1–2 cm long. Aggregate 2.5 cm wide, juicy. July. Mts. Woodland borders and clearings. N.S. and Que. s to Ga. and Tenn.

BLACKBERRY
Rubus betulifolius Small

Stems glabrous and angled with strongly recurved and strongly flattened prickles. Leaf blades glabrous to sparingly pubescent on both sides. Pedicels with thorns but not stipitate-glandular; petals elliptic-ovate, 12–15 mm long, flowers small. Similar to *R. argutus*, but the leaves are not velvety pubescent. Apr.–July. Mts., Pied., Coast. Pl. Swamps and wet, sandy woods. Va. s to Fla. and Miss.

HIGH BUSH BLACKBERRY
Rubus argutus Link.

Stems erect to arching, angled and furrowed, armed with stout, spreading, flattened prickles. Leaflets velvety pubescent beneath, margins serrate. Upper 3 leaflets of primocanes 2× to 3× as long as broad, acuminate. Pedicels not stipitate glandular; flowers few in short racemes, with a single flower in upper leaf axils; sepals 4.6 mm long, densely pubescent; petals 2–2.5 cm long. Apr.–July. Mts., Pied., Coast. Pl. Thickets, fencerows, overgrown pastures. N.S. to Man. s to Ga. and Miss. (Plate 16).

The cultivated CRYSTAL WHITE BLACKBERRY, *Rubus louisianus* Berger, with amber-white fruits, occasionally escapes from cultivation. W. Va. s to S.C. and La.

SPINELESS BLACKBERRY   *Rubus canadensis* L.
Main stems stout, 1–3 m tall, angled, usually unarmed. Leaves large, blades of leaflets glabrous, prickles straight and terete; primocanes with smooth petioles. Inflorescences without thorns; pedicels not stipitate-glandular. Flowers racemose, numerous. Aggregate small. June–Aug. Mts. Nfld. to Ont. s to Ga. and Tenn. Restricted to higher mountains.

BLACKBERRY   *Rubus laciniatus* Willd.
Somewhat lax shrub with glabrate angled stems and many thorns. Leaves with 5 deeply dissected leaflets, sparcely pubescent above, but pubescent beneath. Inflorescence is a compound paniculate cyme; sepals 8–10 mm long, acuminate and tomentose; petals 2–2.5 cm long. May–July. Mts. Introd. Naturalized in waste places. W. Va. to N.C. Rare.

Three additional references to this complex genus: Fernald, 1950; Davis et al, 1967; Strausbaugh and Core, 1971.

PRAIRIE ROSE   *Rosa setigera* Michx.
Climbing stems, several meters long, glabrous, arching or trailing, armed with stout, straight to slightly curved prickles. Leaflets 3, occasionally 5, acute and sharply serrate, ovate, 2.5–7 cm long, base rounded, stipules entire, or finely toothed, attached for more than half their length. Flowers 4–8 cm broad, in a corymb, sepals pointed, petals pink, 2–3 cm long. Hip red, globular, 8–12 mm in diameter; sepals and fruit with glandular hairs. May–Oct. Coast. Pl., Pied., Mts. Open woods, thickets, clearings and banks. W. Va to Kans. to Fla. and Tex.

The PRAIRIE ROSE makes a satisfactory groundcover for retaining steep banks or on barren slopes. Its clean, healthy foliage forms a dense mat, and in late spring the stems are clothed in immense clusters of pink flowers (Plate 17).

MULTIFLORA ROSE   *Rosa multiflora* Thunb.
Erect shrub with stems several meters long, climbing and recurving. Leaflets usually 7, sometimes 9, obovate to oblong, glabrous above, often slightly pubescent beneath, 1–3 cm long; hypanthium usually glabrous; stipules comblike, fringed; flowers white or red, 2–4 cm broad; sepals ovate, quickly acuminate; petals 1–1.5 cm long. Hip red, 6–9 mm long; May–Oct. Coast. Pl., Pied., Mts. In roadside thickets, used as livestock fences and plantings for wildlife food and cover. N.Y. s to Fla. and Tex. It may become an escaped pest, so thought should be given before planting it (Plate 17).

The MEMORIAL ROSE, *Rosa wichuraiana* Crepin, differs in having smaller, rounder, and firmer leaflets that are semi-evergreen; petals larger, to 2 cm long; achenes 4–5 mm long. May–Oct. Coast. Pl., Pied., Mts. Road and rail embankments. Introd. s to Fla. and La.

CHEROKEE ROSE   *Rosa laevigata* Michx.
A high-climbing glabrous rose, with stout recurved prickles and ternately compound evergreen, leathery, finely toothed leaflets that are shiny green above and netted veined beneath. Leaflets 3; stipules entire, free. Sepals glandular-bristly; petals cuneate-obcordate, 3–4 cm long, white or uncommonly roseate. Hip red, pyriform, with a tapered base. Apr.–Oct. Coast. Pl. and Pied. Roadsides, waste places. S.C. s to Fla. and Miss. This introduced species has been designated the state flower of Georgia, a surprising designation for an exotic.

MACARTNEY ROSE   *Rosa bracteata* Wendl.
A shrub forming dense, symmetrical haycocklike thickets. Bushier than the CHEROKEE but the 5–8 obovate to oval leaflets are shorter. The evergreen leaf blades are rounded at the apex. The inflorescence is a few-flowered corymb; sepals tomentose on both sides, 1.5–2 cm long, lanceolate; petals white or pink, about 3 cm long, deeply obcordate. Hip black, 2–2.5 cm long, densely silky pubescent. Apr.–Oct. Coast Pl. and Pied. Pastures, fencerows, waste places, a serious weed. Introd. Va. s to Fla. and Tex.

SWEETBRIER   *Rosa eglanteria* L.
Slender and glabrous shrub with arching branches forming bushes 1–2 m tall armed with stout, recurved prickles. Leaflets 5–7, doubly serrate, glandular-pubescent and resinous beneath; aromatic; stipules glandular-ciliate. Flowers 3–5 cm wide, pink to white, sepals 1.5–2 cm long, entire, glandular-ciliate, petals 1.5–2.5 cm long; style pubescent. Hips ellipsoid, 1.5–2 cm long, red. May–Oct. Mts., Pied., Coast. Pl. Thickets and rocky pastures, old house sites. N.Y. to Fla. and Tex. Introd. from Europe and escaped from cultivation.
The DOG ROSE, *Rosa canina* L., also introduced from Europe, is similar but lacks glands on leaflets and pedicels and has glands on the tips of leaf serrations. s to N.C. and Tenn. Rare.

SWAMP ROSE   *Rosa palustris* Marshall
Stems to 2.5 m high, stout and straight, glabrous, plant spreading by rhizomes. Leaves compound, with 5–9 leaflets dull green and smooth above, paler and downy beneath, 2–6 cm long, 1–3 cm wide, finely serrate; hypanthium ovoid to globose; infrastipular prickles curved. Flowers pink, solitary or corymbose on erect branches, 4.5–5 cm broad, the bracts resembling stipules or leaves; sepals lanceolate, 2–3 cm long; petals 2–3 cm long. Fruit globose to slightly pyriform, red, glandular-hispid, 8 mm long; May–Oct. Pied. and Coast. Pl. Swamps and low grounds, often in standing water, beaver ponds. N.S. to Minn. s to Fla. and Miss. (Plate 17).
Two of the wild roses worthy of cultivation are *Rosa palustris,* the SWAMP ROSE, and *Rosa carolina,* the CAROLINA ROSE. The SWAMP ROSE always grows in wet areas so it is best massed in low, moist soil at the edge of a pond or low ditch. It is valuable because of its attractive stems and fruits. It is easily cultivated and grows rather tall and is a great plant for gardens with drainage problems. It grows well in moderate shade.
The CAROLINA ROSE, on the other hand, is a low-growing plant preferring full sun and well-drained soil. Its delicate pink flowers are rather graceful. This rose is suitable along roadsides, under power lines and on dry knolls and in places too rocky to cultivate (Plate 17).

CAROLINA ROSE   *Rosa carolina* L.
A low semi-upright shrub to 1 m tall, spreading from underground roots. The stems armed with straight prickles are at first bristly but glabrous with age. Stipules narrow and toothed, the leaves compound with 5, rarely 7, leaflets, with blades 1–3 cm long, glabrous above and paler and pubescent on the veins beneath, tips of the serrations without glands. Flowers few to solitary, 3–5.5 cm; pedicels glandular-hispid; pink petals slightly notched; sepals glandular and reflexed; May–Oct. Mts., Pied., Coast. Pl. Dry woods, pastures, rocky hillsides. N.S. to Minn. s to Fla. and Tex.

FRENCH ROSE   *Rosa gallica* L.
   A rose with stipitate-glandular stems and glandular-ciliate rugose leaves.
Introduced and escaped from cultivation. Rare.
   The species of roses, both native and introduced, frequently will hybridize,
producing individuals not well marked by distinctive features and thus confusing
to the person attempting to make an identification.

SHADBUSH   *Amelanchier spicata* (Lam.) K. Koch.
   Colonial shrub, 0.3–2 m tall, spreading by rhizomes. Leaves deciduous, alternate, oval to suborbicular, when young, tomentose beneath, 2–6 cm long, 1.5–3.5
cm broad, with 7–11 pairs of veins. Racemes erect, 1.5–5 cm long; calyx 5-lobed;
sepals reflexed, lanceolate, 2–3 mm long; petals less than 10 mm long; stamens
numerous. Fruit a pome, berrylike, 7–10 mm in diameter, globose, purplish black.
Mar.–July. Mts., Pied., Coast. Pl. Rocky, schistose and sandy upland woods and
thickets. Que., Me., s to Ga. and Tenn. Fruit sweet and juicy (Plate 18).

SERVICEBERRY   *Amelanchier arborea* (Michx. f.) Fern.
   Shrub or small tree with a nodding, usually lax and reflexed loose infflores-
cence. Leaves deciduous, 4–10 cm long, ovate, serrate, the teeth twice the number
of the leaf veins. Sepals 2–5 mm long; petals 1–1.7 mm long; top of ovary glabrous;
pome red. Mar.–July. Upland and alluvial forests, clearing edges. Ont. s to Ga. and
La. The wood used for tool handles, plants in landscaping (Plate 18).

ROUUND-LEAVED SHADBUSH   *Amelanchier sanguinea* (Pursh) DC
   Slender shrub, with a few arching to solitary stems. Leaves broad and blunt,
2.5–7 cm long, 2.5–4 cm wide, coarsely toothed, with rounded base and apex, 15–
32 teeth on each side, densely woolly beneath, deciduous. Panicles drooping, 4–7
cm long, loosely flowered; petals linear, 10–15 mm long. Fruit a purplish black
globose pome, 6–8 mm in diameter, sweet, juicy. Apr.–Aug. Dry rocky and
gravelly soil. Ont. to Minn. s to Tenn. and N.C. Rare.

SHADBUSH   *Amelanchier obovalis* (Michx.) Ashe
   A rhizomatous colonial shrub with elliptic to oblong leaves 2–6 cm long, acute
to obtuse, base rounded to widely cuneate. Leaves densely woolly white beneath
when young, smooth when mature, with a prominant midrib, deciduous. Petioles
woolly, long, slender. Flowers in erect racemes, blooming before the leaves are
out. Pome dark blue to purple. Mar.–June. Coast. Pl., rare in Pied. N.J. s to Ga., Ala.
   A related SHADBUSH is *Amelanchier canadensis* (L.) Medicus, which is similar
but not stoloniferous. Pedicels are longer, to 10–20 mm instead of 2–5 mm.
Swamps, bogs, upland woods. Coast. Pl. and Pied. Me and Que. s to Ga.
   Shadbushes are difficult to identify due to hybridization, polyploidy, and
apomixis. As a group, the *Amelanchier* species make excellent landscape plants and
are most pleasing when used in a natural situation. They blend in well at the edge
of woods or in shrub borders. They are among the first native shrubs to bloom,
announcing the arrival of spring, and even though their flowers are rather short-
lived, they are worth growing. Their orange autumn coloration is excellent and
birds are attracted to the soft, juicy fruits.

NEVIUSIA   *Neviusia alabamensis* A. Gray
   Rare shrub with showy greenish white, single or clustered flowers on slender
pedicels. Leaves ovate to lanceolate, doubly serrate, 1.5–4 cm long, 1.2–3 cm wide,

deciduous. Sepals 5-pointed, toothed; stamens numerous; styles elongated, achenes naked, drupelike. On shale and limestone soils. Disjunct colonies in Ala., Ga., Miss., Ark. and Mo. (Plate 18).

Forms large, very showy colonies. Often cultivated. Endangered. An unusual landscape plant for the shrub border with flowers that are quite showy and interesting. A great plant to challenge your friends to identify.

NINEBARK   *Physocarpus opulifolius* (L.) Maxim.

Shrubs to 3 m tall with simple, palmately lobed leaves and flowers in terminal corymbs with recurved branches. Bark readily peeling and shredding. Leaves somewhat cordate, 3 lobes and 3 main veins, doubly crenate to serrate, stellate-pubescent toward base, 4–7 cm long. Corymbs many flowered with white or pinkish flowers. Carpels inflated, forming bladdery, reddish fruits splitting into two valves. May–Sept. Mts., Pied., Coast Pl. Moist cliffs, riverbanks. Que. to Wis. s to Fla., Ala., Ark. and Mo.

The landscape value of NINEBARK has long been recognized. Since it blooms later (May–June) than many flowering shrubs, it is best used in masses where a later flowering effect is needed.

MEADOWSWEET   *Spiraea alba* DuRoi

Shrubs with simple deciduous leaves; stem erect, 3–20 dm tall, with tough, yellow-brown twigs. Leaves finely serrate, elliptic-lanceolate to oblanceolate, 5–7 cm long. Flowers 6–8 mm broad, in panicles, the inflorescence densely puberulent; petals 5, white, 2–3 mm long; sepals 5, spreading; stamens numerous. Seeds light brown, 1.5–2.5 mm long. June–Oct. Mts. and Pied. Bogs, stream banks and wet pastures. Nfld., Que. s to N.C. and Mo.

Another MEADOWSWEET, *Spiraea latifolia* (Ait.) Borkh., has oblanceolate, broad, glabrous leaves and follicles and an elongate inflorescence. Flowers white or pinkish in the bud. Moist slopes and meadows. Nfld. to Mich. s to N.C.

HARDHACK   *Spiraea tomentosa* L.

Shrub about 2 m tall with angled twigs, pubescence of rusty color. Leaves 2.5–5 cm long, variably serrate, dark green and glabrous above, gray-tomentose beneath, deciduous. Rose to purple flowers about 4 mm broad, in panicles that are often leafy near the base; follicles densely and permanently tomentulose; seeds 1.2–1.5 mm long. July–Oct. Mts., Pied., Coast. Pl. Swamps and low ground. N.S., Que., to Man. s to Ga., Tenn. and Ark.

In the Upper South or at higher elevations, HARDHACK, with its dusty pink spires along low roadsides mingled with various other wildflowers, is a delightful plant, one suitable for use in a natural garden at home.

The introduced JAPANESE SPIRAEA, *Spiraea japonica* L. f., has flowers in a corymb, stems to 2 m high with terete, gray-pubescent twigs, sharply serrate deciduous leaves 7–9 cm long; pink to deep rose color petals 3mm long. June–Aug. Mts. and Pied. Thickets, roadsides, house sites, forming large colonies and rapidly becoming naturalized. N.E. s to N.C. and Ga. (Plate 18).

Spiraea thunbergii Siebold, the Bridal Wreath, has escaped and become naturalized and is common around old house sites.

CORYMBED SPIRAEA   *Spiraea betulifolia* Pallas.

Erect shrub, less than 1.5 m high with simple dark purple, terete, glabrous stems. Leaves elliptic, oblanceolate to ovate, 2.5–5 cm wide, deciduous. Flowers in a compound corymb 4–10 cm broad; calyx glabrous; petals white, 1–4 mm long; longer stamens about twice as long as the sepals; seeds 1.8–2 mm long. June–Oct. Mts. Rocky banks and acid soil. Md. s to Ala. and Ky. Rare.

The VIRGINIA SPIRAEA, *Spiraea virginiana* Britton, has narrower leaves, to 1.6 cm broad, mucronate and glaucous beneath. The stem is much branched, and the white flowers are 6 mm wide. June–Sept. Mts. Stream banks and rocky places. Va., Tenn., N.C. and Ga. Rare.

FIRETHORN   *Pyracantha coccinea* Roem.
Evergreen shrub with slender spreading purple spines or spine-tipped branches. Leaf blades oblanceolate, 1–3 cm long, crenulate. Petals white, 3 mm long. Pomes scarlet, bitter, 4–6 mm long. Fencerows, old house sites. Mts., Pied., Coast. Pl. Escape from cultivation. Pa. s to Fla. and Tex.

A residual at abandoned house sites is *Kerria japonica* (L.) DC., the GLOBE-FLOWER, an alternate-leaved deciduous shrub with greenish branches, 5 yellow petals, numerous stamens, and 5–8 dryish drupelike achenes. The flowers are sometimes double. Introduced from Asia (Plate 19).

SOUTHERN CRAB-APPLE   *Malus angustifolia* (Ait.) Michx.
Shrub to small tree with simple unlobed leaves. Young twigs densely pubescent, later glabrous. Leaves crenate, elliptic-lanceolate, 2.5–8 cm long, 1–4 cm wide, round-tipped, blunt, or short mucronate. Flowers in simple corymbs, each flower with 5 petals, 5 sepals and 5 styles, at first pink, fading to white, 2.5 cm broad. Fruit a pome. Apr.–Sept. Mts., Pied., Coast. Pl. Borders, old fields. Md. to W. Va. s to Fla. and Mo. Forms thickets from root sprouts. Valuable wildlife food. This and the next species are in need of study, and may not be distinct (Plate 19).

When in full flower, few other shrubs or small trees can approach the beauty of our native crab apples. They are best used at the edge of woodlands or massed in a natural drift. Cedar-apple rust can cause the leaves of crab apple to become unsightly.

The WILD CRAB-APPLE, *Malus coronaria* (L.) Mill., is also a deciduous shrub or tree that forms thickets from root sprouts. The leaves are serrate and usually some are lobed at the base, and acute, rather than blunt, at the tip. They are wider, 2.5–6.5 cm broad, and the mature branchlets are red-brown. Flowers are larger, 3–4 cm broad. Apr.–Sept. Mts., Pied., Coast. Pl. Bottoms, wooded slopes, thickets Ont. to Wis. s to Tenn.

The introduced SIBERIAN CRAB, or CRAB APPLE, *Malus baccata* L. has small fruit, less than 1 cm in diameter and white, oblong petals; leaves glabrous, oblong-ovate, acuminate and sharply serrate. The COMMON APPLE, *Malus pumila* Miller, often escapes or is persistent after cultivation.

RED CHOKEBERRY   *Aronia arbutifolia* (L.) Ell.
Rhizomatous colonial shrub, with slender ascending to spreading branches, simple leaves. Lower leaf surfaces, young shoots, and pedicels are soft-pubescent. Leaves oblong-oblanceolate, glandular-serrate, tomentose beneath, with small reddish trichomes along the midrib above, 4–10 cm long, 1.5–4.5 cm broad, deciduous. Flowers 5-merous, white or pink tinged, 8–12 mm broad; sepals 1–2.5 mm long, sometimes with stipitate glands. Two color forms of the fruit may be found; red and bluish-black. The pomes are 5–7 mm in diameter. Mar.–Nov. Mts., Pied., Coast. Pl. Swamps and wet woods, bogs, springheads and savannas. N.S. to

Mich. s to Fla. and Tex. The berries have been used to treat scurvy (Plate 19).

Aronia arbutifolia can be effective in the landscape when used in groups in moist soil. It has a tendency to become leggy but when massed the leggy character is quite exciting. Brilliant fruit displays and red to crimson fall color highlight this species. Birds enjoy the fruit. The shrub merits more consideration in the land-scape than it usually receives.

BLACK CHOKEBERRY   *Aronia melanocarpa* (Michx.) Ell.
Small, nonrhizomatous shrub with broadly elliptic leaves which are glabrous beneath when mature. Rachis and pedicels glabrous. Leaves deciduous, 3–9 cm long, 1.5–5 cm wide, with reddish brown trichomes scattered along the midrib above. Flowers 8–12 mm broad, white to pinkish; calyx and sepals glabrous on outside, 1–2 mm long, petals 5–8 mm long. Pome purple-black to black, 7–10 mm May–Sept. Mts. Bluffs and cliffs, bogs and balds. Ont. to Minn. s to Ga. and Tenn. Wine red fall color and the purplish black fruits provide incentives for planting this highly adaptable species (Plate 20).

The MOUNTAIN ASH, *Sorbus americana* Marsh., is a deciduous shrub or small tree with pinnately compound leaves with 13–17 leaflets and glutinous winter buds. The inflorescence is 6–15 cm wide with glabrous sepals and obovate petals 3–4 mm long. The fruit is orange-red. Mts. Moist to wet soils, heath balds. Nfld. to Minn. s to N.C., Ga. (Plate 20).

The EUROPEAN MOUNTAIN ASH, *Sorbus aucuparia* (L.) Gaertn, has villous buds and may escape from cultivation. Other escapes are the QUINCE, *Cydonia oblonga* Mill. and the FLOWERING QUINCE, *Chaenomeles speciosa* (Sweet) Nakail, which may persist about deserted home sites.

CHICKASAW PLUM   *Prunus angustifolia* Marsh.
Shrub or small tree to 5 m tall, commonly with thorny stems, forming dense thickets. Leaves deciduous, lanceolate to elliptic lanceolate, 4–8 cm long, acute at the apex, glabrous, serrulate, the marginal teeth tipped with red glands; leaves tending to fold inward and become troughlike. Flowers umbellate, appearing before the leaves; petals white, 5–8 cm long. Drupe red or yellow. 1.5–3 cm long. At flowering, lower leaves are red-glandular. Mar.–July. Pied. and Coast. Pl. N.J. and Kans. s to Fla. and Tex. Makes delicious jelly (Plate 20).

BLACK SLOE or HOG PLUM   *Prunus umbellata* Ell.
A large shrub to small tree to 8 m tall sometimes forming thickets. Leaves glabrous, acute to accuminate, elliptic, oval or oblong, cuneate to rounded at the base, simply and finely serrate, without red-glands on the margins, deciduous. Flowers small, 8–12 mm across, petals 4–6 mm long. Drupe 1.2 cm long, usually black, but populations with red fruits are known. Mar.–Sept. Coast. Pl. and Pied. Dry sandy woods. N.C. to Fla., La. and Tex. A variable species; now regarded to include *Prunus injucunda* Small.

WILD PLUM   *Prunus americana* Marsh.
Deciduous shrub to small tree with somewhat thorny stems, fleshy fruits, and umbellate flowers. Leaves oblong, oval elliptic to slightly obovate, abruptly acumi-nate, usually doubly serrate, 7–12 cm long. Flowers appearing with the leaves; flowers and fruits on slender pedicels 12–20 mm long; flowers large, to 2.5 cm across; petals 1–1.5 cm long. Drupe to 2.5 cm long, usually red, but populations with blue fruits are known. Mar.–Aug. Mts., Pied., Coast. Pl. Stream and woods

borders, fencerows. Ont. to Minn. s to Fla. and N. Mex. A variable species.

The SAND CHERRY, *Prunus pumila* L., is a low-growing rhizomatous shrub with lanceolate deciduous leaves and petals less than 1 cm long. Leaves 3–7 cm long, 1–3.5 cm wide, acute, crenate-serrate, with a cuneate base. Drupe black, edible, 1–1.5 cm long. Apr.–Sept. Mts. Sandy and rocky outcrops. Me. and Ill. s to Va. and N.C. Rare.

The PERFUMED CHERRY, *Prunus malaleb* L., an introduced plant from Europe, has flowers in a short 4–10 flowered raceme; lower pedicels with bracts; leaves slightly cordate to nearly truncate at base. Md. s to N.C. and Tenn. Uncommon escape, widely used as a dwarfing rootstock for sweet and sour domestic cherries.

The WILD GOOSE PLUM, *Prunus hortulana* Bailey, has rather thick deciduous leaves conspicuously veiny beneath, gland-tipped at each tooth. Usually does not sucker to form thickets. Flowers white, opening when leaves are half grown. Drupe red to yellow, often with bloom, 2–3 cm long. Mar.–Aug. Coast. Pl. and Pied. Rich bottomlands. Ill. s to Ga. and Tex. Fruit is aromatic, acid, and very good for preserves. Uncommon.

The ALABAMA CHERRY, *Prunus alabamensis* Mohr, is a shrub to small crooked tree with purple drupes and a pubescent rachis of racemes, dull deciduous leaves, pubescent beneath. Mts. Ga. and Ala.

The WILD BLACK CHERRY, *Prunus serotina* Ehrhart, is normally a tree but may be shrublike in ruderal situations (Plate 20).

CHOKE CHERRY   *Prunus virginiana* L.
    A low shrub to small tree with smoky gray bark. Young shoots, rachis, and pedicels glabrous. Leaves elliptic to obovate, sharply serrate, thin, smooth yellow-green above, 5–10 cm long; twigs aromatic with prussic acid odor when crushed. Racemes 5–9 cm long, at ends of short leafy branchlets. Flowers small, blooming after the leaves, in dense cylindrical clusters; sepals triangular, 1 mm long, deciduous; petals white, 4–7 mm long. Drupe dark red. Apr.–Aug. Mts. and Pied. Rocky hardwoods, shores, and fencerows. N.S. to Sask. s to N.C., Tenn. Uncommon to rare. The hydrocyanic acid content of the bark makes it a poison to be used with care. Extracts are a basic ingredient of cough syrups and other medicines. The leaves are deciduous and poisonous to cattle. The fruits are used by many wildlife forms.

FIRE CHERRY   *Prunus pensylvanica* L. f.
    Slender shrub to small tree, with young shoots reddish and shining; bark light brown. Leaves elliptic-lanceolate, serrate, shining, smooth on both sides, acuminate, deciduous. Flowers white, in umbells, from previous season's wood, on long pedicels. Fruit a small red drupe, 4–6 mm in diameter, thin and sour. Apr.–Sept. Mts. Rocky woods and clearings, often following fire; heath balds. Lab. to S.D. s to N.C., Tenn. and Ga. Fruit used by more than 25 kinds of birds. Commonly a shrub on poor soils. Wilted leaves are poisonous to livestock.

ALLEGHENY SLOE   *Prunus alleghaniensis* Porter
    Low, straggling shrub to small tree with ovate-oblong, sharply serrate, acute or acuminate, deciduous leaves. Flowers white, 1–1.5 cm broad; petals 4–6 mm long; style 4–7 mm long, usually hidden among the stamens. Drupe dark purple, 1 cm in diameter. Apr.–Sept. Mts. Thickets, woods borders, dry slopes. Conn. to W. Va.,

disjunct colony in Tenn. Uncommon to rare. Threatened species.

The WILD GOOSE PLUM, *Prunus munsoniana* Wight and Hedr., a deciduous shrub or small tree to 6 m tall, forms dense thickets. The usually thin leaf blades are lanceolate, 5–10 cm long, and the glands are located next to the sinus on the leaf margins rather than at the tip. Sepals glandular on the margins; petals 6–7 mm long. Mar.–Sept. Pied. and Coast. Pl. Well-drained, sunny sites. Ky. and Mo. s to Ga., La., Tex. Uncommon, colonies disjunct. Very variable species.

The MEXICAN PLUM, *Prunus mexicana* S. Watson, rarely forms thickets and is usually treelike. Leaves ovate, broadly oval, rarely obovate, with a rounded base and the apex acute to abruptly acuminate, velvety tomentose beneath and dull green above, deciduous. Flowers in nearly sessile umbels; sepals obscurely glandular on the margins; petals 6 mm long. Drupe purplish to red, 3 cm long. Apr.–Aug. Coast. Pl. and Pied. Open woods, rich bottoms and prairies. Ind. and Iowa s to Tenn., Ala., Ark., Miss. and Mex.

CAROLINA CHERRY LAUREL — *Prunus caroliniana* Ait.

Thicket-forming shrub or small tree with evergreen elliptic to oblanceolate leaves which are leathery, thick, lustrous, pale beneath and pointed at both ends. Racemes from leaf axils of previous year's growth, 1.3–3 cm long; sepals 1–1.5 mm long; petals 2–3 mm long; stamens 10. Drupe 10–13 mm long, dry, dull black; stone ovoid. Feb.–Oct. Coast. Pl. Low woods, fencerows, abandoned gardens, maritime forests. N.C. s to Fla. and Tex. Native, but also escaping from cultivation.

This species has been widely used for screening and for forming hedges. It can grow rather large and also becomes somewhat weedy as it reproduces readily from seeds (Plate 21).

The PEACH, *Prunus persica* (L.) Batsch, often persists in thickets.

The HAWTHORNS, *Crataegus* species, are a most variable and complex group and identification as to species often is difficult. The complex variation pattern has been produced by hybridization, polyploidy, and agamospermy (asexual seed) producing numerous indistinct biotypes. Our treatment follows that of Clark (1971), Radford, Ahles and Bell (1968), and Little (1979).

WASHINGTON HAWTHORN — *Crataegus phaenopyrum* (L.f) Medicus

Shrub or small tree with deciduous leaves 4–6 cm long, 2.5–4 cm wide, triangular-ovate, coarsely toothed, and prominently lobed. Twigs shiny with slender spines. Fruit 4–6 mm diameter, shiny red, globose, with a ring from fallen calyx lobes. May–Oct. Pied., Mts., Coast. Pl. Riverbanks, low woods, moist areas. Pa. s to Fla., Ark. Mo.

The bright, glossy red fruit makes an attractive display on specimens of this species planted on the University of Georgia Campus. Best used in landscape as a specimen plant or in mass in screening or to direct foot traffic.

In general, the stems of Hawthorns show character in the form of zigzag branches and long thorns. They are valuable to wildlife by providing long-lasting fruits as well as places for birds to nest. Small Hawthorns often are cut at Christmas time and made into decorative gum-drop trees; the gum drops are placed on the thorns.

The LITTLE-HIP, *Crataegus spathulata* Michaux, has smaller leaves, 2–4 cm long, 1–2.5 cm wide, deciduous, frequently toothed, sometimes 3-lobed, with veins running to both sinuses and points of the lobes. Twigs mostly with straight spines 0.5–4 cm long. Fruit 4–6 mm in diameter, with dry pulp. Apr.–Oct. Pied. and Coast. Pl. Wet or moist soils, stream banks, swamps, borders of woods. Va. s to Fla., Tex. and Mo. (Plate 21).

ONE-FLOWERED HAWTHORNE *Crataegus uniflora* Muenchh.
    Shrub 0.5–4 m tall with spines 1–6 cm long. Leaves obovate, elliptic or ovate, toothed, with sunken veins, cuneate to attenuate at the base, deciduous. Twigs stiff-hairy, with many slender spines. Flowers solitary; sepals glandular-serrate, persisting on fruit. Fruit 7–12 mm in diameter, reddish to brownish, pulp mealy. Apr.–Oct. Mts., Pied., Coast. Pl. Dry woodlands, rocky uplands, fields. N.Y. s to Fla. and Tex.
    The COCKSPUR HAWTHORN, *Crataegus crus-galli* L., is a deciduous shrub to tree with elliptic to oblanceolate leaves, 2.5–10 cm long by 1–5 cm wide, sharply toothed beyond the middle, with gland-tipped teeth. Twigs brown, stout, usually with many long brown, spines, the largest of any HAWTHORN. Inflorescence compound, mostly more than 3-flowered. Fruit 10–12 mm in diameter, dull red or greenish. Apr.–Oct. Mts., Pied., Coast. Pl. Moist soils, thickets, woods, fencerows. Ont. s to Fla., Miss. and Kans. (Plate 21).

GREEN HAWTHORN *Crataegus viridis* L.
    Shrub or small tree 8–10 m tall with ovate, elliptical, toothed leaves basally cuneate to attenuate, 2.5–6 cm long, 1.2–4 cm wide, dull above with tufts of pale hair in the veins beneath, often lobed, turning scarlet in the autumn. Twigs gray, glabrous, usually spineless. Inflorescence glabrous; sepals entire. Pome red, globose, 6–8 mm in diameter, with juicy pulp, borne in many drooping clusters. Apr.–Oct. Coast. Pl. and Pied. Moist alluvial woods and swamp forests. Del. to Ind. s to Fla. and Tex.

DOTTED HAWTHORN *Crataegus punctata* Jacq.
    Shrub to small tree up to 10 m tall. Leaves oblanceolate, elliptic, oblong, toothed, 5–10 cm long, 2–5 cm wide, broadest beyond the middle and shallowly lobed, deciduous. Sunken veins impressed on the upper leaf surface. Cymes simple or compound, few- to many-flowered, the branches of inflorescence pubescent. Fruit 12–19 mm in diameter, dull red to yellow, with whitish dots. May–Oct. Mts. and Pied. Riverbanks, moist soils in valleys, especially on limestone soils. Que. and Nfld. s to Ga. and Okla.
    The FLESHY HAWTHORN, *Crataegus succulenta* Link, also has shallowly lobed deciduous leaves, with 4–7 sunken veins on each side, entire sepals, and a glabrous inflorescence. May–Oct. Mts. Woods and stream banks. Can. to Mo. s to N.C. Rare.
    The PEAR-SHAPED HAWTHORN, *Crataegus calpodendron* (Ehrhart) Medicus, is similar but more prominently hairy, with larger leaves; the fruit are borne in upright cluster. Fruit globose to pear shaped, usually with 2–3 pyrenes. May–Oct. Mts. Small rocky streams. N.Y. to Ga. and Ark. Rare.

YELLOW HAWTHORN *Crataegus flava* Ait.
    Shrub or small tree with broad open crown of stout spiny branches. Leaves deciduous with black gland-tipped teeth extending to base of blade; blades cuneate to attenuate; sepals serrate, persisting on fruit. Fruit globose, 8–17 mm in diameter, orange, brown or yellow, in drooping clusters. Mts., Pied., Coast. Pl. Sandy or rocky woodlands, dry sites. Va. and Tenn. s to Fla. and Miss.

FAN-LEAF HAWTHORN   *Crataegus flabellata* (Bosc) K. Koch.
    Much-branched shrub or small tree. Leaves deciduous, broadly ovate to fan shaped, rounded at base, doubly toothed with 4–6 shallow lobes; veins not running to the sinuses; petioles glabrous. Spines long, curved. Pome red, 8–13 mm in diameter, in drooping clusters. May–Oct. Mts., Pied., Coast. Pl. Stream banks, pastures, woodland edges, old fields. Nfld. to Minn. s to Ga., La. A common and variable species with many synonyms. Abundant in the Appalachians (Plate 21).

PARSLEY HAWTHORN   *Crataegus marshallii* Eggl.
    Deciduous shrub or small tree with slender thorny or thornless branches and parsleylike foliage. Leaves broadly ovate, divided nearly to midvein into 5–7 toothed lobes. Leaves truncate or shallowly cordate at base; veins running to sinuses and lobes of leaves; inflorescence pubescent. Pome red, ellipsoid, 5–10 mm long, 4–5 mm in diameter. Apr.–Oct. Pied. and Coast. Pl. Moist valley soils, swamp forests. Va. s to Fla., Tex. and Mo. One of the easiest hawthorns to identify (Plate 22).

MAY HAW   *Crataegus aestivalis* (Walter) T.& G.
    Deciduous shrub often with straight spines 1.5–4 cm long. Leaves ovate to elliptic, basally cuneate to attenuate, coarsely toothed above the middle; veins with tufts of hairs beneath. Inflorescence simple, 1–3 flowered; sepals entire, persisting on fruit. Pome red, 8–10 mm in diameter, edible, maturing in summer. Mar.–July. Coast. Pl. Shallow ponds, wet woods. N.C. s to Fla. and Miss. Excellent Jelly.
    The BLUE HAW, *Crataegus brachyacantha* Englem. & Sarg., has leaves glabrous beneath and fruit that are glaucous blue, 8–12 mm in diameter, maturing in late summer. Coast. Pl. Swamps and streams, prairies. Ga. to Ark. and Tex.

SCARLET HAWTHORN   *Crataegus coccinea* L.
    Shrub or tree with broadly ovate leaves, rounded, truncate, or widely cuneate at base, deciduous, doubly toothed; veins not running to sinuses; petioles not glandular, or remotely glandular with stalked glands. Sepals glandular-serrate. Pome shiny red, with many dark dots. Apr.–Oct. Pied., Mts. Upland woods, moist soils, valleys and hillsides. Que. to Minn. s to Ga. and Ala. Uncommon to Rare.
    The DOWNY HAWTHORN, *Crataegus mollis* (T.& G.) Scheele, has foliage and inflorescence copiously tomentose, is sometimes considered a synonym of the SCARLET HAWTHORN.

CHRYSOBALANACEAE

GOPHER APPLE   *Licania michauxii* Prance
    Low colonial shrub to 4 dm tall, unbranched, spreading by underground stems. Leaves elliptical to oblanceolate, simple, alternate, evergreen, 4–10 cm long. Flowers white in terminal cymes; sepals pubescent, 1–1.5 cm long; petals 1.5–2.5 cm long, densely pubescent; stamens 10–15, filaments united. Fruit an ovoid drupe. May–Oct. Sand dunes, ridges, turkey-oak woods. S.C. to Fla., Miss. (formerly known as *Chrysobalanus oblongifolius* Michx.) (Plate 22).

MIMOSACEAE

MIMOSA   *Albizia julibrissin* Durizzini
    Small deciduous tree with gray bark and unarmed greenish branches. Leaves even bipinnate, 1–2 dm long, with as many as 24 pinnae each with 20–40 sessile

leaflets with an apparent midvein at one edge; leaves fold up at night. Flowers light to dark pink, in globular heads, at the ends of branches, fragrant, with many exserted stamens. Fruit a broadly linear, flat legume, indehiscent, 8–18 cm long; seeds elliptic, 3.5–4.5 mm wide. May–Nov. Mts., Pied. Coast. Pl. Pinelands, hammocks, and roadsides, introduced from tropical Asia and Africa. Del. and Ind. s to Fla. and Tex. Much visited by hummingbirds.

The SWEET ACACIA, *Acacia farnesiana* (L.) Willd., is a stout deciduous shrub, armed with short stout spines. Leaves twice pinnately compound; flowers yellow, in small globose clusters; legumes woody, 4–7 cm long. Coast. Pl. Edge of live oak woods, maritime areas, coastal islands. Ga. and Fla. to Mex.

SMALL'S ACACIA *Acacia smallii* Isely, is similar. Coast. Pl. Fla.

The PRAIRIE ACACIA, *Acacia angustissima* (Miller) Kuntze, is a small semiwoody shrub bearing whitish flowers in globose clusters. Coast. Pl. Sandy soils. Okl., Mo., La. and Tex. Rare.

CAESALPINACEAE

RED-BUD   *Cercis canadensis* L.
Deciduous shrub or tree with simple, cordate, entire, palmately veined, leaves, 8–10 cm long, 12–15 cm wide, cordate. Twigs reddish brown. Flowers several together, in umbellate clusters, blossoming before the leaves; corolla red-purple, 8 mm long, clawed. Legume flat, 6–10 cm long, late-deciduous. Mar.–Nov. Mts., Pied., Coast. Pl. Rich soils, especially neutral or slightly alkaline ones. Conn. to Wis. s to Fla. and Tex.

A plant often used as an ornamental tree. *Cercis canadensis* can be used in the landscape as a single specimen or in groupings at the edge of woodland. A relatively short-lived tree, plants frequently are destroyed by canker. Numerous cultivars are found in the nursery trade, e.g., 'Forest Pansey' with purple leaves; 'Flame', a double pink form; 'Royal', white flowering; 'Pinkbud', a true pink; and 'Silver Cloud', a variegated leaf selection.

GOLDEN-SHOWER   *Cassia corymbosa* Lam.
Shrub 2–4 m tall. Flowers showy, borne in terminal panicles. Leaflets mostly 6, lanceolate to linear-elliptic, 2–5 cm long, glabrous. Flowers bright yellow, petals 5, obovate, about 1 cm long, perfect; stamens usually 7. Legume stout, thick, indehiscent, 7–15 cm long with convex sides and furrowed sutures. Mar.–Oct. Coast. Pl. Waste places, woods, and fencerows. Tenn. to Ga. and La. Introduced from Argentina: often cultivated.

The CROWN-OF-THORNS, *Parkinsonia aculeata* L., is another introduced shrub or small tree. Leaves 2–4 dm long with a winged rachis, phyllodelike; leaflets small, 2–9 mm long; stems armed. Flowers bright yellow. Legume 5–10 cm long. Mar.–Sept. Coast. Pl. Roadsides, hammocks. N.C. to Fla. and Tex. Grown as an ornamental or hedge plant. Uncommon.

FABACEAE

SCOTCH BROOM   *Cytisus scoparius* (L.) Link
Stiff, wiry deciduous shrub with broomlike, angled branches. Leaflets 3 or 1 in the upper leaves. Flowers glabrous, campanulate, 2-lipped; petals bright yellow, 1.5–2.5 cm long, the wing and keel petals clawed. Legume flat, ciliate on the

margins, 4.5–5 cm long. Apr.–July. Mts., Pied., Coast. Pl. Deserted house places, roadsides where escaped from cultivation. N.S. to N.Y., s to Ga. Prefers sandy soil; drought resistant (Plate 22).

FALSE INDIGO   *Amorpha fruticosa* L.
Bushy deciduous shrub to 4 m tall, with odd-pinnate leaves 1–3 dm long and small flowers in dense terminal panicles. Leaves distinctly petioled, the petioles longer than the width of the lowest leaflets; leaflets 11–25, 1–5 cm long with exerted midvein. Racemes dense, 7–15 cm long with violet-purple flowers 6–8 mm long. Legume 2-seeded, dorsally curved, less than 3 mm wide, glandular-punctate. Apr.–Oct. Mts., Pied., Coast. Pl. Swamps and riverbanks, wet places, especially in calcareous soils. Penn. to Wis. s to Fla. and Tex. (Plate 22).
A variable species, with several named varieties. It has long been cultivated as an ornamental plant; the beauty of the violet-purple flowers is set off by the brilliance of the orange stamens.
The OUACHITA INDIGO, *Amorpha ouachitensis* Wilbur, differs from *A. fruticosa* by having petiolules which are conspicuously pustulate. Mts. Ark. and Okla.
Amorpha paniculata T. & G., is distinctive in appearance with an inflorescence grayish to the unaided eye. Thickets, bogs, swampy woods and ditches. Ark. Tex. and La.
Another MOUNTAIN INDIGO, *Amorpha glabra* Desf., is identified by very short, almost obsolete calyx lobes, a straight legume with large distinct glands and a leaf midvein terminating in a small knob. Mts. Hardwood slopes. Tenn. s to Ga. and S.C.

SCHWERIN-INDIGO   *Amorpha schwerinii* Schneider
A bushy deciduous shrub to 2 m tall, with a petiole longer than the width of the lowermost leaflet, deep rose to purple petals and densely fine-pubescent branches. Leaflets brown-villous beneath. Racemes solitary or two together, 4–6 cm long, thickly pubescent; calyx lobes nearly as long as the tube; legume 5–6.5 mm long; 2.2 mm broad, densely short-pubescent and glandular. Apr.–Oct. Pied. Rocky river bluffs and woods. N.C. s to Ga. and Ala.
The LEADPLANT, *Amorpha canescens* Pursh. is a deciduous undershrub scarcely 1 m high with the leaves mostly sessile, the petioles shorter than the width of the lowermost leaflet. Racemes clustered, dense, 5–25 cm long, the flowers on very short pedicels; calyx lobes lanceolate to subulate, only half as long as the tube. Pied. Sandy hills; prairies. Mich., Sask. s to Ark. and Tex. A prairie ecotone species more common west of our range. Frequently grown as an ornamental, its silvery leaflets contrasting with the violet-blue flowers.

INDIGO-BUSH   *Amorpha georgiana* Wilbur
Small deciduous shrub to 1 m high, scarcely branched. Petioles of the upper leaves usually shorter than the width of the lowermost leaflets. Racemes terminal and usually solitary. Corolla purple to bluish; calyx with numerous conspicuous glands. Legume straight on the back, broad, conspicuously punctate with a lateral beak. May–Oct. Dry ridges, sandy field borders and open woods. Coast. Pl. N.C. to S.C. and Ga.
Another FALSE INDIGO, *Amorpha nitens* F. E. Boynton, with glabrous branches, grows to 4 m high. The petioles are longer than the width of the lower

leaflets; leaflets thin, lustrous, broadest below the middle and pubescent beneath. Legumes without resinous dotting. Coast. Pl. Thickets and stream banks. Ill. to Ark., Ala. and Ga.

Amorpha herbacea Walter, is a small, grayish-pubescent deciduous shrub less than 1 m tall with very short petioles so the lowest pair of leaflets appears very close to the stem; leaflets 11–37; midvein terminates in a swollen glandular nob. Racemes as many as 20, clustered, 4–30 cm long; flowers bluish white; calyx with numerous striking punctate glands. May–Oct. Coast. Pl. Pinelands, sandy fields. N.C. to Fla.

LESPEDEZA BICOLOR   *Lespedeza bicolor* Turcz.
Deciduous shrub to 3 m or more tall. Leaves trifoliate, leaflets elliptic or ovate, 1.1–6.5 cm long, pubescent below on the midrib; stipules linear or subulate. Flowers purple in a loose, showy, paniculate cluster up to 40 cm long. Pedicels strigillose, to 5 mm long; corolla 1–12 mm long. Legume elliptic to oval, narrowed at both ends, 7–8 mm long, 1-seeded, indehiscent. June–Nov. Pied. and Coast. Pl. Roadsides, fields, power and fire lanes, pine plantations. Va. s to Fla. and Tex. Widely planted as a bob-white quail food and for erosion control. Introduced from Japan.

PURPLE-SESBAN   *Daubentonia punicea* (Cav.) DC.
Shrub to 3 m tall, with deep red to purple flowers. Leaves even pinnate, with 12–40 leaflets 1–3 cm long, deciduous. Racemes densely flowered, to 10 cm long, axillary; calyx tube 3–4 mm long, lobes 0.5–1 mm long; purplish red corolla 1.2–2.5 cm long, with keel petals tapering into the claw. Legume with a beak, stipitate, 5–8 cm long, coriaceous, 4-winged, constricted at intervals where several to numerous seeds are separated by partitions. June–Nov. Coast. Pl. Sandy waste places and in cultivated areas, roadside ditches. N.C. s to Fla. and Tex. (Plate 23).

The RATTLE-BUSH, *Daubentonia longifolia* (Cav.) DC., is similar but bears yellow flowers and the calyx lobes are acute with the keel petals abruptly narrowed into a claw. Legume long-stipitate. Coast. Pl. Fla. to Tex. Also called POISON BEAN because seeds are very poisonous to sheep and goats.

KUDZU   *Pueraria lobata* (Willd.) Ohwi
Climbing and trailing semiwoody vine up to 30 m long with trifoliate leaves and densely villous young stems. Panicles axillary, 0.5–3 dm long, densely appressed-pubescent; petals violet purple, usually tinged with bright scarlet; legumes 4–5 cm long, brownish-villous, soon dehiscent; fruiting infrequent. July–Oct. Mts., Pied., Coast. Pl. Road cuts and fills, abandoned mine lands, waste places. Pa. s to Fla. and Tex. Introduced from East Asia for erosion control and widely naturalized; often becoming a forest and utility line pest (Plate 23).

WISTERIA   *Wisteria frutescens* (L.) Poiret
Attractive low-climbing woody vine with racemes of light lavender flowers. Leaves deciduous odd-pinnate, usually with 5–7 pairs of leaflets. Flowers on short, stout pedicels; calyx 8–10 mm long, lower lobe shorter than the tube; lower spur of the wing much shorter than the claw; ovary and legume glabrous; club-shaped glands present on the rachis and calyx. Apr.–Sept. Coast. Pl. and Pied. Banks of creeks and rivers and along woodland borders. Va. and Md. s to Fla. and Tex. Now considered to include *Wisteria macrostachya* Nuttall, as the two taxa blend together.

Wisteria frutescens is an excellent flowering vine and is recommended for use

Pachysandra procumbens

Ceratiola ericoides

Cyrilla racemiflora

Cliftonia monophylla

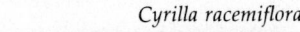

PLATE 25

Acer leucoderme

Cotinus obovatus

Toxicodendron radicans
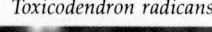

Toxicodendron quercifolia

PLATE 26

Rhus aromatica

Rhus glabra

Rhus typhina MILLER

Rhus copallina

PLATE 27

Illex cassine

Ilex opaca

Ilex myrtifolia

Ilex glabra

PLATE 28

Ilex verticillata GALLE

Nemopanthus mucronata MILLER

Celastrus orbiculatus

Ilex montana KRAKOW

PLATE 29

Euonymus americanus

Staphylea trifolia

Aesculus parviflora

Aesculus sylvatica

PLATE 30

Ampelopsis arborea

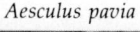

Aesculus pavia

Ceanothus americanus

Rhamnus caroliniana

PLATE 31

Vitis aestivalis   MOORE

Vitis rotundifolia

Vitis cinerea

Vitis vulpina

PLATE 32

over patios. Nowhere near as aggresive as the exotic Wisterias, this attractive vine performs best in moist, fertile soil. It is regrettable that *Wisteria frutescens* has not been used more often by southern gardeners (Plate 23).

Two other WISTERIAS, introduced from Asia and escaped from cultivation, are *Wisteria sinensis* (Sims) Sweet, the CHINESE WISTERIA, and *Wisteria floribunda* (Willd.) DC., the JAPANESE WISTERIA. The former has 7–13 leaflets, while the latter has 13–19 leaflets on the largest leaves. Both are high-climbing vines climbing by twining. Introduced WISTERIAS can become a nuisance.

CLAMMY LOCUST   *Robinia viscosa* Vent.

Deciduous shrub or small tree with pinnately compound leaves; twigs and flower stalks clammy and glandular-viscid with sessile or subsessile glands. Leaflets 12–27, 2–4 cm long. Racemes often pendant, to 1 dm long; flowers crowded; petals light rose to white with a yellow spot on the standard. Legume oblong, 5–8 mm long, glandular-bristly, bearing 5–10 seeds. May–Sept. Mts. and Pied. Rocky woods, hardwood slopes. Pa. and W. Va. s to Ga. and Ala. Includes var. *hartwigii* (Koehne) Ashe, a fruiting form known from N.C.

BRISTLY LOCUST   *Robinia hispida* L.

Shrub to 3 m tall, spreading from rhizomes and thicket-forming, covered with long, straight hairs and stiffer bristles on wood of the previous season. Leaves pinnately compound, to 3 dm long; leaflets 7–13, glabrous above and beneath, deciduous. Racemes of 3–6 odorless pink flowers. Stipular spines lacking but each leaflet bears a spine at the end of the midrib. Legume 5–8 cm long, densely hispid, with 3–5 seeds. May–Oct. Mts., Pied., Coast. Pl. Dry woods and slopes. Va. and W. Va. s to Fla. and Ala. (Plate 23).

A recent taxonomic revision of the LOCUSTS includes in *R. hispida,* the following: ELLIOTTS LOCUST, *Robinia elliottii* (Chapman) Ashe ex Small, *Robinia nana* Elliott, BOYNTONS LOCUST, *Robinia boyntonii* Ashe, and *Robinia kelseyi* Hutchinson. See Iseley & Peabody (1984).

The species of *Robinia* survive and do well along roadsides on steep fills and road cuts. They are quite showy when in flower and are useful in stabilizing banks. Bacteria live on the roots of these plants and fix atmospheric nitrogen so the supply of this essential growth element is increased. The pea-shaped flowers are attractive: both species have been cultivated for many years.

Another legume is a climbing woody vine, *Dioclea multiflora* (T. and G.) Mohr, with 3 leaflets, a racemelike panicle of purple flowers with standards 1.2–1.5 cm long; leaflets 6–15 cm long, blades oval or reniform. Coast. Pl. River and stream banks. Ky. s to Ga., La. and Ark.

RUTACEAE

TOOTHACHE TREE   *Zanthoxylum americanus* Miller

Colonial deciduous shrub to 3 m tall with pinnate leaves and stems with paired prickles near the leaf bases. Leaflets 7–13, ovate, sessile, 4–5 cm long, dotted, pubescent beneath. Flowers small, greenish, borne on wood of the previous season in sessile axillary cymes, appearing before the leaves; petals 4–5; pistils 2–5. Follicle red, 4–5 mm in diameter. Mar.–Aug. Mts. and Coast. Pl. Rich woods riverbanks, often on neutral or basic soils. Que. to N.D. s to Ga. and La. Uncommon to rare. The bark is used to relieve toothache.

The HERCULES'-CLUB, *Zanthoxylum clava-herculis* L., is a well-armed shrub or small tree covered with thornlike prickles on a raised corky base. Leaves 1–3 dm long, dotted. Leaflets ovate, 4–5 cm long, glabrous beneath. Flowers yellow-green, in large terminal cymes. Apr.–Sept. Coast. Pl. Sand dunes, shell deposits, woods, and hammocks. Va. s to Fla. and Tex. Chewing the bark leaves a peppery, burning sensation; has caused livestock poisoning.

The dark green foliage of the two species of *Zanthoxylum* is strikingly handsome. The yellow-green flowers appear before the leaves. *Zanthoxylum clava-herculis* is found on sand dunes along the coast and appears resistant to salt-spray damage. Its unusual growth habit and attractive foliage make it potentially useful in coastal landscaping.

WAFER-ASH   *Ptelea trifoliata* L.
Shrub or small tree with alternate, mostly trifoliate deciduous leaves. Leaflets 6–12 cm long, glabrous to densely pubescent beneath, sessile. Leaves resemble those of the AMERICAN BLADDERNUT, *Staphlea trifoliata* L., (STAPHYLEA-CEAE) with mostly opposite leaves. *Ptelea* flowers are greenish white, in terminal compound corymbs; sepals 1.5 mm long; petals 4–6 mm; samara waferlike, 2–2.5 cm long. Apr.–Aug. Mts., Pied., Coast. Pl. Rich woods, rocky riverbanks. Que. and Neb. s to Fla., Tex. and Mex. Forms of *Ptelea trifoliata* show striking variations. The species has been divided into several subspecies but intermediate forms are common (Plate 24).

This species bears curious light green waferlike fruits that contrast markedly with its dark green leaves. In autumn, the leaves turn yellow or yellow-green, making *Ptelea* a bright fall background at the rear of borders of lower shrubs or in the foreground of a dark Loblolly, Shortleaf, or Virginia Pine woods.

TRIFOLIATE ORANGE   *Poncirus trifoliata* (L.) Raf.
Shrub or small tree with long, (1–5 cm) pointed thorns and ternately compound leaves, green branches. Leaves deciduous, 3–10 cm long, trifoliate, petioles winged. Flowers in axillary fascicles on old wood; petals mostly 5, white. Fruit orange, berrylike, sour, pubescent. Mar.–Oct. Mts., Pied., Coast. Pl. Va. s to Fla., La., Tex. An escape about old house places. Used as a grafting stock for citrus (Plate 24).

Other species of citrus are the LIMEBERRY, *Triphasia trifolia* (Burman f.) P. Wilson, with 6–10 stamens, trifoliate leaves with toothed blades, Coast Pl., and the BITTER-SWEET ORANGE, *Citrus aurantium* L., with 1-foliate leaves and winged petioles, Coast. Pl., Fla. and Ga. The latter of Asian origin, the seeds brought in by the Spanish, later hybridized.

SIMAROUBACEAE

TREE OF HEAVEN   *Ailanthus altissima* Swingle.
Colonial shrub or small tree with staminate and pistillate flowers on separate plants. Leaves deciduous, odd-pinnate, with 15–35 leaflets. Flowers small, yellow-green, in large terminal panicles; staminate flowers ill-scented. Fruit a winged samara, with a seed in the center. May–Oct. Mts. and Pied. Roadsides, woods, and waste places. Mass. to Ia. s to Ga.

Introduced from Asia and becoming a pest, as it coppices freely. Fast-growing, wood used in cabinetmaking.

EUPHORBIACEAE

ALABAMA CROTON
Croton alabamensis E. A. Smith

An evergreen shrub to 3 m tall, with leaf blades elliptic-lanceolate to elliptic, 6–12 cm long, glabrate above with silvery imbricated scales beneath. Stems with white or grayish bark. Petioles and twigs also silvery scaled. Flowers in terminal racemes, staminate above, pistillate below. Capsule 6–8 mm long; seed oval, 5–7 mm long. Appalachian Plateau. Thinly wooded river bluffs on shale and limestone. Tenn., Ala. Rare. May grow so densely that colonies are known as "privet brakes" (Plate 24).

A handsome and interesting shrub, useful as a specimen or in a mass planting. This plant is greatly underused and should be propagated by nurserymen.

CORKWOOD
Stillingia aquatica Chapman

Shrub to 2 m tall, with stout stems and wood lighter than cork. Branches reddish or purplish, more or less glaucous. Leaves alternate, finely crenate, the teeth pointed, callous. Leaves 3–8 cm long, cuneate, some usually overwintering; petioles 1–4 mm long. Flowers in a terminal yellow, green or sometimes red, spike, the rachis with many glands smaller than the bracts; flowers unisexual. Capsule 5–6 mm long, with coarse seeds 4–4.5 mm across, silver-gray, with pinnaclelike tubercles. May–Sept. Coast. Pl. Flatwoods ponds, ditches, shallow water. S.C. s to Fla., Ala. and Miss.

CHINESE TALLOW TREE
Sapium sebiferum (L.) Roxb.

A large shrub to small tree, with broad rhombic-ovate leaf blades, 3–9 cm long, with long-acuminate tips. Plant glabrous throughout, with milky sap. Leaves alternate, deciduous, stipulate, a pair of glands where the petiole meets the blade. Flowers without petals; staminate flowers numerous, borne on fascicles with as many as 15 blossoms; pistillate flowers few, solitary. Fruit a 3-locular capsule; seeds white. Coast. Pl. Waste places, shores, uplands. N.C. s to Fla. and Tex. Introduced from China and escaped from cultivation. The waxy seeds are used to make candles (Plate 24).

SEBASTIAN-BUSH
Sebastiania fruticosa (Bartram) Fernald

Shrub to 2.5 m high with entire elliptic to oval leaves ciliate toward the apex and on the base of the blade, borne on petioles 1 cm or less in length. The leaf with a pair of glandular stipules at the base of the petiole. Racemes green or yellowish, 1–4 cm long, shorter than the leaves, with 1–5 pistillate flowers below numerous staminate ones. Sepals 3; petals absent; stamens 3; stigmas 3. Fruit a 3-sided capsule, seeds subglobose, 4–5 mm long. May–Oct. Coast. Pl. Swamps, stream banks, hammocks, and pocosins. N.C. s to Fla. and Tex.

ANDRACHNE
Andrachne phyllanthoides (Nuttall) Muell-Arg.

A small, straggling, much-branched shrub up to 1 m high, nearly glabrous, with oval to broadly obovate membranaceous leaf blades 1–2.5 cm long on short petioles. Inflorescence of axillary-solitary, monoecious, pedicellate flowers. Fruit dry, splitting into three, 2-valved carpels. July–Oct. Limestone soils or washes of rocky stream beds. Ala., Mo., Ark., Tex., Okla. Rare.

BUXACEAE

ALLEGHANY SPURGE
Pachysundra procumbens Michx.

Evergreen semishrub with stems 1–2 dm in length which die following development of new growth. Leaves grouped near the stem apex, in winter green mottled with purple; blades 5–8 cm long, coarsely serrate. Flowers white in dense spikes. Apr. Usually in fertile and moist soils. Ky. and N.C. s to Fla. and La. (Plate 25).

A highly desirable evergreen groundcover, more attractive than the commonly grown *P. terminalis* Siebold and Zucc. The ALLEGHANY SPURGE forms a soft carpet of gray-green mottled leaves in shaded situations. It appears free from dieback, scale, or leaf spot which sometimes infect *P. terminalis*. It should be propagated, widely promoted and planted in our gardens.

EMPETRACEAE

SANDHILL ROSEMARY
Ceratiola ericoides Michaux

Evergreen, aromatic shrub, resembling a heath, to 1.5 cm tall; bark rough, brownish. Leaf blades almost tubular, appearing needlelike, in crowded whorls; petioles short, yellow. Reddish or yellowish flowers in axillary clusters of 2 or 3; sepals 2, about 1 mm long; petals 2; stamens 2. Drupes red or yellow, subglobose, 2–3 mm in diameter. Nov. Coast. Pl. Sand dunes, sand hills, scrub, soils often acid. S.C. s to Fla. and Miss. Easily destroyed by fire (Plate 25).

CYRILLACEAE

TITI
Cyrilla racemiflora L.

Large, semi-evergreen shrub with thick, membranous, oblanceolate leaves with rolled edges, lustrous above. Leaves partly evergreen, to 10 cm long and 2.5 cm wide, short petioled, with lateral reticulate veinlets on both surfaces. Slender racemes to 15 cm long, on the preceding year's growth; pedicels 1–2.5 mm long; sepals 5, lanceolate, white, keeled, to 1.5 mm long; stamens 5. Fruit a brown or olive drupe about 2.5 mm long, ovoid. May–Oct. Coast. Pl. Swamps, stream banks, and bay forests. Va. s to Fla. and Tex. (Plate 25).

The drooping flower clusters of the TITI are showy and make this an unusual shrub for naturalistic plantings. It will do well if grown in moist soil, in full sun, along streams, ditches, and ponds.

BUCKWHEAT-BUSH
Cliftonia monophylla Gaertner

A shrub or small tree to 8 m tall, often forming dense thickets or stands. Bark dark and scaly. Leaves leathery, evergreen, thick and glossy, dark green above, with a pale and chalky bloom beneath, especially with age; petioles short, 2.5–10 cm long. Racemes 1 to several at the summit of twigs of the previous season, terminal or axillary; flowers fragrant; sepals unequal; petals 5, pink or white, clawed at the base; stamens 10. Anthers orange-colored. Fruit a winged corky drupe. May–Sept. Coast. Pl. Swamps, bays, acid bogs, Ga. to Fla., La. The flowers are an important source of honey (Plate 25).

A beautiful shrub with shiny leaves and clusters of attractive white to pinkish flowers that are followed by yellowish buckwheatlike fruits. *Cliftonia* prefers full sun and moist soils and can be planted along streams, on the shores of ponds, or in low seepages.

ACERACEAE

CHALK MAPLE   *Acer leucoderme* Small

Large deciduous shrub or small tree with 3 or more basal stems, whitish bark, 3-lobed acute to acuminate leaves yellow-green below, pubescent or glabrate, broader than long. Flowers terminal, appearing with the leaves; fruits reddish to tan, mature in midsummer. Pied. Rocky woods, river bluffs. Va. s to Fla. and Tex.

The leaves are a brilliant red in autumn and in the Georgia Piedmont the CHALK MAPLE puts on a fall color display that is dazzling to the eye. The shrublike trees vary from yellow-orange to deep crimson. It is tolerant of dry soils and performs best at the edge of woodlands. A species that is definitely underused (Plate 26).

Two species of MAPLE from the higher mountain elevations of the Southeast are *Acer spicatum* Lam., the MOUNTAIN MAPLE, with flowers in an erect panicle and bark not striped, and *Acer pensylvanicum* L., the STRIPED MAPLE, with flowers in a pendulous raceme and with striped bark. Both species occur south from New England along the mountains into Georgia.

ANACARDIACEAE

SMOKE-TREE   *Cotinus obovatus* Raf.

Deciduous shrub or small tree with broadly ovate, simple, alternate leaves; twigs purple at first, turning dark orange; bark gray, furrowed, scaly on surface. Flowers in loose panicles with plumose branches; heartwood orange. Ga., Ala., and Tenn., Mo., Ark., Okla., Tex. Named for the smokelike appearance of the fruiting sprays (Plate 26).

The bluish green leaves of the SMOKE-TREE become yellow to orange, red or purple in the fall. In spring the plumose branches become smoky pink in color and in winter the bark is a beautiful gray to gray-brown. The SMOKE-TREE often is used as a single specimen for accent in the landscape but is perhaps better used when massed or grouped.

POISON SUMAC   *Toxicodendron vernix* (L.) Kuntze

A deciduous shrub or small tree with pinnately compound leaves, of 7–13 oblanceolate to elliptic, glabrous leaflets. Flowers in axillary panicles. Fruit a grayish white drupe, 4–6 mm broad. May–Sept. Coast. Pl. Pied., Mts. Swamps, bays, and pocosins. Me. to Ind. s to Fla. and Tex. Contact poison. Avoid any Sumac in swampy habitat with entire leaves, grayish white berries and axillary flower clusters.

POISON IVY   *Toxicodendron radicans* (L.) Kuntze

Climbing vine with many adventitious roots with 3-leaflet leaves that are thin, deciduous, glabrous, and often shining above, pubescent on the veins beneath. Flowers in axillary panicles. Fruit a grayish white glabrous drupe, sometimes short-pubescent, 4–6 mm in diameter. Apr.–Oct. Mts., Pied., Coast. Pl. Woodlands, fencerows, waste places. N.S. to Minn. s to Fla. and Tex. The poison is an oil, toxicodendrol (Plate 26).

The POISON OAK, *Toxicodendron quercifolia* (Michaux) Greene, is an erect plant, with thick, densely pubescent, often oaklike leaves. The fruit is a yellowish white drupe, densely pubescent when young, 5–7 mm in diameter. Flowers are greenish white in dense panicles. Apr.–Oct. Pied. and Coast. Pl. Thickets, old fields, woodlands, dry sites. N.J. s to Fla., Tex. and Okla. (Plate 26).

FRAGRANT SUMAC   *Rhus aromatica* Aiton.

Upright, low-thickety nonpoisonous shrub to 2 m tall resembling Poison Oak. Deciduous leaves with 3 leaflets, pubescent when young, later glabrous, the terminal leaflet sessile. Flowers yellowish green in small clusters, produced before the leaves. Fruit a densely hairy scarlet drupe. Feb.–June. Pied. Roadbanks, dry rocky sites, often associated with igneous or basic rocks. Que. and Vt. s to Fla., Tex., Okla. The plant is aromatic (Plate 27).

This low-growing shrub bears orange to reddish leaves in the fall, especially colorful when grown on dry sites. It is an excellent choice for planting on road cuts and fills and other sloping areas where it aids in control of soil erosion.

COMMON SUMAC   *Rhus glabra* L.

Rhizomatous shrub or small tree to 6 m tall. Leaves deciduous, pinnately compound, with 11–20 sessile leaflets. Rachis not winged, branchlets strongly angled, leaflets serrate to the base. Plant glabrous and glaucous. Greenish white flowers are in dense terminal panicles to 2 dm long. Drupes red, densely pubescent, 3–4 mm in diameter. May–Oct. Mts., Pied., Coast. Pl. Roadsides, fencerows, abandoned fields. Me. to B.C. s to Fla., Tex. Seeds used by many birds, perhaps to secure small grubs inside (Plate 27).

Also called the SMOOTH SUMAC, this plant forms colonies and grows luxuriantly wherever the soil has been disturbed, so it is especially suited to mass plantings on sloping road cuts and fills. It bears velvet red fruit in late summer, and the leaves turn early in the fall to a bright red. It is a species at its best on dry, poor-quality soils; its landscape value has long been overlooked.

The WINGED SUMAC, *Rhus copallina* L., also is a deciduous rhizomatous shrub but the stems are densely short-pubescent, the leaflets number 7–21, and the rachis is winged. July–Oct. Mts., Pied., Coast. Pl. Fencerows, thickets, old fields. Me. to Ill. s to Fla. and Tex. (Plate 27).

A species, like other sumacs, valuable for poor soils of low moisture; one that requires little attention but produces masses of reddish fall color.

The STAGHORN SUMAC, *Rhus typhina* L., is a larger rhizomatous shrub or small tree with densely pubescent branches and petioles. Leaflets glabrous, glaucous beneath, rachis not winged. Terminal panicles to 3.5 dm long, conelike, of greenish white flowers; fruit are soft-bristly drupes in velvety maroon, dense clusters; May–Sept. Mts. Meadows and borders. N.S. and S.D. s to Ga., Ala.

This picturesque sumac tolerates dry, sterile soils producing heads of red fruit in summer and yellow to crimson vegetative color in the fall. Like other sumacs, it can be rejuvenated by cutting back to the ground in winter (Plate 27).

The rare MICHAUX'S SUMAC, *Rhus michauxii* Sargent, is a dwarf rhizomatous pubescent shrub. Pied. and Coast. Pl. Sandy or rocky woods. N.C., S.C., Ga. Endangered.

AQUIFOLIACEAE

YAUPON   *Ilex vomitoria* Aiton.

Large evergreen shrub with crenate leaves and usually bright red fruit; Twigs puberulent. Leaves leathery, margins revolute, oval to elliptic, to 3 cm long; petioles short, broad and grooved; drupe globose, 4–6 mm in diameter. Mar.–Nov. Maritime forests, sandhills, Va. s to Fla. and Tex. Leaves used as tea, high in caffeine. An easily grown holly that is suitable for screening, hedges, specimens, or barrier plantings. Scarlet fruits are borne in large quantities on the fast-growing plants. Commonly planted for landscaping, and several cultivars have been selected. Among them are 'Folsoms Weeping' and 'Pendula', weeping forms; 'Nana' and 'Schellings Dwarf', dwarf, compact forms.

The DAHOON, *Ilex cassine* L., also is an evergreen shrub or small tree with a usually bright red drupe, leaves at least 1.5 mm in diameter. May–Nov. Coast. Pl. Bogs, cypress ponds, bays, pocosins. Ur common. N.C. s to Fla. and Tex. (Plate 28).

Of importance to horticulture because of the hybrids selected from crosses of *Ilex cassine* with *Ilex opaca*, the AMERICAN HOLLY. The former seldom is grown in American gardens but it has contributed genes to a number of economically important cultivars, including 'Fosteri', 'East Palatka' and 'Savannah'. It is tolerant of salt spray.

The AMERICAN HOLLY, *Ilex opaca* Aiton, with spiny-margined teeth, often is found in shrublike habit (Plate 28).

The MYRTLE HOLLY, *Ilex myrtifolia* Walter, has leaves not more than 0.8 cm wide. It is reputed to hybridize with *Ilex cassine* (Plate 28).

INKBERRY   *Ilex glabra* (L.) Gray.
An evergreen rhizomatous shrub with black drupes and pubescent twigs. Leaves elliptic to obovate with margins with 1–3 appressed-crenate teeth near the apex, not spinulose, deep green and lustrous above, with punctate glands beneath, to 6.5 cm long; petioles 3–8 mm long, canescent. Pedicels 1–5 mm long. Drupe 5–7 mm in diameter. May–Nov. Coast. Pl. Savannas and pine barrens. N.S. s to Fla. and Tex. (Plate 28).

This species is characterized by light green foliage and dark black fruits. It can be used for foundation plantings or for massing. Several cultivars have been selected, including 'Compactor', a dwarf selection; 'Ivory Queen' and 'Leucocarpa', both with white fruit; and 'Nigra', which has purplish foliage in winter.

The LARGE GALLBERRY, *Ilex coriacea* (Pursh) Chapman, has evergreen leaf blades with entire margins or with a few bristlelike teeth. The fruit is black, 6–9 mm in diameter. Apr.–Oct. Swamps, pocosins, and bays. Va. s to Fla. and Tex.

Taller growing than *I. glabra*, *I. coriacea* has darker green leaves and larger fruit than the INKBERRY. Attempts should be made to select cultivars from this species. It has been overlooked by the nursery industry.

POSSUM HAW   *Ilex decidua* Walter.
Large shrub or small tree with deciduous leaves, blades predominately oblanceolate, strongly cuneate basally, margins appressed-crenate, the teeth gland tipped. Flowers pedicellate, in sessile clusters. Drupes scarlet, lustrous, 6–8 mm in diameter, on stalks 3–5 mm long, persisting after leaf fall into the winter. Apr.–Oct. Pied. and Coast. Pl. Upland woods and thickets. Md. and Ill. s to Fla. and Tex.

The orange to scarlet fruits ripen in October and may persist over winter. This species is useful in an informal shrub border at the edge of woods. It grows particularly well under partial shade in good soils. Several cultivars have been named including 'Reed' and 'Warrens Red', both of which are heavy fruiting.

Ilex longipes Chapman, the GEORGIA HOLLY, has fruiting stalks 1–2.3 cm long.

Ilex amelanchier M.A. Curtis, the SARVIS HOLLY, is a large shrub with deciduous leathery leaves, pubescent above, and predominetely reticulate veined beneath, the veins distinctly raised; staminate flowers clustered; the pistillate solitary; drupe dull red, 8–9 mm in diameter. Apr.–Nov. Coast. Pl. Stream banks, swamp forests, river flood plains. N.C. s to Fla. and Tex. Rare.

WINTERBERRY   *Ilex verticillata* (L.) Gray
Tall shrub with deciduous leaves, greenish white staminate and pistillate flowers on pedicels of about equal length; flowers in short-stalked whorls in the leaf axils; sepals ciliate. Drupe bright red, 5–7 mm in diameter. Apr.–Nov. Pied. Coast. Pl, Mts. Wet woods, bogs, streamsides, springheads. Also called "Black Alder" from the color of the autumn leaves. N.S. to Minn. s to Fla., Miss., and Ark. (Plate 29).
The clusters of bright red fruit ripening in early autumn and persisting into late winter make this an excellent plant for massing in large plantings especially along garden borders. So outstandingly showy are its fruits, it is a shrub every gardener should grow. Among the better cultivars are 'Sparkleberry', 'Winter Red', and 'Christmas Cheer'.
The SMOOTH WINTERBERRY, *Ilex laevigata* (Pursh) Gray., is similar, but the sepals are not ciliate and the drupe usually is orange-red. Coast. Pl. Va. to Ga. *Ilex ambigua* (Michaux) Torrey, is a highly variable deciduous holly of upland woods, often in xeric habitats. It has membraneous and only faintly rugose leaf blades. Pied. Coast. Pl. W. Va. s to Ga., Ala. LARGELEAF HOLLY, *Ilex montana* T. and G., is woolly with large leaves. Mass. to Tex. (Plate 29).

MOUNTAIN HOLLY   *Nemopanthus mucronata* (L.) Trel.
Erect, much branched shrub to 3 m. Leaves deciduous, obtuse, mucronate, to 5 cm long, margins entire or remotely serrate. Flowers bisexual or unisexual; pedicels long and slender; petals 4–5, yellowish; stamens 4–5. Drupe red, with 4–5 bony nutlets. May. Mts. Damp woods, bog margins. N.S. and Wis. s to W. Va. and Ind. A northern species. Uncommon (Plate 29).
Related is *Nemopanthus collinus* (Alexander) Clark, with acuminate leaves, glandular at the tip, with glandular-serrate margins. Moist areas. Mts. W. Va., Va., N.C. Some authorities place *N. collinus* in *Ilex.*
The MOUNTAIN HOLLY is a densely branched, neatly constituted shrub native to cool, damp upland woods. It has abundant light green leaves, ashen gray branches and twigs and crimson red berries.

CELASTRACEAE

BITTERSWEET   *Celastrus scandens* L.
Deciduous woody vine with alternate leaves and a panicle of numerous small green flowers at the branch tips. Leaves 5–11 cm long, 3–7 cm wide. crenulate, smooth on both sides; petioles 1–2 cm long. Sepals, petals and stamens 5. Fruit in drooping clusters of 3-valved orange to scarlet capsule bursting to display the scarlet, long-persisting arils. May–Sept. Mts. Rocky woodland slopes. Que. to Man. s to Ga. and Ala. The roots are used medicinally and the plant for decorations.
An Asian introduction, *Celastrus orbiculatus* Thunberg., usually has 2–3 flowers in short axillary cymes. N.Y. so to Ala. (Plate 29).
Celastrus scandens is a vigorous vine that can engulf other plants. It should be planted in poor sites so it will not overgrow its bounds. It is best used in rough places over rocks or on old fences or in waste corners of the garden. Its fruits are used in flower arrangements.

MOUNTAIN-LOVER   *Paxistima canbyi* Gray.

Low, decumbent, rhizomatous shrub with evergreen opposite leaves and small green flowers solitary or in fascicles in the leaf axils. Leaves 0.5–2.5 cm long, linear to linear-oblong, obtuse, serrate and smooth, with very short petioles. Sepals and stamens 4. Capsule 2-celled, the arils white. Apr.–Sept. Mts. Calcareous rocks, slopes. W. Va. Introduced to N.C. Rare. *Paxistima* is a neat evergreen ground cover but one rarely seen in gardens. Not recommended for the deep south.

STRAWBERRY BUSH   *Euonymus americanus* L.

An erect to somewhat straggling shrub to 2 m tall with green stems and branches, and thin, lanceolate to ovate, subsessile, opposite, deciduous leaves. Flowers 1–3, usually terminal on axillary peduncles; petals 5, light apple green. Capsules are muricate or warty, red, and split open to expose scarlet seeds when ripe; when dry, the capsule and seeds are black. May–Oct. Mts., Pied., Coast. Pl. Woods, ravines, and stream sides. N.Y. to Ill. s to Fla. and Tex. The seeds are used by wild turkeys, and the leaves and stems by deer and rabbits (Plate 30).

The STRAWBERRY BUSH is useful in the landscape in a natural woodsy setting. It will withstand dense shade, but fruits best in very light shade. It is the fruit that elicits interest, focusing attention on what otherwise might be a rather obscure plant. The warty, scarlet capsules never fail to attract attention when they open to expose the scarlet seeds. During early summer the delicate, graceful, symmetric and diminutive yellow-green flowers look ready to be picked and carried by a child's doll.

The RUNNING-STRAWBERRY BUSH, *Euonymus obovatus* Nuttall., is similar but has trailing and decumbent stems. Mts. N.Y. and Mich. s to N.C., Ga. Rare.

BURNING-BUSH   *Euonymus atropurpureus* Jacquin

Shrubs to 6 m tall with opposite, deciduous, long-petioled leaves 5–12 cm long; blades elliptic to ovate-oblong, abruptly pointed, thin. Flowers dark purple, 6–8 mm broad, in cymes; sepals and petals usually 4. Capsule smooth, purple, irregularly 4-lobed; seeds brown, not exposed when ripe. May–Oct. Mts. and Pied. Rich woods. Ont. to Mont. s to Fla. and Tex. Indians used the bark as a cathartic.

STAPHYLEACEAE

BLADDERNUT   *Staphylea trifolia* L.

Deciduous shrub or small tree to 5 m with long-petioled, opposite, 3-foliate leaves. Flowers perfect, white, in axillary or terminal panicles. Pedicels jointed; sepals, petals and stamens 5. Fruit a large bladdery inflated capsule. Apr.–Sept. Mts. and Pied. Rich woods, stream banks. Que. to Minn. s to Ga. and Ala. The 1–4 hard seeds in the bristle-tipped bladder are a favorite food of woodland mice.

The inflated balloonlike fruit and attractive green foliage of the BLADDERNUT can add interest to the landscape. For best effect, use this shrub in the shade at the edge of natural woodland settings or at the rear of the shrub border. It is easy to transplant and makes a fine appearance (Plate 30).

HIPPOCASTANACEAE

YELLOW OR GEORGIA BUCKEYE   *Aesculus sylvatica* Bartram.

Deciduous shrub or small tree with opposite, palmately compound leaves; leaflets 8–16 cm long, to 7 cm wide. Pedicels tomentose, the trichomes glandless;

calyx companulate; petals yellow-green to pinkish; stamens 6–7, usually shorter than the lateral petals. Capsule leathery, with dark lines separating the larger appressed scales, less than 4 cm broad; seeds large, brown and smooth. Apr.–Aug. Pied. Rich woods and stream banks. Va. s to Ga. and Ala. (Plate 30).

The chief landscape value of *Aesculus sylvatica* is it use in shady, mesic woodlands, where is at home on slopes and bluffs.

The BOTTLE-BRUSH BUCKEYE, *Aesculus parviflora* Walter, is a graceful colonial shrub growing to nearly 5 m tall. Leaves deciduous, with 5–7 toothed leaflets. Flowers white, small, in an erect spike resembling a bottle brush; stamens longer than the lateral petals. Capsules to 3 cm in diameter. Coast. Pl. and Pied. S.C. to Fla. and Ala. Low woods. Rare. Often grown as an ornamental (Plate 30).

An excellent plant for massing, or as a single specimen plant; it stands out when in flower. It is used to best advantage in full sun or light shade at a woodland border. When grown alone, it makes a broad, spreading specimen with upright spikes of flowers resembling tall candles.

RED BUCKEYE   *Aesculus pavia* L.
Deciduous shrub or small tree to 4 m high with red flowers. Leaflets usually 5, obovate to oblanceolate; calyx tubular, swollen on one side; petals stipitate-glandular on the margin; stamens longer than the lateral petals. Capsule usually more than 4 cm broad. Apr.–Aug. Coast. Pl. N.C. s to Fla., Tex. and Ark. The seeds are poisonous to cattle. Hybrids are known between *A. sylvatica* and *A. pavia;* the flowers are a blend of red and yellow (Plate 31).

Although at its finest in full sun, it will flower in dense shade. It grows well in fertile, moist, well-drained soil. In full sun it takes on a treelike form or becomes a round-topped shrub. The landscape value is for massing or clumping along woodlands or as shrub borders. Several cultivars have been selected but are seldom available.

SAPINDACEAE

WESTERN SOAPBERRY   *Sapindus saponaria* L. var. *drummondi* (H. & A.) L.
Berson
A large shrub to tree with 4–9 pairs of pinnately compound leaves with winged leaf rachises and small white flowers in a large panicle. Fruit globose, 1–2 cm. in diameter. Limestone bluffs. Mo. s to La., Tex. and Mex. Contains large quantities of saponin, once used as a fish poison.

RHAMNACEAE

BUCKTHORN   *Rhamnus lanceolata* Pursh
Deciduous shrub to 2 m tall with alternate elliptic to elliptic-lanceolate leaves; blades 2–9 cm long, fine-toothed, downy and light green beneath with 7–9 pairs of veins. Flowers 4-merous, in axillary clusters, expanding with the leaves. Drupe globose, black, 6 mm in diameter; nutlets 2, grooved. Plant unarmed. May. Coast. Pl. Pa. and Ohio s to Ala. and Tex.

The ALDER-LEAVED BUCKTHORN, *Rhamnus alnifolia* L'Her., has unisexual 5-merous flowers and crenate-serrate leaves which are glabrate beneath. Mts. Nfld. to B.C. s to W. Va. and Tenn. Rare.

CAROLINA BUCKTHORN   *Rhamnus caroliniana* Walter
    Deciduous shrub with alternate leaves 5–12 cm long, elliptic or occasionally
obovate, with 8–10 pairs of veins and faintly toothed or entire margins. Flowers 5-
merous, green, perfect, appearing after the leaves; petals shorter than the sepals;
the berrylike drupe is at first red, then black, sweet, 3-seeded, ungrooved. Plant
unarmed. May–Oct. Pied. Coast. Pl. Moist deciduous woods, or on alluvial soils.
Va. and Ohio so to Fla., Tex. and Mo. (Plate 31).
    This species is quite handsome in fruit and would appear to have possibilities
in the landscape. However, a word of caution, it self-sows and becomes as weedy
as privet hedge—care should be exercised in planting this native species.
    R. frangula. Introduced.

RATTAN-VINE   *Berchemia scandens* (Hill) K. Koch.
    A woody climbing vine with alternate, oval to elliptic-lanceolate, deciduous
leaves, 3–7 cm long, pinnately veined, the lateral veins nearly straight, evenly
spaced and parallel. Flower cluster a terminal thyrse or panicle. Flowers green or
greenish white, inconspicuous, 5-merous. Fruit an ellipsoidal blue-black drupe 6
mm long. Apr.–Oct. Coast. Pl. Moist woods, river bottoms. Va. s to Fla. and Tex.,
Mo. The principal stems may reach a diameter of 18 cm.

BUCKTHORN   *Sageretia minutiflora* (Michaux) Mohr
    Straggling shrub with slender stem to 3 m tall, with many short, pubescent
branches ending in thorns. Leaves deciduous opposite, ovate-lanceolate, finely
serrate, glabrescent, 1–4 cm long. Flowers white, scented, 5-merous; petals orbicular, ovate, about half as long as the sepals. Drupe subglobose, 7–9 mm in diameter,
Coast. Pl. Along the coast on shell mounds, sand dunes. S.C. to Fla. and Miss. Rare.
    Zizyphus jujuba Mill., is a large introduced shrub with spiny branches, incon-
spicuous flowers and a pulpy, edible drupe, red to black, 1.5–2.5 cm long. Coast. Pl.
Ala. to La.

NEW JERSEY TEA   *Ceanothus americanus* L.
    Deciduous shrub to 1 m tall, with leaves 3-nerved from the base; blades 2–9
cm long. Flowers white, borne on leafless peduncles on leafy shoots of the season.
Apr.–July. Mts., Pied., Coast. Pl. Me. to Man. s to Fla. and Ala. Leaves and roots were
used medicinally and for tea during the Revolution, and a lotion from leaves is sup-
posed to remove freckles (Plate 31).
    The showy white flowers of this low shrub make it ideal for massing in low-
maintenance naturalistic landscapes in light shade or at the edge of woodlands. It
thrives in poor dry soil and transplants readily. The plume-like white flower
clusters make quite a show when the massed plants cover barren areas.

RED ROOT   *Ceanothus herbaceous* Raf.
    Shrub, with leaves 3-nerved from the base; blades narrowly elliptic or oblong-
lanceolate, 1.5–6 cm long, deciduous. Flower clusters terminating the leafy shoots
of the season. Que. to Colo. s to Ark., Tex., and Mex. The LITTLE LEAF RED ROOT,
Ceanothus microphyllus Michaux., has leaves 3-nerved from the base; leaf-blades 3–
8 mm long and entire; a green to yellow stem. Coast. Pl. Dry pinelands and sandhills. Ga. to Fla. and Ala.

VITACEAE*

PEPPERVINE   *Ampelopsis arborea* L.

Woody vine with leaf blades bipinnate, or partly tripinnate, toothed, deciduous, green and lustrous above, reticulate veined beneath. Flowers 5-merous, borne in clusters much shorter than the leaves in compact subumbellate groupings. Drupes blue-black, 6–10 mm in diameter. June–Oct. Coast. Pl. Swamps. Va. and Ill. s to Fla and Tex. (Plate 31).

Seldom cultivated, the PEPPERVINE has reddish purple fall color and is quite beautiful in fruit. Used in full sun, this vine can be effectively integrated into the landscape by growing it on fence or near rock outcrops it can cover.

The CORDATE CISSUS, *Ampelopsis cordata* Michaux., has simple unlobed leaves and first-year stems are glabrous. The pith is white. Pied. Riverbanks and woods. Va. and Ill. s to Fla. and Tex.

An escape from cultivation is *Ampelopsis brevipedunculata* (Maxim) Trautv. with a pubescent first-year stem and simple, but usually lobed, leaves. Mass. s to N.C. and Ga. Rare.

Another escape is *Ampelopsis aconitifolia* Bunge, with glabrous stems and leaves palmately 3–5–parted. N.C.

MARINE IVY   *Cissus trifoliata* L.

Fleshy to woody vine with warty stems, sprawling over shrubs and small trees; young stems succulent to subsucculent, pith white; leaves deeply 3-lobed or with 3 leaflets on stout petiolules, succulent to subsucculent, evergreen, margins coarsely dentate. Flowers small, green, in a 3-parted cyme. Inedible berry 6–12 mm long, black. May–July. Coast. Pl. Salt marshes, maritime woodlands, and rocky inland woods. Fla. to Ark., Tex., Mo., and Ariz. Uncommon to rare.

May be confused with the Asian *Cayratia japonica* (Thunb.) Gagnepain, an uncommon herbaceous, not succulent, escape with compound leaves with 3–5 leaflets. Coast. Pl. La.

VIRGINIA CREEPER   *Parthenocissus quinquefolia* (L.) Planchon

Tree-top climbing vine with palmately compound leaves, usually with adhesive, disk-bearing tendrils, or sometimes coiling; twigs and tendrils glabrous; pith white. Leaves glabrous above to sparsely pubescent beneath; leaflets 3–7, usually 5, stalked, 5–15 cm long, acute or acuminate, coarsely toothed, scarlet in autumn. Flowers in a panicle of cymes; petals 5, yellow-green, 2–3 mm long. Berries blue, 6–9 mm in diameter, inedible. Twigs, tendrils, and leaves glabrous. May–Aug. Mts., Pied., Coast. Pl. Woods, thickets, sand dunes. Me. to Minn. s to Fla. and Tex.

The gorgeous reddish purple fall color of VIRGINIA CREEPER makes this native vine an excellent candidate for use as a groundcover or climber on trees or masonry walls.

Plants with pubescent twigs, tendrils, and leaves have been considered as *Parthenocissus hirsuta* (Donn.) Small.

An Asian ornamental with pubescent 3-lobed leaves and leaves of the basal sprouts 3-foliate is BOSTON IVY, *Parthenocissus tricuspidata* Planchon. Often seen on rock and brick walls.

*contributed by Mike Moore, University of Georgia.

MUSCADINE   *Vitis rotundifolia* Michaux

High climbing or trailing vines with adherent bark and prominent lenticels; simple tendrils, a tendril or inflorescence present at only two consecutive nodes; brown pith continuous through the node; branchlets of the season usually glabrous. Mature leaves simple, cordate, unlobed to shallowly 3-lobed, glabrous beneath except at axils and along veins, deciduous. Berries 1–2.5 cm in diameter, purple except golden green in plants commonly called SCUPPERNONGS. May–Oct. Mts., Pied., Coast. Pl. Swamps, riversides, woods, rocky and sandy areas. W. Va. s to Fla., Tex., and Mo. Many cultivars developed for home use, some for commercial juice and wines. An important wildlife food (Plate 32).

This woody vine may be used in landscaping when grown on an arbor in the yard or along rustic fences marking the edge of a bed of annuals. It will provide both shade under the arbor and, wherever grown, enjoyable fruit.

DOWNY OR SWEET WINTER GRAPE   *Vitis cinerea* Engelm. ex Millardet

Vine, mature bark shredding, lenticels absent or inconspicuous; tendrils forked, a tendril or inflorescence present at only 2 consecutive nodes; branchlets of the season covered by dense, short, straight hairs; branchlets angled in cross section, with brown pith interrupted at nodal diaphragms, nodes not glaucous. Leaves deciduous cordate, unlobed to 3-lobed, simple, crenate, not glaucous beneath but with whitish cobwebby hairs and short straight hairs along the veins and in their axils. Berries 0.4–0.9 cm in diameter, black. June–Oct. Rich bottomlands. Mississippi Basin. Ill. s to Tenn., Tex. Disjunct colonies in Ala., Fla. (Plate 32). The var. *floridana* Munson differs by more dense cobwebby hairs on lower leaf surfaces; branchlets of the season only slightly angled, covered with dense cobwebby hairs. Coast. Pl. Va. s to Fla. and Ala.

FOX GRAPE   *Vitis labrusca* L.

Woody vine with bark on the older stems shredding; lenticels absent or inconspicuous, tendrils forked; a tendril or inflorescence present at 3 or more consecutive nodes; branchlets of the season terete, glabrous or with cobwebby hairs, black prickles, pith brown, interrupted at the nodes, nodes not glaucous. Leaves deciduous, cordate, unlobed or 3-lobed, simple, crenate to dentate, with a dense matting of rusty, tawny to whitish, cobwebby hairs beneath. Berries 1–2.5 cm in diameter, purple to black. May–Oct. Mts. and Pied. Rich woods and stream banks. Me. to Ill. s to Ga. and Ala. This grape has a tendency to trail more than to twine. From it, many American-cultivated grapes, such as the Concord and Catawba, have been derived.

The MUSTANG GRAPE, *Vitis mustangensis* Buckley., has hairs on the underside of the leaves whitish to cream colored; leaves sometimes deeply 5-lobed; tendrils present at only two consecutive nodes; stipules 2–3 mm long. Coast. Pl. Ala. La. Rare.

The CALUSA GRAPE, *Vitis shuttleworthii* House, is similar but has minute stipules less than 1 mm long and promptly deciduous.

PIGEON GRAPE, SUMMER GRAPE   *Vitis aestivalis* Michaux

Vine with mature bark shredding on older stems, lenticels absent or inconspicuous; tendrils forked, a tendril or inflorescence present at only 2 consecutive nodes; branches of the season terete, glabrous with cobwebby hairs, pith brown, interrupted at nodes; nodes frequently glaucous. Leaves cordate, shallowly to deeply 3–5 lobed, simple, crenate to dentate, deciduous. Mature leaves somewhat glaucous beneath, with some whitish to reddish cobwebby hairs. Berries 0.6–1.2 cm in diameter, purple to black. May–Oct. Mts., Pied., Coast. Pl. Stream banks and low woods. Mass. to Wis. s to Fla. and Tex. A variable species (Plate 32).

FROST OR CHICKEN GRAPE *Vitis vulpina* L.

Vine with mature bark shredding, lenticels absent or inconspicuous: tendrils forked, a tendril or inflorescence present at only 2 consecutive nodes; branchlets of the season terete, glabrous, or with sparse cobwebby hairs, brown pith interrupted at nodes by diaphragms 1.5 mm or thicker; nodes not glaucous. Leaves deciduous, cordate, unlobed to rarely 3-lobed, simple, dentate; mature leaves not glaucous beneath, glabrous with simple, short, straight hairs along veins and axils. Berries 0.5–1 cm in diameter, black. Apr.–Oct. Riversides, open thickets. N.Y. to N.D. s to Fla. and Tex. (Plate 32).

THE RIVERSIDE GRAPE, *Vitis riparia* Michaux, has leaves with two lateral, forward-pointing lobes, coarsely dentate margins, and nodal diaphragms of branchlets less than 1 mm thick. Que. s to Va., Tex. and Mo. The RED OR CATBIRD GRAPE, *Vitis palmata* Vahl., has leaves more frequently deeply lobed, the central lobe long-acuminate; branchlets deep purple; nodal diaphragms 2–5 mm thick. Wet lake margins, floodplains. Ill. and Ind. s to Fla., Tex. and Mo. Occasional.

The SAND OR SUGAR GRAPE, *Vitis rupestris* Scheele, is a sprawling vine with tendrils, if present, confined to opposite the uppermost leaves. Leaves reniform, wider than long, conduplicately folded. Dry, rocky habitats. W. Va. to Tex. and Ark. Rare.

MALVACEAE

ROSE-OF-SHARON *Hibiscus syriacus* L.

This Mallow is a large, deciduous, branching shrub with 3-lobed leaf blades (sometimes unlobed), cuneate at the base. The calyx is densely but finely stellate-pubescent. Petals white or rose-purple, darker at the base. The fruit is a capsule; seeds are ciliate. Conn. s. to Fla. and Tex. Occasionally escapes to woodland borders or is a relic about abandoned house sites.

THEACEAE

MOUNTAIN CAMELLIA *Stewartia ovata* (Cav.) Weatherby

Large shrub or small tree with perfect, showy, axillary, white flowers and deciduous, alternate, simple leaves 6–15 cm long. Petals 5, rarely 6–7, to 4.5 cm long, with erose margins; stamen filaments purple or white; styles 4–5, distinct. Fruit a capsule. Seeds dull, angled or narrowly winged at one end. June–Sept. Mts. and Pied. Wooded stream margins, flood plains. Va. and Ky. s to Ga. and Ala. Rare. When in flower, a most luxuriant woodland shrub (Plate 33).

Both Stewartias grow best under light shade in moist soil. They are specimen plants, and should be placed in a conspicuous location whether it be in shrub borders or at the edge of woods. The flowers are spectacular.

SILKY CAMELLIA *Stewartia malacodendron* L.

Smaller shrub like the Mountain Camellia but with united styles, purple filaments, lustrous seeds without angles or winged margins. The leaves are smaller, from 5–10 cm long. May–Oct. Coast Pl. Pied. (uncommon) Mts. (rare). Rich woods. Va. to Ark. s to Fla. and La.

The CAMELLIA, *Camellia japonica* L., an ornamental shrub introduced from Japan, has evergreen waxy leaves and white to red single or double flowers. It will occasionally be found as an escape. Coast. Pl. The Alabama State Flower.

The SASANQUA, *Camellia sasanqua* Thunberg, also introduced, commonly escapes, and should be looked for.

The LOST GORDONIA, *Franklinia alatamaha* Marshall, is a shrub or small tree with smooth black bark, deciduous leaves, and large white flowers; the leaf blades are obovate and long-cuneate at the base. Apparently extinct in the wild, it is preserved in cultivation from seeds collected in 1765 by John and William Bartram who found it along the Altamaha River near the Georgia Coast where it was associated with *Pinckneya bracteata* (Bartram) Raf., the FEVER-TREE. William Bartram first saw *Franklinia* blossoms during the summer of 1773 or 1776. It was last seen in the wild in 1790 by Dr.Moses Marshall and in 1803 by botanist John Lyon (Harper, 1958). Dr. Marshall was the nephew of Humphrey Marshall who named *Franklinia*. Also called the FRANKLIN TREE, it tends to be short-lived when cultivated in the South (Plate 33).

A handsome aristocrat in the garden with large, luxuriant white flowers and orange to red fall color. This species often does not perform well in the Piedmont and Lower South due to soil-borne wilt and dieback disease. It is best grown in the Upper South away from the historical cotton belt. Slow release spikes containing "Subdue," a fungicide, have proven useful for control of the disease causing organism (*Phytophthora*).

LOBLOLLY BAY   *Gordonia lasianthus* (L.) Ellis

An evergreen shrub or small tree with gray bark and oblong, long-elliptic or ovate-elliptic leaf blades 6–15 cm long. The leaves are glabrous, dark green, and have blunt appressed teeth. The flowers are long-pedicelled and the filaments of the stamens are yellow to cream. Coast. Pl. Bays, low hammocks, swamps. N.C. s to Fla. and Miss. The bark has been used for tanning (Plate 33).

The LOBLOLLY BAY is a magnificent evergreen wetland species of the Coastal Plain that grows well in the Piedmont and middle Atlantic States in moist, fertile soil in full sun. Most often used in the landscape in a group of three to five. The treelike habit, showy white flowers and evergreen leaves demand a place of prominence in a large garden.

TAMARICACEAE

TAMARISK   *Tamarix gallica* L.

A large shrub or irregularly branching small tree with tiny, scalelike, imbricated, evergreen leaves. The white or pinkish flowers are borne in terminal panicles. Coast. Pl. Va. to Fla., Tex. and Ark. Introduced from Europe; an occasional escape. Planted as an ornamental and for sand binding; apparently tolerant of saline conditions.

HYPERICACEAE or GUTTIFERAE

ST. ANDREWS CROSS   *Ascyrum hypericoides* L. var. *hypericoides*

A small smooth shrub to 2.5 dm tall with opposite, thin, stalkless, oblanceolate leaves 1–8 mm long. Branches flattened, 2-edged; bark brown, shreddy.

Flowers terminal or axillary, 12–18 mm broad; sepals 4 in 2 pairs, the outer broad and round, the inner small and narrow; petals 4, yellow, forming a cross; styles 2, very short. Seeds black, 1 mm long. May–Aug. Coast. Pl., Pied., Mts. Woods and thickets, often dry. Mass. and Neb. s to Fla. and Tex. The leaves have minute black dots (Plate 33).

A decumbent plant is *Ascyrum hypericoides* L. var. *multicaule* (Michaux) Fernald, which forms mats; its pedicels remain erect in fruit. W. Va. and Ky. s to Ga. and Miss.

The related *Ascyrum pumilum* Michaux, is a tiny decumbent shrub 6–15 cm tall with solitary flowers and reflexed pedicels. Coast. Pl. N.C. s to Fla., Miss.

ST. PETER'S-WORT   *Ascyrum stans* Michaux
Sparingly branched shrub with 3 or 4 styles and smaller inner sepals; the stems are erect, 2-edged, reaching 6 dm tall. Leaf blades elliptic to oval, coriaceous, somewhat clasping, to 3 cm long and 1.4 cm wide. Flowers terminal, axillary, or in cymules; sepals cordate or ovate, obtuse or rounded at the apex, inner ones lanceolate, acute or acuminate; the four petals showy, longer than the sepals, bright yellow, obovate, 7–10 mm broad. Capsule ovoid, seeds brown; June–Oct. Coast. Pl. Pied. Moist to dry sandy woods, pinelands and barrens. N.Y. and Ky. s to Fla. and Tex.

Ascyrum tetrapetalum (Lam.) Vail, is related but differs by having outer sepals that are acute or acuminate at the apex. Coast. Pl. Low pineland, swamps. S.C., Ga. and Fla.

Members of the Genus *Hypericum* are a confusing complex of intergrading taxa. Perhaps half of the 35-odd species occurring in the Southeast commonly called St. John's-Worts, may be considered woody. The name alludes to St. John the Baptist Day, June 24, when many are flowering. All have yellow flowers that are terminal, axillary, or in cymes. Most differ from *Ascyrum* by having 5 petals and sepals versus 4 in *Ascyrum*.

HYPERICUM   *Hypericum microsephala* (T.& S.) Gray ex S. Wats.
Branching evergreen shrub less than 1 m tall with 4 nearly equal sepals and long styles, numerous stamens with distinct filaments. Leaves sessile, linear-cuneate to elliptic, 6–14 mm long. Flowers with 4 showy yellow unequal petals; sepals linear to elliptic, obtuse. Capsules 7–8 mm long with striate and pitted seeds. Apr.–June. Coast. Pl. Pine flatwoods edges. Fla. and Ga.

SAND-WEED   *Hypericum fasciculatum* Lam.
Erect evergreen shrub, about 1 m tall; bark spongy, exfoliating. Leaves numerous, linear-subulate or linear, to 2 mm wide, about 1.5 cm long, with many smaller ones clustered in the axils; blades with 2 longitudinal grooves beneath, the base notched, sessile. Sepals linear, similar to the leaves; petals 5, 6–9 mm long. Capsule ovoid, 4–5 mm long. May–Sept. Coast. Pl. Low pinelands, swamps. N.C. s to Fla. and Miss.

The evergreen *Hypericum galioides* Lam. has wider leaves not fascicled. Coast. Pl. N.C. to La.

Hypericum myrtifolium Lam., also evergreen, bears foliaceous sepals and leaves that are auriculate and clasping on the stem. Coast. Pl. Ga. to Fla. and Miss.

MOUNTAIN ST. JOHN'S-WORT   *Hypericum buckleyi* Curtis
A decumbent, spreading shrub to 3 dm tall. Leaf blades obovate to elliptic, to

Stewartia ovata

Franklinia alatamaha

Ascyrum hypericoides

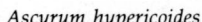

Gordonia lasianthus

PLATE 33

Hypericum frondosum

Opuntia humifusa

Dirca palustris

Dirca palustris

PLATE 34

Edgworthia papyrifera

Decodon verticillatus

Aralia spinosa

Elaeagnus umbellata

PLATE 35

Cornus amomum

Nyssa ogeche

Cornus florida

Cornus drummondii

PLATE 36

Cornus candensis MILLER

Cornus candensis MILLER

Clethra alnifolia

Clethra acuminata

PLATE 37

Chimaphila maculata

Befaria racemosa

Elliottia racemosa MILLER

Rhododendron maximum

PLATE 38

Rhododendron catawbiense

Rhododendron minus

151.
Rhododendron vaseyi

Rhododendron austrinum

PLATE 39

Rhododendron bakeri

Rhododendron alabamense
GALLE

Rhododendron flammeum GALLE

Rhododendron calendulaceu

PLATE 40

1.2 cm long, 3–8 mm wide, sessile or with petioles 1 mm long or less. Petals delicate, about twice as long as the 5 sepals; stamens numerous, clustered; styles 3, capsule conic, 3-celled. Seeds brown. June–Aug. Mts. Cliffs, balds, and mountain summits and seepages. N.C. to Ga. Rare.

This low-growing, decumbent, bright yellow-flowered spreading shrub is useful where a groundcover is needed in the landscape.

Hypericum brachyphyllum (Spach) Steudel, has leaves less than 1 cm long and 1 mm wide in fascicles; stems 2-winged, erect, to 1.5 m tall. The new leaves are lustrous above. Flatwoods, cypress pond margins. Ga. to Fla. and La.

A semi-decumbent related shrub is *Hypericum reductum* P. Adams, only reaching 0.5 m tall with stem 6-angled below the nodes, dull new leaves, and capsules 5–9 mm long. Flatwoods, dunes, sandhills. N.C. to Fla. and Ala.

The related *Hypericum lloydii* (Svenson) P. Adams, a somewhat decumbent shrub, has longer notched leaves and sepals. Pied. Dry pine woods, rock outcrops. N.C. to Ala. An erect shrub with leaves more than 13 mm long and sepals longer than 4.5 mm not deeply longitudinally grooved is *Hypericum nitidum* Lam. Its main stem has thin, hard, firm bark broken into thin furrows; seeds brown. Ditches and pools in wet pine woods. N.C. to Fla. and Ala.

SPHERICAL-FRUITED ST.JOHN'S-WORT   *Hypericum cistifolium* Lam.
Erect shrub to 6 dm tall with a 4-angled winged stem. Leaves with slightly clasping base to 4 cm long and 10 mm wide, sessile, not notched. Sepals 5, minute, 2–4 mm long; stamens less than 55, clustered; stigmas 3, Capsule 1-celled, globose-ovoid; seeds brown. Ditches, low pinelands. Coast. Pl. Ga. to Tex.

Hypericum dolabriforme Vent., also has numerous stamens, minute stigmas, and 1-celled larger capsules, to 5–8 mm long; corolla larger, to 18 mm or more broad. Often on thin soils over limestones. Ind. s to Ga., Ala.

SHRUBBY ST. JOHN'S-WORT   *Hypericum prolificum* L.
Relatively tall shrub with few flowers in narrow panicles; Leaves and sepals are distinctly notched at the base. Leaves 7–14 mm wide, elliptic to linear, to 5 cm long, sessile or short-petioled. Sepals 5, to 8 mm long, obovate; petals 5, the corolla 2–2.5 cm broad; stamens numerous; ovary 3-locular. Capsules conic to ovoid, to 13 mm long; seeds black. Mts. and Pied. Rocky and sandy woods. N.Y., Iowa, Mo., s to Ga. and La.

Hypericum densiflorum Pursh is similar, but the largest leaves are 3–7 mm wide, the flowers are more numerous in corymblike panicles, and the corolla is less than 1.5 cm broad. Swamps, bogs, and balds. N.Y. and Mo. s to Ga., La., Tex. Those with 5 styles and 5-celled capsules are var. *lobocarpum* (Gattinger) Svenson. Mts. N.C. to Mo. s to La.

Hypericum prolificum has value in the landscape when planted in masses for yellow summer flowers. It blooms over a relatively long period of time and the flowers are quite attractive.

Hypericum nudiflorum Michaux ex. Willd. is an erect shrub with wing-angled stems, numerous stamens, leaves not notched, and sepals less than half as long as the petals. Pied. and Coast. Pl. Sandy soils. Va. s to Fla. and Tex.

The GOLDEN ST. JOHN'S-WORT, *Hypericum frondosum* Michaux, has very showy, usually solitary flowers with oblique petals to 23 mm long and foliaceous sepals. Pied. and Mts. Bluffs; riverbanks; thin, rocky soils. Ga. to Tenn. and Tex. Often cultivated as an ornamental (Plate 34).

The cultivar, 'Sunburst' of the GOLDEN ST. JOHN'S WORT is more attractive than the native species. It can be used in mass plantings in situations where bright yellow flowers are needed over a long blooming season.

CISTACEAE

BEACH HEATH, GOLDEN HEATH   *Hudsonia ericoides* L.
Low-spreading dune, pineland or mountain shrub with evergreen leaves and terminal, sessile, bright yellow flowers. Branches and branchlets numerous. leaves scalelike, densely imbricated and appressed, hoary-pubescent, from less than 3 to more than 4 mm long. Sepals densely long-hairy and if acute, sepals pubescent only above the middle. Fruit an ovoid, 3-angled, smooth capsule bearing 1–2 minute, oblong seeds. Includes *H. tomentosa* Nuttall and *H. montana* Nuttall. (Skog and Nickerson, 1972). Sand dunes and blows, Que. to S.C. also inland to shores of Great Lakes; Table Rock and adjacent balds, N.C.; dry sandy pinelands and acidic rocks, Nfld. s to S.C.

Hudsonia ericoides is an attractive mat former which in spring is covered with bright yellow flowers; it should be ideal to cultivate on sandy dunes. However, it is difficult to establish and is rarely planted and is rather short-lived.

CACTACEAE

PRICKLY-PEAR   *Opuntia humifusa* Raf.
Low succulent plant with segmented, spiny stems. Leaves alternate, deciduous, fleshy, to 10 mm long, with or without 1 large spine to 3 cm long from the leaf axil. Leaves bearing tufts of hairlike spines called glochids. Stem segments flattened, ellipsoid to oblanceolate, to 20 cm long. Flowers showy, yellow, with numerous petals and stamens. Berry brown to purple, less than 2.5 cm broad. Pied., Mts. Coast. Pl. Sandy soils, rock outcrops in open or thin woods. May–Oct. Mass. to Ky. s to Fla. and Miss. (Plate 34).

The related *Opuntia pusilla* (Haw) Haw bears 2 or more spines at some nodes and segments that readily break apart. N.C. to Fla. and Miss.

THYMELAEACEAE

LEATHERWOOD   *Dirca palustris* L.
Bushy deciduous shrub to 2 m tall with alternate, oblong-ovate to obovate leaves rounded at the base, 5–8 cm long; petioles 1–2 mm long. Flowers yellow in axillary clusters of 2–3, appearing before the leaves, the floral tube 5–6 mm long. Fruit a reddish to purple drupe, becoming green to yellow in the south, 1–2 cm long. Indians used the twigs for thongs and the bark has been used medicinally. Mts. and Pied. Mar.–July. Rich woods, deciduous thickets, often on neutral soils, north slopes. N.B. to Minn. s to Fla. and La. Rare (Plate 34).

Used in light shade in moist, fertile soil, *Dirca palustris,* with its rich green foliage and pale yellow flowers, forms a picturesque shrub. In the fall the leaves turn to an attractive clear yellow color.

Edgeworthia papyrifera Siebold & Zucc., the PAPERBUSH, is a ternately branched deciduous shrub to 2 m with lance-oblong leaves to 12 cm long; yellow blooms appear before the leaves in dense axillary clusters. Mts. Ga. Naturalized

ELAEAGNACEAE

AUTUMN OLIVE
Elaeagnus umbellata Thunberg

Shrubs with leaves silvery beneath, deciduous, and alternate. The yellow, fragrant, umbellate flowers are in axillary clusters of 3–10. Calyx tube slender, longer than the lobes; stamens 4. Drupes red, 5–8 mm long on pedicels about 1 cm long, juicy. Introduced from Asia, planted for wildlife food and cover. Apr.–Sept. Mts., Pied., Coast. Pl. Fencerows, woods edges, and waste places. Va. s to Fla. and La.(Plate 35).

The RUSSIAN OLIVE, *Elaeagnus angustifolia* L., another Asian introduction, is a deciduous shrub with silvery branches and leaves silvery beneath, and the style covered by disk. Others of Eurasian origin are *Elaeagnus multiflora* Thunberg, with leaf blades that are brown-scaly beneath. Escape from cultivation. The THORNY ELAEAGNUS, *Elaeagnus pungens* Thunberg, has evergreen leaves and stems with thorns. Scattered locations, N.C. to Tex.

LYTHRACEAE

WATER-WILLOW
Decodon verticillatus (L.) Elliott

Aquatic semishrub, woody below, with soft-corky bark under water, exfoliating in strips at the water surface; colonial, the stems rooting at the tips. Leaves deciduous, opposite or whorled, 5–15 cm long and 2–3 cm broad. Flowers axillary in short-stalked cymes; calyx lobes acuminate, petals purplish pink, 8–12 mm long. Capsule 4–7 mm in diameter, seeds 2 mm long, finely reticulate, olive green with a brown spot on one side. July–Sept. Swamps, wet shores, pools, and bogs. Coast. Pl. Me. s to Fla. and Tex., inland to Ill. and Mo. (Plate 35).

The WATER WILLOW is valuable for decorating and colonizing pond edges and other very wet places. When in flower, it is conspicuous and attractive.

The CRAPE-MYRTLE, *Lagerstroemia indica* L., is a small tree or shrub with crisped purple, pink to white petals and exfoliating bark. Residual at old house sites. Native of Asia. Va. s to Fla. and Tex.

ARALIACEAE

ENGLISH IVY
Hedera helix L.

An evergreen trailing and climbing vine with aerial roots and alternate, long-petioled, coriaceous leaves. Leaves roundish, angled, 3–5 lobed, or entire. Flowers small, greenish yellow, in solitary racemose umbels. Fruit a black drupe. Mts., Pied., Coast. Pl. Va. s to Fla. and Miss. From Europe, naturalized about houses, fences, cemeteries. Used medicinally; poisonous if eaten. A varnish resin, dye and tanning substances have been obtained from it.

HERCULES' CLUB, DEVIL'S WALKING STICK
Aralia spinosa L.

A tall, erect shrub, often colonial, with a seldom branched spiny stem and a terminal cluster of deciduous leaves, 1–2 m long, alternate, bipinnately compound, armed with slender prickles; leaflets numerous, (to 250), ovate, 5–10 cm long. Flowers white, in dense umbellate clusters arranged in a large terminal panicle; petals 2–3 mm long. Fruit a black berrylike drupe 4–6 mm in diameter. June–Sept. Mts., Pied., Coast. Pl. Low upland woods, roadside thickets, slopes, bluffs and ravines, coastal hammocks. N.J. to Iowa, s to Fla., Tex. and Mo. Bark and fruits used medicinally; the inner bark poisonous to livestock. Planted as an ornamental and easily propagated from seed or root cuttings (Plate 35).

Aralia spinosa is best used as a specimen focal-point plant or massed at the edge of woods. Its thick, clublike stem, huge compound leaves, white flower clusters and beautiful fruit clusters make this an attractive shrub. Its ability to develop new plants from its roots can create a maintenance problem and should be considered when selecting a site for the shrub.

NYSSACEAE

OGEECHEE-LIME   *Nyssa ogeche* Bartram ex. Marshall

A small tree, or a many-stemmed shrub with alternate, deciduous leaves; leaf blades variable from elliptic to oblong-oval, entire, glabrous above and soft-pubescent below. Staminate flowers in compact round clusters; pistillate flowers borne singly on short stalks. Drupes rose red, 2–4 cm long, usually longer than their stalks; stones attached by papery wings to the skin of the fruit. Apr.–Oct. Coast. Pl. Swamps, sloughs, river banks, and bay forests. S.C. to Ga. and Fla. The fruits are used in preserving and for an acid drink. One of the sources of Tupelo honey (Plate 36).

The OGEECHEE-LIME is lovely when naturalized about ponds and in very wet places. Largely neglected by horticulturists, it has purplish to scarlet fall color and attractive, purplish, plum-sized fruit.

CORNACEAE

FLOWERING DOGWOOD   *Cornus florida* L.

A small tree, sometimes shrublike, with brownish, checkered bark and opposite leaves. Leaves ovate to broadly elliptic, abruptly acuminate or acute at the apex. Flowers small, greenish yellow, tightly clustered and surrounded by 4 white or rarely pink, petal-like, involucral bracts usually notched at the apex. Flowering before the leaves. Drupes in clusters, the fruits scarlet and shiny, crowned by 4 persistent calyx lobes, 8–18 mm long. Mar.–Oct. Mts., and Pied. Coast. Pl. Me. to Ill. and Kans. s to Fla. and Mex. Open pine woods, clearings, mesic woodlands, thickets. Drupes are an important wildlife food especially for squirrels and birds; the hardwood has been used for shuttles, tools, and wood engraving; the deciduous leaves have delightful autumn colors: widely planted as an ornamental (Plate 36).

One of the most popular of our native plants, blooming in spring the DOGWOOD extends interest and color into the canopy of the surrounding trees. A plant of many uses, e.g., as a lawn specimen, naturalized in woodlands, near corners of large buildings, in parks, and at the edge of woods; it should be planted in semishade in moist, fertile soil. Cultivars too numerous to mention have been selected having pink bracts, variegated foliage, double bracts, purple leaves, dwarf habit, and yellow fruit. The handsome bracts, scarlet fruit, consistent red to purple fall color, make *Cornus florida* highly desirable in the landscape. When growing the native species, local seed sources usually yield plants best suited to local conditions and give superior results. Few sights are more beautiful than a forest with naturalized dogwood in full bloom.

PAGODA DOGWOOD   *Cornus alternifolia* L. f.

Shrub to 6 m tall. Leaves alternate but crowded near the end of branches giving an appearance of being in whorls or opposite. Pith of second-year twigs white. Leaves deciduous, whitish beneath,and prominately ribbed. Petioles 2–6 cm long. Drupes dark blue to black. May–Sept. Mts., and Pied. Balds, rich woods, and stream banks. Nfld. to Minn. s to Fla., Ala. and Mo.

An interesting dogwood, best used for naturalizing in light shade, but overshadowed by *C. florida.* Of some value where a horizontal, low-branched effect is needed.

SILKY-CORNEL   *Cornus amomum* Miller
Spreading shrubs to about 5 m tall; branchlets of the current growth copiously pubescent with rusty or silvery hairs; pith of twigs brown or tawny. Leaves deciduous, opposite; lower leaf surfaces covered with long, appressed reddish hairs; upper surface glabrous and smooth; leaf petioles pubescent. Flowers in pubescent, cymose inflorescences covered by colorless to reddish hairs. The drupe is pale blue or spotted with cream, subglobose, sparsely pubescent, about 8 mm in diameter. May–Sept. Coast. Pl., Pied., Mts. Borders of swamps, stream banks, and springheads. Que. to Minn. s to Fla. and Miss. A variable group, with several named subspecies. The inner bark was used by the Indians to mix with tobacco to make kinnikinnik (Plate 36).

Tending to be a bit coarse in texture, it is little used in landscaping. However, it is of value if massed at the edge of low woods. The same might be advocated for several of the other native CORNELS. All of the native bush dogwoods are readily transplanted and will thrive in many diverse situations. The blooms are much alike but the handsome fruits vary from white to blue.

ROUGH-LEAF DOGWOOD   *Cornus drummondii* C. A. Meyer
Shrub to small tree to 6 m tall; sometimes colonial. Twigs of the current season copiously pubescent; pith brown. Leaves deciduous, 6–10 cm long, usually ovate; upper surface pubescent, scabrous, the lower softly pubescent. Mature drupes white, rarely faintly bluish, subglobose, about 5 mm in diameter. Stones 1–2, flattened laterally, broader than long. Stream banks, floodplains, limestone bluffs. Ohio to Neb. s to Ga. and Tex. (Plate 36).

ROUND-LEAVED DOGWOOD   *Cornus rugosa* Lam.
Shrub to 3 m high, loosely branched, with round to ovate, acuminate leaves. Twigs yellowish green, often mottled with red; pith white. Leaves deciduous woolly beneath, with 7–9 pairs of veins. Cymes dense, flat topped, on peduncles to 4 cm long. Drupes light blue. May–Oct. Mts. Sandy to rocky slopes. Que. to Ia. s to Va. Uncommon.

Another mountain species is the RED OSIER DOGWOOD, *Cornus stolonifera* Michaux, a deciduous, stoloniferous shrub with white pith, deep red, smooth branches; fruit white or lead colored. Mts. Nfld. to Alaska s to W. Va., Va., Ill. and N. Mex. More common north of our range.

SWAMP DOGWOOD   *Cornus foemina* Miller
Shrub or small tree to 6 m tall. Twigs reddish, becoming grayish with age; pith white. Leaves opposite, variable in shape from broadly to narrowly elliptic, to oblong-elliptic to ovate or lanceolate, deciduous. Cymes convex to flat-topped, sparsely pubescent with appressed colorless hairs; flowers small, white. Drupes bright blue, globose, about 6–7 mm in diameter. Pied. and Coast. Pl. Swamps and uplands. Del. to Ill. s to Fla. and Tex. A highly variable species with two named varieties.

A rare species is *Cornus racemosa* Lam., a thicket-forming shrub with brown pith, white fruit on red pedicels and elongate paniculatelike cymes. May–Sept. Pied. and Coast. Pl. Wet areas. Ont. to Ky., s to N.C.

Another CORNEL with white pith is *Cornus asperifolia* Michaux, with scabrous leaves, brown woolly or closely pubescent branchlets and white fruit. The inflorescence is a convex cyme, pubescent, often with reddish hairs. Along streams and rivers, thickets. Minn. to Ala. and Tex. A hybrid between this species and *Cornus amomum* is widely cultivated as an ornamental.

The BUNCHBERRY, *Cornus canadensis* L. is a small partly woody plant with greenish flowers and bright red fruit (Plate 37).

The BUNCHBERRY is a beautiful native groundcover that perhaps can be used at higher elevations in the Southeast. It inhabits cool, moist, acid woodlands and can best be transplanted as strips of sod; it will need frequent watering until well established.

For information about *Cornus* see Wilson, (1965) and Tehon, (1942).

CLETHRACEAE

MOUNTAIN PEPPERBUSH   *Clethra acuminata* Michaux
Shrub to 4 m tall with alternate, deciduous, simple, elliptic to oblong, acuminate leaves 7–18 cm long, serrulate. Flowers in erect terminal racemes with pubescent pedicels; flowers white, fragrant; 5-merous; stamens 10, the filaments pubescent; Capsule hairy, 3-locular, 3–4 mm in diameter. July–Oct. Mts. and Pied. Acid woods, ravines, and riverbanks. At higher elevations. Pa. and W. Va. s to Ga. (Plate 37).

A loosely proportioned shrub best used in full sun. The stems are unusual, sometimes exfoliating or presenting a polished, brownish color. The MOUNTAIN PEPPERBUSH is larger in every way than the SWEET PEPPERBUSH and its flowers are rather showy. It is best used as a background plant in the shrub border.

SWEET PEPPERBUSH   *Clethra alnifolia* L.
Shrub to 3 m tall with alternate, deciduous, simple, obovate-oblong to oblanceolate or elliptic oblanceolate leaves to 8 cm long with acute, subacute or obtuse apexes. Flowers white, fragrant, in erect terminal racemes with pubescent pedicels, 5-merous, stamens 10, filaments glabrous. Capsule hairy, subglobose, about 3 mm in diameter. Some plants may have leaves that are densely tomentose beneath. Pink-flowered forms occur. June–Oct. Coast. Pl. and lower Pied. Wet pine savannas, bays, bogs and pocosins (Plate 37).

An excellent plant for landscaping a damp area although SWEET PEPPERBUSH will grow in almost any soil. Under cultivation it becomes a shrub of remarkable beauty at all seasons. When grown in full sun, the alluring perfumed flower clusters and the striking foliage in summer make it a desirable shrub for any garden. SWEET PEPPERBUSH should be grouped in clumps at the edge of woods or in and about the banks of a winding small watercourse.

ERICACEAE

A large diversified family containing many species of shrubs called heaths. They are typically plants of acid soils and are abundant in the Southeast on mountain slopes, hillsides, and bogs and in the swamps and thickets of the coastal plain. Among them are many forms useful for food, landscaping, and medicinal products for man and wildlife. Their roots are associated with micorrhiza.

Woody shrubs, vines, or trees with alternate evergreen or deciduous leaves; urceolate or campanulate flowers; calyx and corolla each of 4–5 united or distinct segments; stamens distinct, often twice as many as the petals; anthers usually opening by terminal pores; ovary superior or inferior; fruit a capsule, berry, or drupe.

PIPSISSEWA   *Chimaphila maculata* (L.) Pursh.

Low semishrub to 2 dm tall. Leaves evergreen, lanceolate, 2–6 cm long, leathery, sharply serrate to serrate-dentate, deep green with white band along midrib. Flowers fragrant, waxy, petals white. Pied., Mts., Coast. Pl. Pine and pine-hardwood forests. N.H. and Mich. s to Ga. and Ala. (Plate 38).

The related *Chimaphila umbellata* (L.) Barton differs, lacking the white band on leaves; petals pink or white. May–Oct. Similar habitats. N.S. to Alaska s to Ga., Calif. *Chimaphila* is placed by some authorities in the family Pyrolaceae.

TAR-FLOWER   *Befaria racemosa* Vent.

Slender, sparsely branched, erect evergreen shrub. Twigs with long, spreading hairs. Leaves sessile, elliptic to ovate, 2–4 cm long and 6–20 mm wide. Flowers showy, fragrant, in terminal racemes on wood of the current season; petals 7, separate, white to pink, glutinous, spatulate to oblanceolate, 2–3 cm long; stamens 12–14. Capsule 6–8 mm in diameter, with amber-colored seeds to 1.5 mm long. Coast. Pl. Wet pine flatwoods and sand scrub. Ga. into Fla. (Plate 38).

GEORGIA PLUME   *Elliottia racemosa* Muhl.

A large shrub up to 6 m tall, spreading by rootstocks and often forming large colonies; twigs glabrous. Leaf blades elliptic to elliptic-ovate, 6–12 cm long, deciduous. Flowers numerous, in racemose panicles; calyx with 4–5 lobes; petals white, 6–14 mm long. June–July. Coast. Pl., one Pied. station. Oak ridges and sand-hills. Ga., (S.C.?). One of the rarest of flowering shrubs in the Southeast, known only from a few stations in southeastern Georgia. Fertile seeds are rare, but it can be propagated from root cuttings. Extensive sprouting from rootstocks occurs following site disturbance. Threatened species (Plate 38).

Although seldom seen in America's gardens, *Elliottia racemosa* is magnificent in flower and has striking reddish-purple color in the fall. Use it as a conversation piece in full sun in shrub borders.

ROSE BAY, GREAT LAUREL   *Rhododendron maximum* L.

Evergreen shrub to 10 m tall with thick, coriaceous leaves to 20 cm long, glabrous bright green above, pale green beneath, gradually narrowed to an acute to acuminate apex. Flowers in an umbel-like cluster of 10–30 opening after the new leaves; pedicels stipitate-glandular; calyx lobes 2–4 mm long; corolla white to pinkish, often with a greenish throat with yellow or orange spots; stamens 10. Capsules stipitate-glandular, 1–1.5 cm long; seeds tapered, to 2.0 mm long. June–Oct. Mts. and Pied. Acid woods, slopes, and stream banks. N.S., Ont. to Ohio, s to Ga. The state flower of West Virginia (Plate 38).

In early summer, when its masses of flowers are in bloom, it is a most attractive shrub. It should be planted along streams or other watercourses at the higher elevations and lattitudes of the Upper South. It requires moist, cool, acid soil and blooms best in light shade. If planted with proper regard for natural and harmonious effect it will beautifully clothe a shady slope rising above a stream. It can become leggy and underplantings of *Leucothoe* may be desirable.

MOUNTAIN ROSE BAY, PURPLE LAUREL   *Rhododendron catawbiense* Michaux

Evergreen shrub to 6 m tall with thick, coriaceous leaves to 16 cm long, rounded to an obtuse or slightly acute apex. Flowers numerous, in an umbel-like group, larger than *R. maximum;* calyx lobes 1 mm or less long; corolla widely bell shaped, to 5 cm broad, lilac-purple, with olive green spots on the upper lobe; stamens 10. Capsules densely hirsute, eglandular, to 2.5 cm long; seeds to 2.5 mm long. Apr.–Oct. Mts. and Pied. Acid soils on mountain summits, bluffs, and cliffs. Va. to Ky. s to Ga. and Ala. Particularly abundant on Roan Mountain, N.C. Introduced to Europe in 1809 by John Fraser (Plate 39).

Much more compact than *R. maximum,* the habit of *R. catawbiense* is neater and more dense. It is an outstanding plant for groupings in light shade in acid soil in the Upper South. Plant material from the lower reaches of the Piedmont and Cumberland Plateau appears to be better adapted to landscaping. The dark green foliage and the lilac-purple flowers should be welcome in any garden. Several cultivars are available in the nursery trade.

DWARF RHODODENDRON   *Rhododendron minus* Michaux

Straggling but upright evergreen shrub to 3.5 m tall with lower surface of leaves, calyx, corolla, pedicels, and twigs resinous dotted. Leaves thick, coriaceous, to 10 cm long. Flower clusters of 7–10, appearing after the leaves; calyx lobes 2 mm long, resinous, deltoid; corolla rose, spotted with green, rarely with a yellow spot on the upper lobe; stamens 10. Capsule lepidote, to 12 mm long. Apr.–Oct. Mts., Pied., Coast. Pl. Stream banks and wooded slopes. N.C., Tenn. and Ga. Once thought to be distinct, the CAROLINA RHODODENDRON, *Rhododendron carolinianum* Rehder, is now considered synonymous with *R. minus* (Plate 39).

CHAPMAN'S RHODODENDRON, *Rhododendron minus* Michaux var. *chapmanii* (Gray) Duncan & Pullen, is similar, but has white filaments instead of pink and magenta tubes and spotted lobes instead of rose. The leaf apices of this variety usually are obtuse, while those of *R. minus* are acute or acuminate. Pinelands, northwest Fla. Considered endangered by the Federal Government and Florida. Also known as *R. chapmanii.*

Rhododendron minus is a desirable plant for light shaded areas of the Piedmont and northward. Group it in a woodsy setting. It has a light, airy aspect that is more pleasing than the heaviness of the other two species. The flowers are borne in abundance.

The remaining members of the Genus *Rhododendron* are commonly called AZALEAS. They have deciduous, usually serrulate or ciliate leaves, a corolla that is decidedly 2-lipped and funnel-shaped, and only 5–7 stamens. Azaleas readily hybridize in nature, and many artificial crosses have been made by plant breeders. For additional information see Galle (No Date), Galle (1985), and Roane and Henry (1983).

PINKSHELL AZALEA   *Rhododendron vaseyi* Gray

Deciduous shrub to 5 m tall. Leaves stipitate-glandular above and often below, narrowly to widely elliptic, up to 12 cm long. Flowers appearing before the leaves in 5–8 flowered clusters; pedicels stipitate-glandular, to 1.5 cm long; corolla various shades of rose pink with reddish-orange dots at the base of the upper petals, lacking the distinct tube of most azaleas and appearing to have separate petals; stamens usually 7, sometimes 5 or 6. Capsules stipitate-glandular. May–Oct. Mts. Mountain bogs; spruce forests. N.C. (Plate 39).

Highly regarded as a graceful, spreading shrub with charming, clear pink flowers lightly speckled on the upper lobe, it should be grown in the Upper South by all lovers of beautiful flowers. The autumn color of its foliage is brilliant. It needs acid soil and is intolerant of drought.

FLORIDA AZALEA   *Rhododendron austrinum* (Small) Rehder
Deciduous shrub to 4 m tall with fragrant golden yellow flowers; twigs red-brown; in winter, the flower buds have soft, gray pubescence. Flowers in umbel-like racemes, in clusters of 8–15 blooms, opening before or with the leaves; pedicels pubescent. The corolla tube is glandular, yellow to reddish. Capsule cylindric-ellipsoidal, to 2.5 cm long, glandular-pubescent. Mar.–Apr. Coast. Pl. River terraces, flood plains on sandy, acid soils. Fla., Ga., Ala., Miss. Plants with reddish corolla tubes may indicate hybridization with *R. canescens* (Plate 39).

One of the earliest to flower, this Coastal Plain native with its abundant yellow to orange flowers is one of the easiest native azaleas to grow.

OCONEE AZALEA   *Rhododendron flammeum* (Michaux) Sargent
Deciduous, stoloniferous shrub to 2 m tall; twigs orange-brown. Flowers salmon to deep pink or yellow on strigose pedicels, opening with the leaves; corolla with a large bright orange or scarlet spot on the upper lobe, the tube slender, nonglandular, pubescent, longer than the lobes, dialated at the apex; stamens 5, more than twice as long as the tube, filaments rose pink. Capsule 2–3 cm long, narrowly ovoid. Apr.–May. Pied. Woods and sand hills. S.C. to Ala. Hybridizes with *R. canescens*, *R. alabamense* and *R. viscosum*, producing interesting color variants (Plate 40).

Formerly known as *R. speciosum*, the OCONEE AZALEA is noted for its range of flower color. It will tolerate somewhat drier soils than some of the other azaleas.

BAKER'S AZALEA   *Rhododendron bakeri* (Lemmon & McKay) Hume
Shrub to 3 m tall with red, yellow, or orange flowers in clusters of 3–9, flowering in June and July after the leaves have expanded; pedicels villous, stipitate-glandular; the corolla tube is gradually dialated, as long as the lobes, ridged, and glandular; the lobes without yellow or red spot; the stamens are exserted, much longer than the tube, the exserted part red. Capsule cylindric, to 1.5 cm long, covered with glandular trichomes. Mts. Cumberland Plateau, Ky. Tenn.; Blue Ridge above 3000 ft. elevation. N.C., Ga. Hybridizes with *R. calendulaceum*, especially in the Great Smoky Mountains. The flowers are smaller than those of *R. calendulaceum*, the corolla tube is thinner and blooms generally occur 2–4 weeks later (Plate 40).

Although little known and difficult to find at nurseries, *R. bakeri* has showy flowers, varying somewhat in color, but always attractive. Its later blooming habit is advantageous in providing color between midseason azaleas and *R. prunifolia*.

FLAME AZALEA   *Rhododendron calendulaceum* (Michaux) Torrey
Upright, tall, nonstoloniferous shrub to 5 m tall. Flowers red to yellow or orange, large, up to 6 cm wide. Leaves oblong to obovate or lanceolate, finely pubescent above, mucronolate at the apex, 2–8 cm long. Flowers appearing with or shortly after the leaves in clusters of 5–7; pedicels usually setose and stipitate-

105

glandular; corolla funnelform, the tube glandular-pilose and pubescent; stamens long-exserted, to nearly 3 times as long as the tube; filaments yellow to orange. Capsule ovoid-oblong, 1.5–2 cm long, setose and pubescent. May–June. Mts. Dry open woods, especially on west-facing slopes, along streams. Pa. and Ohio s to Ga. and Ala. John Bartram thought this "the most gay and brilliant-flowered shrub yet known" (Plate 40).

Bartram was right because the FLAME AZALEA is the showiest of all native azaleas, distinguished not only by its flower color, ranging from pure yellow to scarlet, but also the large size of both the flowers and the plant. It is an excellent lawn specimen or is striking when employed in masses. Rather slow-growing in nature, the FLAME AZALEA responds readily in cultivation and can be grown in a partially shaded area or in the open. As with most azaleas, when heavily shaded, flowering decreases, so thinning the overstory to increase sunlight striking the azalea will usually result in increasing the number of blooms. There is no more gorgeous sight in the world than a fine planting of FLAME AZALEA.

PINXTER-BLOOM   *Rhododendron periclymenoides* (Michaux) Shinners
Stoloniferous shrub 1–3 m tall, with white, pink, to violet-red fragrant flowers. Twigs sparingly pubescent, strigose; winter buds glabrous. Leaves glabrous to glabrescent. Flowers appear before or with the leaves, pedicels strigose but usually glandless; corolla 3.5–5 cm in diameter, tube finely pubescent, but rarely glandular, fragrant; stamens exserted, more than 3 times as long as the corolla lobes; styles longer than the stamens. Capsules oblong, 1–2 cm long. Mar.–Oct. Mts., Pied., Coast. Pl. Stream banks, woodlands. Mass. to Ohio s to N.C., Tenn. and Ga. Formerly known as *R. nudiflorum*.

This is a dwarfish, stoloniferous shrub, useful for naturalizing in woodland settings.

ALABAMA AZALEA   *Rhododendron alabamense* Rehder
A low stoloniferous shrub usually less than 2 m tall. Flowers white, lemon scented, usually with a yellow spot; corolla tube narrow, glandular. Twigs with glandular pubescence; winter buds brown, glabrous, scales fimbriate at the apex. Leaves 3–6 cm long, with distinct odor when crushed; petioles short, 2–5 mm long. Flowers expanding before or with the leaves in clusters of 5–15; corolla funnelform with cylindrical tube, 3–4 cm across; stamens twice as long as the tube, filaments white. Capsules cylindrical-oblong, 1.5 cm long. Apr. Pied. Dry open woodland slopes. S.C. to Ala. Rare. Hybridizes frequently with *R. canescens*, flowers pink, plants taller and less stoloniferous. North cent. Ala., west cent. Ga. Pure forms uncommon (Plate 40).

The ALABAMA AZALEA is a large-flowered, fragrant, nearly white-blooming shrub. Since it frequently hybridizes with others, pure forms are sometimes difficult to locate.

ROSESHELL AZALEA   *Rhododendron roseum* (Loisel) Rehder
Stoloniferous shrub to 5 m tall with clove-scented pink flowers, pubescent winter buds. Leaves 3–7 cm long with dense grayish pubescence beneath. Flowers expanding before or with the leaves, in clusters of 5–9; pedicels finely villous. Corolla funnelform, the tube with numerous gland-tipped trichomes; lobes as long as the tube; stamens about twice as long as the tube, filaments yellow-brown; style longer than the stamens, purple. Capsule stipitate-glandular, narrower

106

above. 1.5–2 cm long. May. Mts. Deciduous woods, stream banks. N.H. to Ohio, s to N.C., Tenn., Mo. (Plate 41).

This is an attractive native azalea for landscape use and perhaps the finest in the pink color range. Like most Rhododendrons, it is best used in groupings in light shade.

PIEDMONT AZALEA   *Rhododendron canescens* (Michaux) Sweet

Erect shrub to 5 m tall, often stoloniferous, with pure white to pure pink slightly fragrant flowers in clusters of 6–15 that expand before or with the leaves. Twigs yellow-brown; winter buds pubescent. Leaves thinly pubescent above, velvety so beneath, 4–9 cm long; petioles 2–7 mm long. The corolla tube is funnelform, to 4 cm across, deeper pink than the lobes and nearly twice as long; stamens 3 times as long as the tube, filaments pink and pubescent below the middle; style pink, as long or longer than the stamens. Capsule cylindric oblong, narrowed upward, pubescent, 1.5–2 cm long. Feb–Oct. Pied. and Coast. Pl. Streamsides, moist slopes, pocosins, savannas. The most abundant native azalea in the Southeast. Va. to Tenn. s to Fla. and Tex. Hybrids are common with *R. viscosum, R. austrinum, R. flammeum,* and *R. alabamense* (Plate 41).

Widespread, abundant, and extremely variable, the PIEDMONT AZALEA bears smaller, paler flowers than some of the other azaleas but the better color forms deserve to be grown in our gardens. Native along Piedmont streams, it is a superior plant to naturalize in similar habitats.

DWARF AZALEA, COASTAL AZALEA   *Rhododendron atlanticum* (Ashe) Rehder

Low, stoloniferous, erect shrub to 0.5 m tall with white flowers flushed with pink, scented, with or without a yellow spot. Winter buds glabrous or slightly silky pubescent. Leaves obovate to oblong-obovate, to 6 cm long, bright to bluish green. Flowers appearing with or before the leaves, in clusters of 4–10; pedicels with gland-tipped trichomes, to 1 cm long, hirsute; corolla tube funnelform, 1.5–2.5 cm long, with prominent rows of long, stipitate, glandular trichomes; stamens thrice as long as the corolla tube, filaments white to light brown, prominently pubescent below the middle. Style longer, 4.5–5.5 cm, exceeding the stamens. Apr.–Oct. May bloom in the fall. Coast. Pl. Pine barrens, moist woods. Del. to Ga. (Plate 41).

The virtues of this low-growing azalea are many; it is a heavy bloomer, has attractive foliage, and fragrant flowers. A superb shrub in every way, the DWARF AZALEA should be used in great masses where a low azalea is needed.

SWAMP AZALEA   *Rhododendron viscosum* Torrey

Low, stoloniferous shrub 3–5 m tall with white to rarely pink flowers appearing after the leaves. Twigs pubescent, winter buds glabrous to pubescent. Leaves ovate to oblong-lanceolate, usually with ciliate margins. Flowers white, fragrant, spicy scented, in clusters of 4–9; corolla tube slender, funnelform, densely covered with glandular trichomes, tube about 1.5 cm long, quite sticky to the touch; stamens exserted, filaments white, villous below the middle, to 5.5 cm long; style longer than the stamens, white, pubescent below, sometimes violet near the top, 4–6 cm long. Capsules stipitate-glandular, 1–2 cm long. A variable species with several varieties and forms. Taller plants usually found along streams. May–Oct. Mts., Pied., Coast. Pl. Swamps, riverbanks, pond margins. Me. to Ohio s to Fla. and Tex. (Plate 41).

A later bloomer for the landscape is *R. viscosum* with glistening white flowers on a low, stoloniferous plant. With careful selection, a range in flowering time can be obtained, adding fragrance to the garden for a month or more. It is a neat-looking shrub and valuable where later flowering is needed.

HAMMOCK-SWEET AZALEA   *Rhododendron serrulatum* (Small) Millais
Shrub to 6 m tall with clove-scented, very fragrant, white to creamy white flowers in clusters of 6–10 appearing in July and August after winter buds have partly formed. Branches densely strigose; winter buds with more than 15 aristate scales, the margins of the scales fimbriate with a dark outer band. Leaves elliptic, obovate to obovate-oblong, often pubescent beneath, serrulate, the margins cilliate. Corolla tube slenderly cylindric, 2.5–3.5 cm long, twice the length of the lobes, with glandular trichomes making the tube quite sticky; stamens exserted, about 1.5 times the tube length; filaments yellow, villous below the middle. Style purple above, much longer than the stamens. Capsules villous, glandular-setose, to 1.5 cm long. May–Oct. Coast. Pl. Swamps, bogs, and pond edges. Va. s to Fla. and Tex. Sometimes considered a variety of *R. viscosum* (Plate 42).
This Coastal Plain native is less hardy farther north than some of the higher-elevation species, but it does well in more southern areas that may be too hot and humid for some of the horticultural hybrids.

SWEET AZALEA, SMOOTH AZALEA   *Rhododendron arborescens* (Pursh.) Torrey
Tall deciduous shrub to 6 m with fragrant white flowers occasionally with a pink flush, often with a yellow spot and a bright red style. Twigs and winter buds glabrous, the buds fimbriate on the margins. Leaves oblanceolate, bright green. Flowers appear after the leaves, in clusters of 3–8; corolla funnelform, tube 2–3 cm long, with scattered glandular trichomes; stamens exserted, about twice as long as the tube; filaments purple above, pubescent below; style about as long as the stamens. Capsules oblong-ovoid, 0.5–2 cm long. June–Oct. Mts. and Pied. Swamps, stream banks, rocky woods. N.Y. to Ky. s to Ga. and Ala. The dried leaves give off the odor of coumarin, a vanillalike scent (Plate 42).
Possibly one of the most beautiful of our native azaleas, blooming in June. *R. arborescens* should be used in very light shade in natural woodland settings and does well along small streams at middle elevations. It is a desirable species for the garden.

PLUMLEAF AZALEA   *Rhododendron prunifolia* (Small) Millais
A large shrub to 7 m tall with orange to scarlet to deep red flowers in clusters of 4–5, blooming after the leaves appear in mid to late summer. Twigs and winter buds glabrous, margins of buds fimbriate, orange to red-brown. Leaves deep green above, 3–12 cm long, elliptic to obovate. Corolla funnelform, the tube 2–2.5 cm long, sparingly glandular-pubescent; stamens exserted, nearly thrice as long as the tube, filaments yellow, villous below; style red, much longer than the stamens. Capsules ovoid-oblong, to 2 cm long. June–Nov. Occasionally flowering in September. Pied. and Coast. Pl. Moist shaded ravines and streamsides. W. cent. Ga. and E. cent. Ala. (Plate 42).
The PLUMLEAF AZALEA is a graceful shrub for woodland conditions and most valuable for its later blooming period of July to August. It has scarlet to deep red flowers. Since its range is centered along the lower Chattahoochee River it is

not as hardy to the north as some other native azaleas. However, its vibrantly colored flowers produced so late in the season make it an excellent choice for the shady garden.

MINNIE-BUSH   *Menziesia pilosa* (Michaux) Jussieu
Shrub to 3 m tall, with deciduous, alternate leaves; blades entire, 3–8 cm long, mucronate and ciliate. Young twigs pubescent. Flowers appear with the leaves. Flowers small, in small terminal corymbs, 4-merous; corolla greenish red, yellow, or white, 6–9 mm long, urceolate-companulate; calyx persistant, the lobes glandular-ciliate; stamens 8. Pedicels becoming erect when fruiting. Capsule 4-chambered, 4–7 mm long. May–Oct. Mts. Heath barrens, acid woods. Pa., W. Va. s to Ga. The vegetation resembles that of azales and blueberries (Plate 42).

SAND MYRTLE   *Leiophyllum buxifolium* (Bergius) Elliott
Evergreen-leaved shrub 0.2–1 m tall with crowded, alternate, or subopposite leaves with very short petioles. Leaves shining above, dull beneath, 5–12 mm long. Flowers small, 5-merous, white, or sometimes pink tinted, in dense terminal corymbs; pedicels glabrous or stipitate-glandular, longer than the bracts; stamens 10; calyx lobes longer than the tube. Capsule 3-parted. Seeds red-brown. Sometimes divided into two varieties but the characters are not conclusive. Mar.–Sept. Coast. Pl., Pied., Mts. Dry, sandy pine barrens. N.J. disjunct to N.C., Tenn. and Ga. Rocky bluffs in the Mts., Pied. and sandy pinelands in the Coast. Pl. (Plate 43).

This fine-textured evergreen shrub is a dainty and unusual item for the rock garden, and when in flower, it is quite showy.

MOUNTAIN LAUREL   *Kalmia latifolia* L.
Large, evergreen, thicket-forming shrub to 10 m tall with mostly alternate, glabrous, coriaceous leaves. Blades 5–10 cm long, elliptic to elliptic-lanceolate; petioles 1–2 cm long. Flowers numerous in terminal corymbs, pink to white with purple markings; pedicels viscid-pilose to glabrous, ascending when in fruit. Corolla shallowly 5-lobed; calyx 5–6 parted; style 14–18 mm long. Apr.–Oct. Mts., Pied., Coast. Pl. Dry rocky woods, slopes, stream banks, often on acid sandy soils. N.B., Ont. to Ind. s to Fla. and La. The hard root once used to make pipe bowls. The genus is named for Allegheny traveler Pehr Kalm, a student of Linnaeus (Plate 43).

One of the most beautiful of our flowering shrubs but seldom grown in American gardens. Why? Until recently nurserymen found it difficult to propagate, but *Kalmia* now is being produced commercially through micropropagation (tissue culture). Dr. Robert Jaynes has made a number of crosses among the species of the genus, and many of his selections are being propagated commercially. MOUNTAIN LAUREL is an excellent plant for naturalizing and is a terrific evergreen plant for shaded borders. It appears at its best on rocky hillsides where it often produces its finest displays.

LAMB-KILL   *Kalmia angustifolia* L.
A stoloniferous shrub to about 1 m tall, with short-petioled, oblong to lanceolate, mostly opposite or whorled evergreen leaves that are glabrous or pubescent at maturity. Leaves 2–6 cm long, petioles 4–12 mm long. Flowers pink to purplish in axillary to terminal corymbs; corolla 1 cm across; pedicels not pilose, recurving in fruit; filaments 3–4 mm long. Apr.–Oct. Occasionally blooming in the autumn. Bogs, springheads, pocosins. Coast. Pl., Mts. Nfld. and Lab. to Mich. s to N.C. and Ga. The leaves of *K. latifolia* and *K. angustifolia* are poisonous to livestock. The

SHEEP LAUREL, *Kalmia carolina* Small, sometimes considered distinct, has leaves pale-pubescent beneath. Mts., and Coast. Pl. Va., Tenn., N.C., S.C., Ga.

Of smaller stature than *K. latifolia*, LAMB-KILL has soft, olive-green leaves with a dull finish and flowers in lateral clusters along the stem, thus providing a totally different effect in the landscape from *K. latifolia*. LAMB-KILL is recommended for higher elevations in the mountains or in the upper South. It performs best in moist soils and is available in the nursery trade.

The related WHITE-WICKY, *Kalmia cuneata* Michaux, is a small stoloniferous shrub with alternate, deciduous, oblong-obovate leaves that are glandular beneath. Flowers white, 1.5 cm across in umbellate corymbs from the axils of leaves of the preceding year. May–Oct. Pied. and Coast. Pl. Wet thickets and shrub bogs. N.C., S.C. One of our rarest shrubs. The WICKY, *Kalmia hirsuta* Walter, is a straggly, low evergreen shrub with thin, hirsute, alternate leaves. The pink to near white flowers are borne singly in the axils of the leaves. June–Oct. Coast. Pl. Sandy pinelands. S.C. to Fla. and Ala. (Plate 43).

MOUNTAIN FETTER-BUSH   *Pieris floribunda* (Pursh) B. & H.

A handsome, evergreen shrub to 1.5 m tall; twigs strigose. Leaves leathery, alternate; blades usually strigose on the margins. Flowers in dense terminal paniculate racemes. The inflorescences terminate growth of the season in June or July: the small white flowers expand the following April or May. Bracts subtending the flowers are as long as the pedicels; calyx and corolla 5-parted; stamens 10. May–Oct. Mts. Balds and moist slopes at high elevations. W. Va., Va., N.C., Tenn.

This underutilized plant is a low, handsome evergreen shrub with relatively stiff branches and dark green leaves. The flowers are borne in dense upright panicles. In some situations, it is superior to the exotic *P. japonica.* The flower buds are formed in autumn and are attractive over winter. In spring the racemes of bell-shaped flowers are conspicuous. MOUNTAIN FETTER-BUSH is best used as an undershrub in large plantings.

The curious evergreen, *Pieris phillyreifolia* (Hooker) DC., may be a shrub to 1 m tall or may climb to 10 m by growing beneath the outer bark of the Cypress, *Taxodium ascendens.* Flowers white, borne in axillary racemes produced just prior to blossoming in January to March. Coast. Pl. Cypress-gum ponds. S.C. s to Fla. and Ala. (Plate 43).

Grown in shrub form, *P. phillyreifolia* can add interest to landscape plantings. It is a valuable conversation plant to challange visitors as to its identity.

The BOG ROSEMARY, *Andromeda glaucophylla* Link, is a low-creeping, slender evergreen shrub with revolute narrow leaves and pink and white flowers in small umbels. Greenl. and Lab. to Man. s to Cranberry Glades, W. Va.

ZENOBIA   *Zenobia pulverulenta* (Bartram) Pollard

Stoloniferous shrub to 2 m tall. Leaves deciduous to half-evergreen, alternate, leathery, 2–8 cm long, pale green to bluish white to glaucous beneath; petioles 3–6 mm long. Flowers white, showy, nodding, fragrant, in corymbs from axillary buds on the upper part of twigs of the preceding season; corollas relatively large, 8–12 cm long; stamens 4-awned. Fruit an erect, globose, 5-valved capsule; seeds angled, rust colored. Apr.–Oct. Coast. Pl. Bogs, bays, savannas, swamps. Va. s to S.C. A showy shrub with handsome and fragrant flowers, not often cultivated, but a suitable garden introduction.

The glaucous leaves of this gracefully arching shrub are especially attractive. It requires moist, acid soil but is easily grown in the garden.

FETTER-BUSH   *Lyonia lucida* (Lam.) Koch
A showy and handsome evergreen shrub with glabrous lower leaf surfaces; branches are strongly angled. The flowers are in axillary clusters of racemes; corolla usually pink, 5–9 mm long. Apr.–Oct. Coast. Pl., sometimes Pied. Bogs, bays, and swamps in moist situations. Va. s to Fla. and La. (Plate 44).

Seldom seen in gardens, the evergreen species of *Lyonia* are handsome, arching evergreen shrubs readily at home in the sandy, acid soils of the Coastal Plain. They are useful in masses or as specimen plants.

The related STAGGER-BUSH, *Lyonia ferruginea* (Walter) Nuttall, is a rhizomatous evergreen shrub to small tree to 6 m tall with alternate leaves 2–7 cm long. Twigs and lower leaf surfaces scurfy with abundant stipitate-peltate, rusty scales. Flowers white, in axillary fascicles, borne on twigs of the previous year; calyx lobes triangular, to 2 mm long; corolla 2–4 mm long with very short lobes. Capsule 5-angled, 3–6 mm long. Apr.–Oct. Coast. Pl. Oak-pine forests, thickets, evergreen scrub on well-drained soil. S.C. s to Fla. Uncommon (Plate 44).

Another similar species of STAGGER-BUSH is *Lyonia fruticosa* (Michaux) G. S. Torry, which has a shrubby habit, rigidly ascending branchlets, and conspicuously reduced leaves. Flowers usually borne on new shoots of the season. Coast. Pl. Pine flatwoods. S.C., Ga., Fla.

MALEBERRY   *Lyonia ligustrina* (L.) DC
Deciduous shrub to 4 m tall spreading by rhizomes. Twigs terete, with short pubescence and stipitate-peltate scales. Leaves variable in shape, 2–9.5 cm long, minutely serrate. Infloresence subpaniculate; flowers white, axillary, on twigs of the previous season; calyx pubescent to glabrous, persistent; corolla 3–4 mm long, the lobes outwardly curving. Apr.–Oct. Coast. Pl., Pied., Mts. Wet places. Me. to Ohio s to Fla., Tex. (Plate 44).

STAGGER-BUSH   *Lyonia mariana* (L.) D. Don
Rhizomatic deciduous shrub to 1.5 m tall. Leaf blades 3–8 cm long, entire, with sparse, short-headed trichomes. Flowers fascicled, along upper parts of leafless branches of the previous season; calyx lobes elongate, 3–9.5 mm, deciduous; corollas white, 7–14 mm long, more or less cylindrical; anthers without awns. Capsules urn shaped, 4–6.5 mm long. Apr.–Oct. Savannas, bogs, pond edges, pine-oak woods. Coast. Pl. and Pied. R.I. s to Fla., disjunct in La., Tex., Ark., Mo., Okla. *Zenobia* is similar, but has awned anthers, persistent sepals, and a globose capsule (Plate 44). ·

FETTER-BUSH   *Agarista populifolia* (Lam.) Judd
Shrub to 4 m tall with glabrous, evergreen, often revolute leaves. Blades 2.5–9 cm long, lanceolate to ovate-lanceolate, finely reticulate-veined. Flowers in loose, short, axillary racemes borne on wood of the previous season; pedicels slender, 7–8 mm long, subtended by a persistent bract; corolla white, urn shaped, 7–8 mm long; filaments S-shaped, pubescent; anthers awnless. Capsule 4–5 mm long; Apr.–Oct. Coast. Pl. Hammocks, swamps, and springs. S.C. to Fla. Rare. Once known as *Leucothoe populifolia* (Lam.) Dippel (Plate 45).

A superior plant for southern gardens, its arching habit of growth and bright green color give a wonderful texture where it is used. It is one of the better plants for creating a naturalistic effect along cool, shaded streamsides or on bluffs. With proper pruning it can be maintained as a medium-sized foundation plant.

DOG-HOBBLE   *Leucothoe axillaris* (Lam.) D. Don
Evergreen shrub to 1.5 m tall with abruptly pointed leathery leaves, petioles to about 1 cm long, and rather broadly ovate to rounded bracts and broadly ovate sepals. Flowers in axillary racemes; corolla white, 6–8 mm long; filaments short-pubescent, lacking sigmoid curves; anthers with two very short awns. Capsule oblate, to 5 mm broad. Mar.–Oct. Coast. Pl. Swamps, bogs, flood plains. Va. s to Fla. and La. (Plate 45).

A similar species with decidedly long-acuminate leaves, with petioles 8–15 mm long, bracts lanceolate-lanceolate-acuminate, and sepals ovate-oblong and acutish is *Leucothoe fontanesiana* (Steudel) Sleum. Mts. and Pied. Moist woodlands, thickets. Va. to Ga. A graceful evergreen shrub with arching branches and pointed leaves. The branches often appear weighted down with clusters of white, urn-shaped flowers. *Leucothoe axillaris* looks natural when it is planted along small stream watercourses in moist, acid soil in partly shaded areas. It also may be massed or placed at the foot of taller, more leggy, shrubs. Some nurserymen report problems with leaf spot on this species. Landscape uses for *L. fontanesiana* are similar. Several cultivars have been selected from the latter species.

MOUNTAIN FETTER-BUSH   *Leucothoe recurva* (Buckley) Gray
Shrub to 4 m tall, with deciduous, glabrous, light green leaves 5–13 cm long, 1-sided, recurving, racemes, ovate sepals, anthers with two awns, a 5-lobed capsule and winged seeds 2–2.5 mm long. Apr.–Oct. Mts. Ridges, rocky woods and thickets at high elevations. Va. s to Ga. and Ala. The leaves turn scarlet in autumn.

The SWAMP LEUCOTHOE, *Leucothoe racemosa* (L.) Gray, found in the Coastal Plain and Piedmont, is similar but the leaves are smaller, to 9 cm long, the racemes are straight and usually erect, the anthers are 4-awned, the capsule is unlobed and the seeds wingless. Mar.–Oct. Coast. Pl. and Pied. Swamps, bogs, cypress-gum wetlands. Mass. s to Fla. and Tex. (Plate 45).

When in flower, the SWAMP LEUCOTHOE is a handsome, deciduous shrub. Its arching branches are covered with clusters of white flowers. The bright green leaves provide a new texture to the natural scene when these shrubs are used along a pond or stream. It is a species with much promise for the home landscape.

SOURWOOD   *Oxydendrum arboreum* (L.) DC
Medium-sized, deciduous tree often blooming as a shrub, with ridged, fur-rowed, red bark, and deciduous leaves with a sour taste. Flowers white, urn shaped, in 1-sided terminal racemes, on wood of the season. Capsule 5-locular, pendulous. June–Oct. Pa. to Ind. s to Fla. to La. An important source of honey; the tree has considerable ornamental value because of its droopng racemes and early fall color (Plate 45).

The drooping flower clusters, reminding one of flowers of the lily-of-the-valley, literally cover the foliage during the summer months. Coloring early in the fall to reds and purples, SOURWOOD is best used in the landscape in massed clusters or as specimen plants. It can be naturalized along roadsides where it often grows on the poor soils of the highway cuts. One of our best native plants for use in full sun.

LEATHER-LEAF   *Cassandra calyculata* (L.) D. Don
Low, much-branched, rhizomatous evergreen shrub to 1 m tall. Leaves

Rhododendron canescens

Rhododendron atlanticum

Rhododendron roseum
GALLE

Rhododendron viscosum

PLATE 41

Rhododendron prunifolium
GALLE

Rhododendron arborescens

Rhododendron serrulatum GALLE

Menziesia pilosa

PLATE 42

Leiophyllum buxifolium

Pieris phillyreifolia

Kalmia latifolia

Kalmia hirsuta   MILLER

PLATE 43

Lyonia lucida

Lyonia ferruginea

Lyonia mariana   MILLER

Lyonia ligustrina

PLATE 44

Agarista populifolia

Leucothoe axillaris

Leucothoe racemosa

Oxydendron arborteum

PLATE 45

Gaylussacia frondosa

Epigea repens

Vaccinium arboreum

Gaylussacia ursina

PLATE 46

Vaccinium arboreum

Vaccinium stamineum

Vaccinium pallidum

Vaccinium pallidum

PLATE 47

Vaccinium hirsutum

Vaccinium myrsinites

Vaccinium hirsutum

Vaccinium corymbosum

PLATE 48

leathery, 1–5 cm long, alternate, scurfy, peltate scaled but glabrate above, short-petioled. Flowers white, small, nodding, on arching terminal branchlets, the flowers partially developed the previous season. Corolla 6–7 mm long, urnlike, the 5 lobes recurved; calyx persistent; filaments flat, tapered upward. Capsule 5-parted, with a 10-valved inner layer. Mar.–Oct. Coast. Pl. Sphagnum bogs, peaty pond margins. Circumpolar: Nfld. to Alaska s to S.C. Uncommon.

TRAILING ARBUTUS   *Epigaea repens* L.
   A prostrate evergreen shrub with creeping stems. Leaves alternate, oval to elliptic, coriaceus, petiolate. Flowers pistillate or bisexual; corollas white to pink, with 5 spreading or recurving lobes. Stamens 10, filaments slender, with a tuft of hair near the middle. Capsule 5-locular, multiseeded. Feb.–June. Mts., Pied.,Coast. Pl. Dry rocky woods. Lab. to Ia. s to Fla. and Miss. The flowers are fragrant. The roots have a micorrhizal association and the plants are difficult to transplant: the seed are dispersed by ants. Picking has reduced its abundance (Plate 46).

CHECKERBERRY   *Gaultheria procumbens* L.
   Low, rhizomatous shrub with alternate, evergreen leaves 1.5–6 cm long with deciduous bristle-tipped teeth. Flowers solitary, small, white, axillary; stamens 8–10. Fruit an elipsoidal red berry formed by the fleshy glabrous calyx and its base. June–Dec. Mts., Pied., Coast. Pl. Acid woods and swamp edges. Nfld. to Wis. s to Ga. The fruit and plant are wintergreen scented and the oil is extracted for commercial use.
   The CHECKERBERRY makes an excellent groundcover for acid, moist, cool, shady places. Transplant it by using pieces of sod.
   The CREEPING SNOWBERRY, *Gaultheria hispidula* (L.) Bigelow, has white berries and revolute leaves 1 cm or less in length. Mts. Mossy woods, bogs. Lab. to Ida. s to N.C.

HEATH   *Erica tetralix* L.
   Shrub to less than 2 m tall with evergreen whorled, linear leaves less than 5 mm long and fine pink or white flowers in terminal or axillary fascicles. New Engl. s to N.C. European introduction.
   Another Old World species is the HEATHER, *Calluna vulgaris* (L.) Hull, with imbricated opposite leaves 1 mm long in 4 rows and small pink or white flowers. Locally introduced, naturalized on dry sand. Mts. New Engl. s to W. Va. Uncommon.

BLACK HUCKLEBERRY   *Gaylussacia baccata* (Wang.) K. Koch
   Much-branched, stiff, deciduous colonial shrub to 3–8 dm tall. Leaves elliptic to elliptic-oblanceolate with scattered trichomes and dotted with resinous glands. Flowers in axillary panicles from wood of the previous season; calyx 5-lobed, persistent; corolla tubular, 4–5.5 mm long. Fruit a drupe 6–10 mm across, black, not glaucous, glabrous, with 10 nutlike sweet seeds. May–Sept. Mts. Dry to moist pine and hardwood woods. Nfld. to Sask. s to Ga. and La. The fruit and twigs are used by many forms of wildlife.
   One of the more ornamental huckleberries, it also bears the most flavored fruit. The BLACK HUCKLEBERRY is a good groundcover for thin, rocky woods. In autumn, the leaves turn to glowing tints of orange and crimson.
   Gaylussacia may be distinguished by the 10-celled ovary having 10 ovules, the berrylike drupe, the ovules becoming hard, the usual presence of resinous glands

on the underside of the leaves, flowers always in lateral racemes, and anthers awnless. *Vaccinium* has a 5-celled ovary, or with false partitions, 10-celled; numerous ovules and fruit a fleshy berry; the flowers are variously arranged, and the anthers may be awned.

DANGLEBERRY   *Gaylussacia frondosa* (L.) T.& G. var. *frondosa*
    Deciduous shrub to 2 m tall with widely spreading branches, glabrous twigs, and leaves to 6 cm long. Corolla 3–4 mm long, slightly longer than broad, greenish white with tints of pink. Fruit 5–8 mm in diameter, a cadet blue, glaucous, berrylike drupe. Mar.–Aug. Coast. Pl. and Pied. Well-drained to moist woodlands, thickets, bogs, bays. N.H. s to S.C. and Ala. (Plate 46).
    The WOOLLY DANGLEBERRY, *Gaylussacia frondosa* var. *tomentosa* Gray, is similar, but has densely tomentose twigs and lower leaf surfaces. Mar.–Aug. Coast. Pl. Moist pinelands. S.C. to Fla. and Ala. Rare. Also related is the SMALL DANGLEBERRY, *Gaylussacia frondosa* var. *nana* Gray, now considered specifically as *G. nana* (Gray) Small, which grows 2–6 dm tall with leaves 2–4 cm long, strongly glaucous and sparsely pubescent beneath; relatively short branches; corolla 2–3 mm long, broader than long. Coast. Pl. Open woods. Ga. s to Fla. and Miss.

BOX HUCKLEBERRY   *Gaylussacia brachycera* (Michaux) Gray
    A low evergreen shrub with glabrous leaves to 2.5 cm long, completely lacking glandular hairs, the blades elliptic. Racemes short, with 2–6 flowers and deciduous bracts that are shorter than the pedicels; flowers white to pink, 3–5 mm long. Berrylike blue drupe, 6–10 mm long, with a heavy bloom. May–July. Mts. Sandy soils, slopes. Pa. and Del. s to Tenn. and S.C. First found in 1790 in West Virginia by Michaux and reported by Kin and Pursh about 1805, the species was "lost" until rediscovered in 1921 by F. W. Gray who advertized for the "juniper berry" in local newspapers and recieved reports of it from 75 localities! The colonies seem to consist of single, self-sterile individuals and may extend over 8 acres.
    The BOX HUCKLEBERRY is a lovely, interesting groundcover suited to areas under mountain laurels and rhododendrons where the soil is extremely acid, well drained, and high in organic matter. Plant it in the upper South or at higher elevations.

DWARF HUCKLEBERRY   *Gaylussacia dumosa* (Andrz.) T.& G.
    Deciduous, or semi-evergreen rhizomatous shrub 1–3 dm tall, the larger leaves to 3 cm long, elliptic-oblanceolate, the upper surface with scattered hairs and short-stalked resinous glands, lower surface with resinous glands. Raceme bracts longer than pedicels and foliaceous, remaining until the fruits mature. Racemes to 4 cm long, 4–10 flowered; calyx and hypanthium with stalked glandular trichomes; corolla white, 4–7 mm long. The drupe is black, shiny, 6–8 mm in diameter. Mar.–Oct. Coast. Pl., Mts., Pied. Well-drained pinelands, sandy habitats, and sphagnum bogs. Nfld. and Pa. s to Fla. and La.
    MOSIER'S HUCKLEBERRY, *Gaylussacia mosieri* (Small) Small, is taller than the DWARF HUCKLEBERRY, reaching 3–15 dm, with inconspicuous, short-stalked glands. Leaves 3–6 cm long, elliptic-oblanceolate to oblanceolate, at first minutely pubescent on both sides, becoming veiny with age. Corolla 3.5–7.5 mm long; sepals 1.5–2 mm long. Insipid fruit black, conspicuously glandular-hairy, 8–10 mm in diameter. Coast. Pl. Hammocks, bogs, and flatwoods, often with the

preceding. Ga. and Fla. to La.

BEAR-HUCKLEBERRY   *Gaylussacia ursina* (M. A. Curtis) T.& G.

A shrub to 1.5 m tall having stamens with pubescent filaments and leaves with a short, abrupt tip. Twigs, petioles, and the lower side of the leaves on the midrib are tomentose. Leaves green, 5–10 cm long, elliptic to elliptic-oblanceolate. Calyx lobes obtuse. Drupe black, 10–12 mm in diameter, shiny, insipid to sweet. May–Sept. Mts. above 1700 ft. Acid slopes, summits, woodlands. Tenn., N.C., S.C., Ga. (Plate 46).

BLUEBERRIES of the Genus *Vaccinium* are a complex assemblege of a number of polymorphic groups, some possible hybrids, and variable individuals. For many species, identification is difficult at best. Principle sources are Godfrey and Wooten (1981); Clark (1971); Radford, Ahles and Bell (1968); Strausbaugh and Core (1973); and Vander Kloet (1980, 1983, 1983).

SPARKLEBERRY   *Vaccinium arboreum* Marshall

Coarse shrub to 10 m tall with many branches, handsome glossy foliage, and abundant white, bell-shaped flowers in the spring. Leaves semi-evergreen, oval to obovate, elliptic, 1.5–4.5 cm long, leathery. Flowers borne in leafy-bracted racemes, the corolla 5-parted; stamens included within the corolla; anthers awned. Berry black, lustrous, smooth, 5–8 mm long, dry, with scanty pulp, persisting to late winter. Apr.–Dec. Coast. Pl., Pied. Mts. Dry sites in pine or hardwood understories or around openings. Va. and Mo. s to Fla. and Tex. An important wildlife food in late winter; long-lived, fire resistant. The flower sprays are ornamental, the foliage glossy (Plates 46, 47).

Although relatively slow growing, SPARKLEBERRY is a handsome shrub and should be considered for the landscape. It is ideal if planted in full sun in thin woodlands, at the edge of woods, or as a backing to an annual or perennial garden. It sparingly spreads by underground roots and grows well in dry soils. The flowers bloom later than those of most Vacciniums and are abundant.

DEERBERRY   *Vaccinium stamineum* L.

Shrub to 5 m tall with round twigs often branching so as to form flattish fans. Leaves deciduous, glabrous to pubescent, elliptic to oblanceolate, 3–9 cm long, entire. Flowers pendulous on leafy-bracted racemes, the bracts smaller than the true leaves; corollas 5-parted, white, campanulate, 5–8 mm long; stamens exserted, anthers awned, extended into long tubes. Berry green to amber, pink to purple, usually glaucous, tart, bitter, quickly deciduous. Apr.–Oct. Pied. and Mts. Dry woodlands. N.Y. to Mo., s to Fla. and La. Highly variable species, sometimes divided into species or intraspecific taxa (Plate 47).

Adapted to dry, thin woodlands from low to high elevations, the DEERBERRY deserves to be grown in American gardens. Some of the highly glaucous forms may provide potential cultivars to be selected and exploited by nurserymen.

UPLAND LOW BLUEBERRY   *Vaccinium pallidum* Aiton

A low shrub occurring in small to large open colonies. Twigs green to yellow, glaucous and usually angular, pubescent or glabrous. Leaves pale to dark blue-green, usually glabrous but sometimes pubescent beneath with an entire or serrate margin, deciduous. Leaves average 1.7 cm wide and 3.1 cm long. Corolla greenish white, with pink striping; filaments glabrous or marginally ciliate; flower pedicels are glaucous, rarely finely pubescent. The berry is variable, being blue to black, glaucous to shining or dull, 4–8 mm in diameter. Apr.–Oct. Mts., Pied.,

Coast. Pl. Oak or oak-hickory woods, pine savannahs, cut-over lands, rocky ledges. Me. to Minn. s to Ga., Ala. and Kans. Includes *Vaccinium vacillans* Torrey. An important wildlife food especially of the Ruffed Grouse, but used by many songbirds. Fruiting has been increased by controlled burning (Plate 47).

Vaccinium hirsutum Buckley, is a similar species, with gland-tipped trichomes on the fruit. The entire plant is densely hirsute. Mts. Open acid woods. N.C., Ga. and Tenn. Distinguished from all other blueberries by its purplish black pubescent fruits.

EVERGREEN BLUEBERRY   *Vaccinium myrsinites* Lam.

Evergreen colonial shrub to 6 dm tall. Leaves elliptic to oblanceolate, sessile or subsessile, less than 1.5 cm long, green to glaucous, with scattered stalked glandular hairs beneath. Flowers 2–8 in short, axillary racemes before the season's growth; calyx glabrous to glaucous, corolla white to deep pink, urceolate, 6–7 mm long or less. Berry black or blue-black, 5–8 mm in diameter, sometimes slightly glaucous. Coast. Pl. Acid sandy soils, pinelands, scrub. S.C. s to Fla. and Ala. (Plate 48).

A related EVERGREEN BLUEBERRY, *Vaccinium darrowii* Camp, is more markedly glaucous and bluish green and lacks the stalked glands on the underside of its leaves. Leaf margins are thickened and usually somewhat revolute, entire or with appressed, gland-tipped teeth. Its glaucous, blue fruit is only 4–6 mm in diameter. Coast. Pl. Seasonally wet to dry pinelands, scrub. Ga. to Fla. and Tex.

The CREEPING BLUEBERRY, *Vaccinium crassifolium* Andrews, is an evergreen trailing shrub with fruiting pedicels shorter than the fruit. Leaves with leathery blades and slender, short petioles; leaf margins are decidedly thickened; blades less than 1.5 cm long. Bears a 5-parted pink and white corolla, the lobes of which are small in relation to the tube. Berry black to purple, 5 mm long. Coast. Pl. Bog and bay borders. Va. s to Ga. and Ala.

HIGHBUSH BLUEBERRY   *Vaccinium corymbosum* L.

Shrubs generally 2–3 m high but occasionally 1–5 m tall, with 2–5 or more stems from a single crown, occasionally suckering when disturbed or bent, rarely reproducing by root sprouts; twigs angular to rounded, green, yellow or reddish. Leaves ovate to narrowly elliptic, usually deciduous; blades pubescent, glabrous or glaucous beneath, very rarely glandular; margins entire to serrate. Corolla cylindrical, rarely urceolate or campanulate, white, sometimes tinged with pink; berry dull black to blue and glaucous, rarely shining black. Mar.–Nov. Mts. Pied. and Coast. Pl. Open swamps and bogs, sandy lake shores, upland woods, ravines, and summits. N.S. to Ill. s to Fla., Tex. and Okla. Uncommon to rare in Mo., Ky., Tenn. (Plate 48).

The populations of *Vaccinium corymbosum* consist of diploids, widespread in the Southeast, tetrapoids centered in the northeastern United States and adjacent Canada, and a few isolated hexaploids along the Blue Ridge and on the Coastal Plain from South Carolina to Louisiana and north to the Ouachita Mountains in Arkansas. Recent studies by Vander Kloet have resulted in the combining of a number of species into this one high bush type. Vander Kloet has not found any gross morphological features which consistantly divide the population either in the field or herbarium. *Vaccinium corymbosum* L. therefore now includes *V. ashei* Reade, *V. fuscatum* Aiton, *V. amoenum* Aiton, *V. myrtilloides* Ell., *V. elliottii* Chapman, *V. constablaei* Gray.

HIGHBUSH BLUEBERRIES are excellent low screens that can blend into the shrub border. In addition to a most brilliant fall color of scarlet and crimson, they yield a delightful bonus of fruit for pies, muffins, pancakes, and the birds. Vacciniums need moist acid soil and while they do best in full sun, this blueberry will grow well in submature to mature hardwoods although fruiting will be minimum under heavy shade. Numerous cultivars selected for both fruit production and fall color characteristics are available and highly recommended for inclusion in the home landscape. New cultivars for the Deep and Middle South are commercially called "Rabbiteyes." They and cultivars suitable for the Upper South provide edible fruit without use of pesticides.

DWARF BLUEBERRY   *Vaccinium tenellum* Aiton
Erect rhizomatous shrub to 4 dm tall. Young branchlets copiously pubescent. Leaves deciduous, bright green, oblanceolate to oblong-obovate, to 3 cm long, finely ciliate, serrulate, remotely stipitate-glandular beneath, acute at the apex. Flowers pink to white, in fascicles of 5–15, sessile on naked branches, appearing with the leaves; corolla narrow, 5–7 mm long, essentially glabrous; stamens 5 mm long. Berries black with whitish bloom 5–8 mm in diameter. Mar.–July. Coast. Pl. and Pied. Pinelands, dry woodland borders and acid swamp edges. Va. s to Ga., Ala.

EARLY LOW BLUEBERRY   *Vaccinium angustifolium* Aiton
A low colonial shrub with serrate leaves 1–3 cm long. The leaves are bright green on both sides; the lower leaf surface is not glandular although the margin may be glandular-serrulate; the usually white corolla is 3–5 mm long and the berries are bright blue, 5–7 mm in diameter. Mts. Heath barrens, dry, rocky, or sandy soils; bogs. Va. and W. Va. The common blueberry of the mountain region and a variable species with several named subspecies. The earliest to ripen, large quantities are harvested from the wild.

BEARBERRY   *Vaccinium erythrocarpum* Michaux
Erect shrub to 1 m tall, divergently branched, with exfoliating bark. Leaves deciduous, ovate-lanceolate to elliptic-lanceolate, acuminate, bristly-serrate, the teeth with stipitate glands, 3–8 cm long. Flowers solitary on slender pedicels of new growth; calyx lobes 4; the corolla deeply 4-cleft, the tube 2–4 mm long, the 4 lobes narrow, rose, rotate and 7–10 mm long; anthers long-exserted and awnless. Berry dark red to purplish, 5–9 mm in diameter; flavor insipid. May–Sept. Mts. Moist or dry woods, heath barrens. W. Va., Va., N.C., Tenn. Rare to uncommon. Endemic to the Southern Appalachians. Once used to make jelly.

CRANBERRY   *Vaccinium macrocarpon* Aiton
Sprawling shrub 4–15 cm high, with ascending branches. Leaves deciduous, narrowly elliptic, 6–17 mm long, glaucous beneath, margins entire, scarcely revolute. Pedicels with leaflike bracts over 1 mm wide, 2–4 mm long, erect; flowers solitary or axillary at the base of current shoots; calyx 4-lobed; corolla 4-lobed, white to pink; stamens 8. Berry red, acid, 9–15 mm in diameter, globose to pyriform. May–Nov. Mts. Sphagnum bogs, springheads, wet shores and meadows. Nfld. to Minn. s to Tenn. and N.C. Also Coast. Pl. of N.C. The commercial cranberry.

The SMALL CRANBERRY, *Vaccinium oxycoccos* L., is similar, but has slender stems, ovate leaves 5–6 mm long, that are glaucous beneath and strongly revolute. Pedicels with red scalelike bracts less than 1 mm wide. The berry is 6–10 mm in diameter, at first punctate, later deep red. Sphagnum bogs. Circumboreal, s in Mts. Va., W. Va. Rare.

SAPOTACEAE

SOUTHERN BUCKTHORN
Bumelia lycoides (L.) Persoon

Thorny shrub 3–6 m tall with simple leaves glabrous or slightly pubescent beneath, 7–12 cm long, deciduous to partly evergreen. Flower clusters dense and many flowered, glabrous; calyx 5-lobed, corolla white, 5-lobed. Fruit a drupelike berry, 10–12 mm long. Under magnification, veins in the leaves are markedly reticulate. June–Oct. Coast. Pl. and Pied. Dunes, rich woods, river and lake borders. Va. to Ill. s to Fla. and Tex.

FALSE BUCKTHORN, *Bumelia lanuginosa* (Michaux) Persoon, is similar, but has the branchlets and lower leaf surfaces covered with woolly pubescence. The berry is larger, to 10–15 mm long, and the shrub may reach 20 m tall. Coast. Pl. Ga. and Fla. to Tex., Kans., Ill.

The TOUGH-BUCKTHORN, *Bumelia tenax* (L.) Willd., also has pubescence, but it is lustrous white, not woolly, and becomes tawny and coppery. The pedicels and calyx are also rufus sericeous. May–Oct. Coast. Pl. S.C. to Fla.

Bumelia reclinata Vent., has glabrous leaf blades, corolla lobes 2 mm long, and small fruit, to only 6–7 mm long. Coast. Pl. Ga., Fla.

Bumelia thornei Cronquist, is a thorny shrub with obovate leaves 1.5–3 cm long. Coast. Pl. Endemic to Ga. Members of this genus have milky sap, hard wood, and crooked and rough branches often inhabited by lichens, liverworts, and mosses.

SYMPLOACEAE

COMMON SWEETLEAF
Symplocos tinctoria (L.) L'Her.

Erect, mostly evergreen shrub or small tree with thick, leathery leaf blades, 5–15 cm long, short-petioled. Leaves simple, alternate, glabrous or pubescent above, tomentose beneath, and sweet tasting. Flowers bright to creamy yellow, relatively small, borne in conspicuous axillary clusters or at the leafless nodes of wood of the previous season. Fruits are drupelike, reddish brown, becoming dry at maturity, 8–10 mm long. Mar.–Sept. Mts., Coast. Pl., Pied. Upland woods, moist ravines, stream margins. Del. s to Fla., Ark., Tex. Leaves are a favorite cattle food; bark and leaves yield a yellow dye (Plate 49).

The clusters of fragrant flowers are showy in the early spring and the lustrous green leaves are pleasing. Useful for naturalizing on thinly wooded bluffs or as a conversation plant in the shrub border.

EBENACEAE

PERSIMMON
Diospyros virginiana L.

Tree to 35 m tall but often thicket-forming from rhizomes and appearing shrublike. Bark checkered into small brown to blackish blocks. Terminal bud aborted on twigs. Leaves deciduous, alternate, simple, 5–15 cm long, dark green above, often with dark blemishes, glabrous to sparingly pubescent and whitish below. Flowers unisexual, inconspicuous, axillary, the female flowers solitary, the male clustered; corolla greenish yellow, 4–5 lobed. Fruit a globose berry, orange when ripening, later brownish-purple, containing several seeds; fruit astringent at first, flavorful when fully ripe. May–Oct. Pied., Mts., Coast. Pl. Old fields, pinelands, hardwood forests. Conn. and Ia. s to Fla. and Tex. An important food of foxes, opossums, and other wildlife. The dark heartwood is used for utensils (Plate 49).

The PERSIMMON has a yellowish green fall color; the bark on older trees is blackish, thick and divided into blocks. Most ideally used in the landscape as a tree for parks and botanic gardens. The ripe fruit is an ancestral delicacy used in jellies, pies, and savory condiments.

STYRACACEAE

SNOWBELL, STORAX   *Styrax americana* Lam.
Deciduous shrub, occasionally treelike, with elliptic, oval, or obovate leaves to 8 cm long and 4 cm wide; blades glabrate with age above, sparingly pubescent below. Flowers in racemes 5 cm or less in length; corolla white, 5-merous; stamens 10. Fruit globose, densely short pubescent, 7–8 mm long. Apr.–Sept. Coast. Pl. In standing shallow water, alluvial woods, stream banks. Va. to Mo. s to Fla., Tex. (Plate 49).

The STORAX, *Styrax grandifolia* Aiton, has deciduous leaves, oval or broadly obovate to nearly orbicular, 8–15 cm long racemes 5–15 cm long. Va. s to Fla. and La.

Both species of *Styrax* are fine choices for the garden landscape. They are at their best when grown in full sun to very light shade: plant them where visitors can enjoy the pendulous flowers at close range. Storaxes perform well in moist soil along streams and ponds and should be naturalized in these situations.

SILVERBELL   *Halesia carolina* L.
Shrubs to small trees; as the leaves unfold, they bear from the axils of leaf scars, umbels or racemes of pendant, white, 4-merous flowers. Leaves simple, alternate, and deciduous with oblong, elliptic to ovate-oblong, abruptly acuminate blades. Flowers in clusters of 2–5 on slender pedicels; styles as long as the corolla. Fruit 4-winged, dangling from the branches. Mar.–Sept. Mts., Pied., Coast. Pl. Rich woods and stream banks, river bottoms. Va. to Ill. s to Fla., Tex. and Mo. (Plate 49).

The SNOW-DROP TREE, *Halesia diptera* Ellis, bears 2-winged fruit, and the style equals the corolla. Coast. Pl. Woodland floodplains, marsh edges, ravines. S.C. to Fla. and Tex., Ark.

A similar plant is *Halesia parviflora* Michaux, with style exserted from the corolla by nearly half its length; corolla shorter, to 12 mm long, pubescent. S.C. to Fla., Miss. and Okla. See Reveal & Seldin (1976) for a different nomenclatorial interpretation.

Long neglected in American gardens, the SILVERBELLS are commonly encountered in gardens in the British Isles. They are marvelous small native trees and shrubs especially valuable for planting along stream banks in shade or full sun. They may be used in groups or as single specimen trees in parks. Interest is increasing in the SILVERBELLS and they are being grown by several wholesale nurseries in the Southeast. The elegant snow-white flowers appear in earliest spring simultaneously with the leaves. The smaller sizes of plants appear easier to establish.

OLEACEAE

SWAMP-PRIVET   *Forestiera acuminata* (Michaux) Poiret
A weak, leaning shrub or small tree with simple, opposite, deciduous leaves with oblong, obovate to rhombic blades, 4–8 cm long, tapering at both ends but the apex acuminate. Flowers small, greenish yellow in axillary clusters, petals absent.

Fruits wrinkled, oval or ellipsoid drupes, 7–10 mm long. Mar.–May. Coast. Pl. and Pied. Swamp forests, riverbanks, gravel bars. S.C. to Ky. and Ill. s to Fla. and Tex. (Plate 50).

A related species is *Forestiera ligustrina* (Michaux) Poiret, which has elliptic to obovate leaf blades 2–3 cm long, with obtuse to acute tips. Coast. Pl. and Pied. Dry, rocky woods. Ky. to Ga., Fla., Ala.

A related species with evergreen leaves is *Forestiera segregata* (Jacquin) Krug. & Urban. Its blades are elliptic to elliptic-spatulate, 2–4 cm long. Coast. Pl. Hammocks, shell middens, edge of salt marshes. S.C., Ga., Fla.

A new species from Florida and South Carolina is *Forestieria godfreyi* Anderson.

GRANDSIR-GRAYBEARD   *Chionanthus virginicus* L.
Shrub to small tree with opposite, deciduous, simple leaves to 18 cm long, glabrous above, glabrous to densely pubescent below, entire; petioles purple. Flowers in clusters on pendant fringelike inflorescences with green leaflike bracts; corolla white, with petals 4-merous, narrow and elongate. Drupe blue-black, ovoid, 1–1.8 m long. Coast. Pl., Pied., Mts. Apr.–Sept. Dry acid soils, rocky woods and bluffs. N.J. to W. Va. s to Fla., Tex. and Okla. (Plate 50). Widely transplanted ornamental. A related ornamental escape is the LILAC, *Syringa vulgaris* L. which bears fruit in a 2-lobed capsule.

Chionanthus virginicus is of great value in the landscape as a specimen plant. When placed in shrub borders or in a group planting its fantastic flowers and dark green leaves often become the showpiece of the garden. It apparently presents no cultural difficulty and is available in the nursery trade.

WILD OLIVE, DEVIL WOOD   *Osmanthus americanus* (L.) Gray
An evergreen shrub or small tree with pale bark. Leaves leathery, simple, opposite; blades elliptic, oblong-elliptic or lanceolate. Flowers small, greenish to creamy white in axillary panicles on twigs of the previous season. Fruits dark blue drupes 6–10 mm long. Apr.–Oct. Coast. Pl. Forests, bluffs swamps. Va. s to Fla. and La. (Plate 50).

The loose and open habit of the WILD OLIVE makes this a wanted shrub whether used in a naturalized landscape or in a more formal setting as a foundation plant. Readily available in nurseries, *Osmanthus americanus* deserves a place in southern gardens.

CHINESE PRIVET   *Ligustrum sinense* Lour.
Shrub to 10 m tall with semi-evergreen leaves with pubescent petioles and branchlets, leaves to 2–5 cm long. Flowers white or cream colored. Drupes blue, ellipsoid, 4–5 mm long. Coast. Pl., Pied. Mts. Waste places. Ky. to Ga. and Ala.

Other PRIVETS are *Ligustrum japonicum* Thunberg, with glabrous branches and leaves more than 5 cm long; *Ligustrum amurense* Carr, with glabrous branchlets; *Ligustrum ovalifolium* Hasskarl, with glabrous petioles and *Ligustrum lucidum* Aiton, the GLOSSY PRIVET, with flowers in panicles 20–25 cm long. Waste places, river flood plains. Escapes (Plate 50).

LOGANIACEAE

YELLOW JASMINE   *Gelsemium sempervirens* (L.) Aiton f.
Climbing vine, with evergreen, opposite leaves with glabrous blades 2.5–7 cm

long. Flowers fragrant; calyx lobes obtuse, corolla yellow. Capsule oblong, abruptly pointed, the beak less than 2 mm long; seeds winged. Mar.–Nov. Coast. Pl., Pied. Thickets, fencerows, often on granitic or gneissic outcrops. Va. s to Fla., Tex. and Ark. (Plate 51).

The closely related JASMINE, *Gelsemium rankinii* Small, has flowers without fragrance, the calyx lobes are acute to acuminate, the seed wingless, and the rounded capsule beak is more than 2 mm long. Swamps and bogs. N.C. s to Fla. and La. Infrequent to rare.

Often used as a "mail box" plant, *Gelsemium sempervirens* is a twining evergreen vine with wiry stems. When grown in cultivation in full sun, it becomes much denser and attractive than normally seen in nature. It can be used on trellises and as a groundcover, and is especially useful on granitic or gneissic rocky outcrops. The bright yellow flowers are a welcome sight in March; the double-flowered form 'Pride of Augusta' is available from nurseries, but the single-flowered natural form is most attractive.

BUTTERFLY-BUSH   *Buddleia lindleyana* Fortune
Shrub to 2 m tall, branchlets 4-angled, leaves usually opposite, 3–10 cm long, slightly toothed, nearly glabrous. Flowers in a purplish violet terminal spike; flowers and the rachis covered with whitish glands; calyx 4-lobed, the sepals united, to 16 mm long, the tube curved, trumpet shaped. June–Oct. Stream banks and waste places. Infrequently naturalized in our area (Plate 51).

A related introduced species is *Buddleia davidii* Franchet, with a pubescent rachis in the inflorescences; white-tomentose lower leaf surfaces, blades to 25 cm long. Md. s to Ga., Tenn. Introduced from China; an occasional escape.

APOCYNACEAE

CLIMBING DOGBANE   *Trachelospermum difforme* (Walter) Gray
Slender twining vine with smooth stems and milky sap. Leaves deciduous, opposite, 4–10 cm long, petiolate to subsessile, variable in shape and size, lanceolate to broadly obovate on the same plant. Flower clusters with long peduncles, produced in only one axil of a leaf pair; flowers numerous, very fragrant, yellow to greenish; corolla tube 6 mm long, the lobes 3–4 mm. The fruits are slender follicles 15–25 cm long; seed angled, with silky hairs. May–Sept. Coast. Pl. and Pied. Bottomlands, floodplains, thickets. Del. to Ind. s to Fla., Tex. and Mo. The plant may be poisonous.

OLEANDER   *Nerium oleander* L.
Evergreen erect shrub; leaves mostly in whorls of 3, sometimes opposite, oblong-lanceolate, entire. Flowers showy in terminal branching cymes, rose-pink, red, purple, or white to yellowish. Follicles 10–18 cm long. All parts of the plant are extremely toxic if eaten. Residual at old house sites or from roadside plantings.

The GREATER PERIWINKLE, *Vinca major* L., and the COMMON PERIWINKLE, *Vinca minor* L., are trailing, evergreen subshrubs with opposite, entire leaves and solitary, usually blue flowers. Persistent at old house sites, cemeteries. Useful as groundcovers to control slope erosion, but can become pests unless used where they can be controlled. They are shade tolerant.

ASCLEPIADACEAE

CYNANCHUM   *Cynanchum scoparium* Nuttall

A slender, diffuse vine, woody in the south, with linear, deciduous leaves on short petioles. Corolla greenish white, with a crown attached at its base. Coastal hammocks, S.C. to Fla. and Miss.

The SILK-VINE, *Periploca graeca* L., is a partly woody vine with brownish-purple, green-margined corolla lobes 9–11 mm long. Rare Escape. Mass. s to Fla. and Kans.

VERBENACEAE

BEAUTY-BERRY   *Callicarpa americana* L.

Shrub to 2.5 m tall with scurfy, stellate-pubescent twigs. Leaves deciduous, simple, opposite, with stellate pubescence beneath. Flowers in pinkish axillary cymes shorter than the subtending petioles. Drupe 4-seeded, bright purple. June–Oct. Coast. Pl., Pied., Mts. Woodlands. Md. to Fla., Tex. (Plate 51).

Glabrous leaves mark the rare *Callicarpa dichotoma* (Lour.) K. Koch. N.C. and Va.

The BEAUTY-BERRY is a coarse, open shrub; the pinkish flowers are followed by a profusion of bright purple fruit. The fruit clusters encircle the stem and are persistent over a long period. It is an ideal shrub for massing in the light shade of southern pines and grows well in most soils. A white form is available.

LANTANA   *Lantana camara* L.

Shrub, sometimes armed with prickles. Leaves sparsely pubescent and often very scabrous. Flowers in axillary, dense, flat-topped spikes. Corolla orange to yellow, red or lavender. Fruit fleshy. Coast. Pl. S.C. to Fla. and Tex. Escaped ornamental.

The WEEPING LANTANA, *Lantana montevidensis* (Sprengel) Briquet, has leaves usually densely soft, spreading pubescent and sometimes very slightly scabrous. Coast. Pl. Introduced.

Lantana horrida H.B.K., has obtuse calyx lobes shorter than the tube. A rare escape.

Other escaped members of the Verbena Family are the GLORYBOWERS, *Clerodendron bungei* Steud. and *Clerodendron indicum* (L.) Kuntze. Both have white corollas 9–15 cm long. Coast. Pl. S.C. to Fla. and Tex.

The LILAC CHASTE TREE, *Vitex agnus-castus* L., is a garden escape with deciduous, opposite, palmately compound leaves and a strong aromatic odor. Flowers are pubescent, violet and fragrant, in open terminal compound cymes. N.C. to Fla. and Tex.

LAMIACEAE or LABIATAE

WILD ROSEMARY   *Conradina canescens* (T. and G.) Gray

Much-branched aromatic low shrub with opposite linear leaves. Calyx tube densely pubescent with stiff hairs. Coast. Pl. Dunes and scrub. w. Fla. to Miss. It tolerates salt spray making the plant ideal for naturalistic uses in coastal landscapes. Its grayish foliage is unusual and attractive (Plate 51).

The APPALACHICOLA ROSEMARY, *Conradina glabra* Shinners, bears a calyx tube that is glabrous or minutely and inconspicuously puberulent.

Conradina verticillata Tennison, bears short, 2-leaved branches in most axils. Mts. Sandy woods and ravines, sandy river bars. Ky., Tenn. Well suited to rock gardens: easily propagated by cuttings. Repels rabbits. (Jennison, 1933).

RED BASIL   *Satureja coccinea* (Nuttall) Bentham
Shrub to 1 m tall with oblanceolate to spatulate entire leaves 8–14 mm long. Corolla more than 2.5 cm long, scarlet; calyx 7 mm or more long; upper-lip lateral lobes triangular, shorter than those of the lower lip. Coast. Pl. Dry pine barrens and sand hills. Ga. to Miss. It is the correct plant for landscaping Coastal Plain sandhills or sand ridges. Loose, open growth habit.

The GEORGIA BASIL, *Satureja georgiana* (Harper) Ahles, a low shrub, has a pink to lavender corolla 1–2 cm long, elliptic to ovate glabrous petiolate leaves. Coast. Pl. and Pied. Dry woods and bluffs. N.C. to Fla. and Miss. It is usually less than 2.5 dm tall and often is found growing naturally on roadcuts where little else can survive. It should be naturalized in problem areas of dry, thin soil in full sunlight.

Satureja dentata (Chapm.) Briquet, is similar, but has subsessile, densely pubescent leaves. Sandy scrub. Fla.

Satureja ashei Weatherby, has linear, revolute leaves. Scrub oak-pine. Ga., Fla.

SOLANACEAE

CHRISTMAS BERRY   *Lycium carolinianum* Walter
A weakly spiny shrub to 15 dm tall with succulent ligulate or clavate leaves to 3 cm long. Leaves simple, alternate, deciduous, often with short, leafy branchlets in the axils. Flowers usually solitary; corolla blue or lilac, or white. Berry red, to 1.5 cm long. Coast. Pl. Sand spits, shell beaches, mounds, salt marshes. S.C. to Fla. and Tex.

The MATRIMONY-VINE, *Lycium halimifolia* Miller, is a vinelike shrub with elliptical to obovate leaves, not succulent, and a red to orange berry to 2 cm long. Va. to Ky. s to Ga., Tenn. Rare escape.

RUBIACEAE

BUTTONBUSH   *Cephalanthus occidentalis* L.
Disheveled-appearing shrub to 3 m tall. Twigs reddish brown with corky lenticels. Leaves deciduous, opposite, or in whorls of 3–4, the blades oval, oblong-oval, elliptic or ovate, variable in size, 7–15 cm long, 3–10 cm wide. Flowers sessile, in dense globose heads; corolla white, 4-lobed; style long, much exserted from the corolla. Fruit 4–8 mm long, eventually splitting into 2 or 4 nutlets. June–Sept. Mts., Pied., Coast. Pl. Swamps, pond and lake edges, bogs, marshes, often in water. Can. to Minn s to Fla. and Tex. Waterfowl are principle users of the nutlets (Plate 52).

Cephalanthus occidentalis is a straggly, loose shrub with rather interesting flower clusters. It can be used in the landscape in full sun in the shallow waters of ponds or in wet soil at the edge. Every few years it should be cut to the ground and rejuvenated as the young, vigorous stems are much more attractive than the older ones and seem to produce more blooms. Much admired and cultivated in Europe, it is largely unappreciated in the southeastern United States but can be tasteful and useful in the landscape.

RUBIACEAE

FEVER-TREE   *Pinckneya bracteata* (Bartram) Raf.

Handsome shrub or small tree. Young twigs pubescent, becoming reddish brown with raised lenticels. Leaves deciduous, opposite; blades oval, elliptic or ovate, variable in size from 5 to 20 cm long. Flowers in loose, few-flowered, usually terminal cymes; calyx segments 5, at least one enlarged and becoming leaflike, 6–8 cm long, pink, or rarely yellow, and showy: corollas greenish yellow, with brownish or purple spots. Fruit a 2-valved capsule with numerous seed. May–Sept. Coast. Pl. Bayheads, seepage swamps. S.C., Ga., Fla. Often locally abundant. Formerly known as *P. pubens* (Plate 52).

When in flower, The FEVER-TREE is one of the most attractive of our native woody plants, producing a display that can be seen from some distance. It should be planted in moist soil and used as a specimen or accent plant. It is not reliably hardy in the upper Piedmont but is excellent southward.

BIGNONIACEAE

CROSS-VINE   *Bignonia capreolata* L.

High-climbing woody vine; stems with a cross-shaped pith. Leaves semi-evergreen, opposite, compound, usually with 2 leaflets and a branched tendril with adhesive disks at the tips. Flowers axillary, in clusters of 2–5; corolla 4–5 cm long, orange to reddish outside and yellow to red within, the 5 lobes much shorter than the throat. Fruit a flat, beanlike capsule to 15 cm long; seeds winged. Apr.–Aug. Pied. and Coast. Pl. Thickets, low woods, edges of bayheads. Md. to Ill., Mo. s to Fla. and La. Formerly placed in the genus *Aniostichus* (Plate 52).

The showy flowers and mostly evergreen leaves make this an ideal vine for trellises or fences. Seemingly known to few, this is one of our southeastern treasures just waiting to be used in our gardens. The name CROSS-VINE is derived from the appearance of the stem tissue when cut in cross section.

TRUMPET CREEPER   *Campsis radicans* (L.) Seem.

A trailing or climbing vine, ascending by aerial rootlets. Leaves opposite, deciduous, pinnately compound; leaflets 7 or more, acuminate with coarsely serrate margins, without a tendril. Flowers in a crowded terminal cluster; corolla funnelform, 6–8 cm long, orange to red, the 5 lobes much shorter than the tube; stamens included. Fruit a long, pendant capsule, 10–20 cm long, the seed winged. June–Oct. Pied., and Coast. Pl. Fencerows, waste places, upland woodlands. N.J. to Ia. and Mo. s to Fla., La. and Tex. (Plate 52).

A rampant, deciduous vine with rich orange to reddish flowers best used in the landscape on fences or arbors. Several cultivars have been selected with red or yellow flowers.

CAPRIFOLIACEAE

BUSH HONEYSUCKLE   *Diervilla lonicera* Miller

Shrub to 1.5 m tall, with simple, deciduous, opposite leaves 8–15 cm long; blades acuminate at the apex; petioles 3–10 mm long. Flowers in terminal or sub-terminal cymes; corolla 12–20 mm long, yellow to reddish. Fruit a slender long-beaked, capsule. June–Oct. Mts. and Pied. Dry woods, Nfld. to Man., s to Ga., Ala.

The closely related *Diervilla sessifolia* Buckley, has sessile, larger leaves which are glabrous beneath. W.VA. to Ala. This is the best for landscape use. It is a tough, hardy plant, wonderful for naturalizing on road cuts in full sun. Use it in the upper South on sites where few other plants will survive.

Diervilla rivularis Gattinger, is similar but has leaves that are pubescent beneath. N.C. and Tenn.

ELDERBERRY   *Sambucus canadensis* L.

Stoloniferous, deciduous, soft-stemmed shrub to 4 m, with grayish brown bark and prominant lenticels; pith white. Leaves odd-pinnately compound, with 5–11 leaflets, the lower of which are sometimes divided into 3 segments; petioles 3–10 cm long, slender and naked. Flowers small, white, borne in large, flat, many-flowered cymes, having glands in the forks of the cyme. Fruit a purple-black berrylike drupe, 4–6 mm long. Apr.–Sept. Swamp edges, springs, wet woods, fencerows, roadside edges. Mts., Pied., Coast. Pl. N.S. to Man. s to Fla., Tex. (Plate 53).

Sambucus canadensis should be used in full sun in moist soil or planted near a pond or stream or along low roadside ditches. The flat-topped cymes of white flowers are showy and are followed by attractive and useful purple to black fruit. Cutting back to the ground seems to rejuvenate the plant, making it ideal for roadside use, where it can be mowed. It is easily established and is naturally at home in the zigs and zags of an old rail fence.

A similar species is *Sambucus pubens* Michaux, with a paniculate inflorescence, brown pith on second-year wood, with red fruit and without glands in the inflorescence. Rocky woods. Nfld. to Alaska s to Ga. and Tenn. (Plate 53).

CORAL-BERRY   *Symphoricarpos orbiculatus* Moench

Erect, much-branched shrub 1–2 m tall with slender, purplish stems. Leaves oval to ovate, obtuse or rounded at both ends, deciduous. Flowers in dense clusters in the upper leaf axils, sessile or nearly so; corolla greenish, 3–4 mm long, 4–5-lobed. Fruit red berrylike drupes, persistent. July–Nov. Pied. and Mts. Rocky places and woodlands, often on circumneutral soils. Conn. to Colo. s to N.C., S.C., Ala., La. and Tex.

The SNOWBERRY, *Symphoricarpos albus* (L.) Blake, has a pinkish or pink to white corolla 5–9 mm long. The fruits are white, berrylike drupes, 6–12 mm in diameter. Que. to Neb. s to Va., W. Va.

The two species of *Symphoricarpos* are sometimes used as ornamentals but their value is rather limited.

TWINFLOWER   *Linnaea borealis* L.

A slender, creeping, evergreen woody plant with 2 delicate, white, nodding, fragrant flowers, borne in pairs at the end of elongated peduncles; corolla funnelform, 8–15 mm long, hairy inside. June–Aug. Mts. Cool woods, peaty deposits, talus slopes. Circumboreal in distribution. W. Va. Uncommon.

JAPANESE HONEYSUCKLE   *Lonicera japonica* Thunberg

Climbing or trailing vine with hairy young stems and exfoliating older stems. Leaves semi-evergreen, opposite, ovate to elliptic-oblong. Flowers borne on new wood in pairs on a short peduncle bearing two bracts; corolla white to pinkish, becoming yellow with age, distinctly 2-lipped. Fruit a shiny black berry, 5–6 mm long. Apr.–Oct. Mts., Pied., Coast. Pl. Fencerows, thickets, woodlands. Mass. to Kans. s to Fla., Tex. and Mo. Introduced for erosion control, now a troublesome weed overwhelming the native flora (Plate 53).

A valuable deer-food plant in the Piedmont, JAPANESE HONEYSUCKLE can be used as a good, fast-growing bank cover in the Upper South.

RED TRUMPET HONEYSUCKLE   *Lonicera sempervirens* L.
Twining vine with glabrous young stems. Leaves opposite, semi-evergreen, narrowly oblong to broadly oval, the uppermost 1, or rarely 2, pairs of leaves connate-perfoliate, often glaucous beneath, sometimes pubescent, sessile or on short petioles. Flowers in 2–4 sessile, remote whorls forming interrupted spikes; corolla red or slightly yellow outside, yellow inside, nearly regular and not prominently 2-lipped. Berries red. Mar.–Sept. Pied. and Coast. Pl. Fencerows, woods, and thickets. Me. to Neb. s to Fla. and Tex. (Plate 53).
Another excellent vine for the mailbox; when cultivated in the garden the plant is quite vigorous and flowers abundantly if grown in full sun. Several cultivars of *L. sempervirens* are listed in the nursery trade. For fences, one should consider any of the vinelike native honeysuckles; you will not be disappointed.

YELLOW HONEYSUCKLE   *Lonicera flava* Sims
Twining or loosely ascending vinelike shrub, sometimes semi-prostrate, the uppermost 2 pairs of leaves connate, light green or pale to lightly glaucous. Corolla 20–37 mm long, 2-lipped, with a slender tube and yellow-orange lobes. Apr.–Aug. Pied. and Mts. Rocky woods. N.C. to Mo. s to Ga., Ala. and Ark. Local (Plate 54).
The SMOOTH HONEYSUCKLE, *Lonicera dioica* L. is a climbing, vinelike shrub. Leaves elliptic to oblong, the upper several pairs connate-perfoliate. Flowers in a short pedunculate spike; corolla 2-lipped, yellow to purplish, the tube swollen on one side at the base. Berries red, crowded. June–Sept. Mts. and Pied. Rocky banks, woods, thickets. Me. to Man. s to Ga. and Mo. Uncommon.
Lonicera prolifera (Kirchner) Rehder, may be distinguished by its pale yellow corolla and heavily whitened and glaucous upper leaf surfaces. Ont. to Man. s to Tenn., Ark.
The FLY-HONEYSUCKLE, *Lonicera canadensis* Marsh, is a straggling shrub with glabrous leaves, peduncles longer than the greenish yellow axillary flowers 2 cm long. Berries red. Mts. Moist woods. Que. to Sask. s to N.C., Tenn.
Several *Lonicera* species introduced from Asia have become naturalized, including: MORROW'S HONEYSUCKLE, *Lonicera morrowi* Gray; TARTARIAN HONEYSUCKLE, *Lonicera tatarica* L.; WINTER HONEYSUCKLE, *Lonicera fragrantissima* Lindley & Pax; *Lonicera maackii* (Rupr.) Maxim.; and *Lonicera* × *bella* Zabel. Identification often is difficult due to the variable nature of these cultivated taxa.

MAPLE-LEAVED ARROWWOOD   *Viburnum acerifolium* L.
Stoloniferous shrub to 2 m tall. Young twigs pubescent. Leaves palmately 3-lobed, opposite, coarsely dentate, black dotted beneath, and 5–12 cm broad. Cymes slender-peduncled, 2–9 cm broad, the flowering stems with one pair of leaves; flowers creamy white, 5-merous, perfect. Drupe black, compressed, 8–9 mm long. Apr.–Oct. Mts., Pied., Coast. Pl. Dry rocky woods. Que. to Minn. s to Ga., Tenn. (Plate 54).
A shade-tolerant shrub useful for naturalizing in wooded settings. It should be allowed to develop large, loose colonies. The foliage is especially colorful in the autumn.

WITCH-HOBBLE   *Viburnum lantanoides* Michaux
Shrub to 1–4 m tall with cordate, pinnately veined leaves. New growth with rusty-stellate pubescence; lower branches often prostrate and rooting. Leaves deciduous, broadly ovate, short acuminate, serrate, basally cordate; petioles 1.5–3 cm long. Cymes sessile, the exterior flowers showy but neutral, 2.5 cm broad, the inner flowers perfect, 5–7 mm broad; flowering stems with one pair of leaves. Drupes red, changing to black, 10–12 mm long; stone deeply grooved. Apr.–July. Mts. Ravines, coves, and stream banks. Ont. s to Ga., N.C., Tenn. (Plate 54).

A straggly shrub best used naturalized in moist, shady woods in the Upper South. Once known as *V. alnifolium.*

SOUTHERN ARROW-WOOD   *Viburnum dentatum* L.
Shrub to 3 m tall with arrow-straight stems. Leaves deciduous, opposite, mostly ovate, with conspicuous lateral veins, margins sharply serrate, bases sub-cordate, rounded or truncate; petioles 5 mm or more long. Flowers in flat-topped cymes with stalks 2–12 cm long. Flowers small, whitish, 5-merous. Fruits are one-seeded blue-black drupes, 5–8 mm long. Mar.–Sept. Pied., Coast. Pl., Mts. Woodlands, bogs, stream banks, floodplain forests. Me. to Ill. s to Fla. and Tex. (Plate 54).

The related *Viburnum rafinesquianum* Schultes, or DOWNY ARROWWOOD, differs in having the upper leaves sessile or the petioles less than 4 mm long; stipules present. Apr.–July. Pied. Dry basic or neutral soils. Que. to Man. s to Ga., Ky., Mo.

Viburnum dentatum is a highly variable species variously interpreted as made up of several varieties or ill-defined species not worthy of recognition, such as *Viburnum bracteatum* Rehder. *Viburnum dentatum* is a hardy, sturdy shrub for full sun to light shade. The foliage is interesting but highly variable. Selections should be made of superior clones for landscape use. They are good plants throughout the season, with creamy blossoms, light green foliage, and deep blue fruits. The abundance of straight stems gives the plant the name ARROW-WOOD.

SWAMP-HAW   *Viburnum nudum* L.
Shrub or small tree. Leaf blades thick, to 15 cm long, deciduous, abruptly short-acuminate with margins mostly entire or somewhat revolute, glandular dotted, especially beneath; petioles 5–20 mm long, somewhat winged. Cyme stalked, with 4–5 primary branches, to 15 cm across, flowering after the leaves have expanded; flowers small, white to cream colored, 5-merous. Drupe bitter, 6–10 mm long, cream or pink, then deep blue with a bloom. May–Oct. Pied., Coast. Pl., Mts. Bogs, springheads, bays, creek bottoms. Conn. to Ky. and Ark. s to Fla. and Tex. Including *Viburnum cassinoides* L.

A handsome shrub for massing or for the shrub border. The creamy white flowers are followed by most attractive fruit that changes color as the season progresses. This fine native should occupy a place in southern gardens.

BLACK HAW   *Viburnum prunifolium* L.
Shrub or small tree 2–6 m tall. Stems and leaves glabrous or sparsely scurfy-stellate. Leaves deciduous, elliptic to oblong-elliptic, not glandular dotted beneath, sharply serrate. Cymes sessile or nearly so; flowers numerous, perfect. Drupes bluish black, 8–14 mm long, the pulp sweet. Mar.–Oct. Pied., Coast. Pl., Mts. Woodlands. Conn. to Kans. s to Fla. and Tex. (Plate 55).

The rigid, horizontal branches and spurlike twigs give it the name BLACK

HAW. Fast growing and extremely adaptable, it is worthy of landscape use.

The SMALL VIBURNUM, *Viburnum obovatum* Walter, has deciduous leaves only 2–5 cm long and 1–3 cm wide, the blades oblanceolate to spatulate, the upper surface glabrous, the lower glandular dotted. Cymes sessile. Drupes passing from red to black during maturation. Coast. Pl. Stream banks, low woods. S.C. to Ala. Uncommon.

Seldom seen in our gardens, this plant is of interest due to its small leaves.

The BLUE HAW, *Viburnum rufidulum* Rafinesque, has buds, petioles, lower leaf surfaces scurfy with short, wavy, rusty red trichomes. Leaves mostly ovate or elliptic, lustrous above with finely serrate margins, deciduous. Cymes sessile or nearly so. Drupes glaucous blue, 10–14 mm long. Pied. and Coast. Pl. Va. to Mo. s to Fla. and Tex. Somewhat similar to *V. prunifolium,* the BLUE HAW grows taller and larger in all its parts. The rusty red fuzz on its leaves and twigs is unusual and fascinating (Plate 55).

COMPOSITAE or ASTERACEAE

MARSH ELDER   *Iva imbricata* L.
A succulent, low, bushy-branched subshrub, to 1 m tall. Leaves alternate, linear-elliptic to linear-lanceolate, to 4.5 cm long, 4–10 mm wide, glabrous, almost sessile, margins mostly entire. Flowers in solitary, heterogamous heads, in the axils of the upper bracteal leaves, the greenish white unisexual flowers surrounded by involucral bracts, the staminate flowers more numerous than the pistillate. Fruit a yellow-brown achene. Aug.–Nov. Coast. Pl. Coastal sands, dunes. Va. s to Fla., Tex.

The HIGH WATER SHRUB, *Iva frutescens* L. is similar but larger, to 3 m tall, with opposite, appressed-pubescent leaves. Saline marshes and shores. N.J. s to Fla. and Tex.

BUSH GOLDENROD   *Chrysoma pauciflosculosa* (Michaux) Greene
A semiwoody shrub to 2 m tall; new growth viscid. Leaves alternate, narrowly oblong to oblanceolate, conspicuously net veined. Flowers in 5-flowered head, arranged in panicles, involucral bracts and branches of inflorescence appearing varnished; ray flowers yellow. Achenes 2.3–3 mm long. July–Oct. Coast. Pl. Sand scrub, sand dunes. N.C. to Fla. and Ala. (Plate 55).

The BUSH GOLDENROD can be planted on inner sand dunes along the coast or on the deep sands of the sandhills of the Coastal Plain. Sometimes included in *Solidago.*

CLIMBING ASTER   *Aster carolinianus* Walter
Diffusely branched plant with principal stem and branches woody: climbing to 4 m or more or tangling upon its own woody, 1 cm thick stems. Leaves alternate, simple, auriculate-clasping, elliptic, 2–6 cm long. Involucres 7–12 mm high; bracts whitish, green, spreading to squarrose; rays numerous, ligules lavender-pink or lavender to 2 cm long. Achene brown, 3 mm long, glabrous. Coast. Pl. Marshes, shores and edges, often in water. N.C. to Fla. (Plate 56).

GROUNDSEL TREE   *Baccharis halimifolia* L.
Freely branched glabrous shrub to 4 m tall. Leaves dull grayish green with conspicuous amber glandular punctations, evergreen, alternate, leathery, elliptic to obovate, serrate, 2–6 cm long. Flowers in discoid heads, ray flowers lacking. Heads small, many flowered, clustered on distal portions of branches simulating panicles; most of the heads on definite stalks. The pistillate shrub is conspicuous in

Symplocos tinctoria

Diospyros virginiana

Halesia carolina

Styrax americana BARBERS

PLATE 49

Chionanthus virginicus

Forestiera acuminata

Osmanthus americana MILLER

Ligustrum japonicum

PLATE 50

Gelsemium sempervirens

Buddleia lindleyana

Callicarpa americana

Conradina canescens

PLATE 51

Bignonia capreolata

Pickneya bracteata

Cephalanthus occidentalis

Campsis radicans

PLATE 52

Lonicera japonica

Sambucus pubens

Sambucus canadensis

Lonicera sempervirens

PLATE 53

Viburnum acerifolium

Lonicera flava

Viburnum dentatum

Viburnum lantanoides

PLATE 54

Viburnum prunifolium

Viburnum rufidulum

Viburnum rufidulum

Chrysoma pauciflosculosa BELL

PLATE 55

Aster carolinianus

Baccharis halimifolia

Borrichia frutescens

PLATE 56

autumn with its white pappus. Sept.–Oct. Coast. Pl. and Pied. Marshes, swales, shores. Formerly coastal, now can be found inland. Mass. s to Fla., Tex., Okla.

The GROUNDSEL TREE is noteworthy for naturalistic landscapes along the seacoast. It is at home along salt-marsh edges as well as near sand dunes. It can be used in roadside plantings throughout much of the lower Coastal Plain (Plate 56).

The FALSE WILLOW, *Baccharis angustifolia* Michaux, has linear, almost needlelike leaves, 1–3 mm broad, lustrous green. Coast. Pl. Edges of salt and brackish marshes. N.C. s to Fla., Ala. *Baccharis glomerulifolia* Persoon, has clusters of heads scattered along leafy branchlets and paniculate leaf blades without orange glands. N.C. to Fla.

SEA OX-EYE   *Borrichia frutescens* (L.) DC.

Rhizomatous colonial shrub to 1 m tall. Branches ascending, grayish pubescent when young. Leaves oblanceolate to elliptic, opposite, 2–16 cm long, densely gray-pubescent on both sides, margins entire. Flowers in heads surrounded by short-mucronate or spine-tipped involucral bracts; pales with spiny tips; ray flowers yellow; disk flowers brownish yellow. May–Sept. Coast. Pl. Brackish marshes and estuarian shores. Va. s to Fla., Tex., Mex. (Plate 56).

An ideal plant for landscape use along the edge of salt marshes.

Keys to Families of Shrubs

A. Plants semiparasitic upon the branches of trees—LORANTHACEAE
A. Plants not semiparasitic upon the branches of trees, but terrestrial.
   B. Gymnosperms not bearing true flowers.
      C. Branchlets bearing tiny, closely appressed, scalelike or awl-shaped leaves—CUPRESSACEAE
      C. Branchlets bearing alternate, flat, linear leaves about 2.5 cm long with the petioles twisted so the leaves appear more or less in one plane—TAXACEAE
   B. Angiosperms bearing true flowers.
      D. Stems thick and fleshy, or flattened pads usually bearing spines and bristles borne in small clusters—CACTACEAE
      D. Stems of ordinary appearance, not as above—
         E. Monocotyledons with parallel-veined leaves; stems with scattered vascular bundles.
            F. Plants with hollow-jointed bamboolike stems and elongate leaves sheathing at the base—GRAMINEAE/POACEAE
            F. Plants with various stems, but not hollow and jointed.
               G. Plants with palmlike leaves; inflorescences large and drooping, having numerous small flowers; fruit drupelike—PALMAE/ARECACEAE
               G. Plants with linear, strap-shaped leaves, with very sharp, hard points; inflorescences terminal, with numerous white flowers over 3 cm long; fruit a capsule—AGAVACEAE
         E. Dicotyledons normally with net-veined leaves; stems with vascular bundles arranged in a ring.
            H. Stems bearing ochreae at the nodes—POLYGONACEAE
            H. Stems not bearing ochreae at the nodes.
               I. Plants with the flowers in involucrate heads having numerous small flowers surrounded tightly by a cup of bracts—COMPOSITAE/ASTERACEAE
               I. Plants having various inflorescences including tightly rounded heads but the flowers not surrounded by involucral bracts typical of the Compositae family.
                  J. Leaves opposite or whorled—KEY I
                  J. Leaves alternate.
                     K. Leaves compound—KEY II
                     K. Leaves simple.
                        L. Leaves evergreen—KEY III
                        L. Leaves deciduous—KEY IV

KEY I. SHRUBS WITH OPPOSITE OR WHORLED LEAVES

A. Leaves whorled.
   B. Leaves linear, small; flowers sessile in the leaf axils; bark on the older wood gray and shreddy—EMPETRACEAE (*Ceratiola*)
   B. Leaves, broad, not linear; flowers not sessile; bark not gray and shreddy.
      C. Flowers in terminal and axillary, long peduncled heads; native species of swamps and wet lands—RUBIACEAE (*Cephalanthus*)
      C. Flowers in terminal and axillary cymes, sometimes panicle-like; introduced species of well-drained sites—VERBENACEAE (*Clerodendron*)
A. Leaves opposite.
   D. Leaves compound.
      E. Leaves trifoliate; capsule papery, inflated to 3 cm long—STAPHYLEACEAE (*Staphylea*)
      E. Leaves pinnately or palmately compound; fruits various, but not as above.
         F. Leaves pinnately compound; flowers white, in flat-topped cymes—CAPRIFOLIACEAE (*Sambucus*)
         F. Leaves palmately compound.
            G. Leaves strongly aromatic when crushed; flowers blue; fruits 5 mm broad—VERBENACEAE (*Vitex*)
            G. Leaves not aromatic; flowers white, yellow, or red; fruits 3 cm or more broad—HIPPOCASTANACEAE (*Aesculus*)
   D. Leaves simple.
      H. Leaves lobed.
         I. Flowers yellowish, in drooping clusters; fruit a winged schizocarp splitting into samaras—ACERACEAE (*Acer*)
         I. Flowers white, in erect clusters; fruit a capsule or drupe.
            J. Flowers small, in flat-topped cymes; fruit a 1-seeded drupe; bark not peeling—CAPRIFOLIACEAE (*Viburnum acerifolium*)
            J. Flowers large, especially the sterile ones, in drooping paniclelike cymes; fruit a several-seeded capsule; bark peeling—HYDRANGEACEAE (*Hydrangea quercifolia*)
      H. Leaves not lobed.
         K. Flowers and fruits in heads or compact headlike cymes.
            L. Bracts subtending inflorescence large, white, not resembling the leaves; fruit a red drupe; flowers in compact cymes—CORNACEAE (*Cornus florida*)
            L. Bracts subtending inflorescence similar to leaves; individual fruits small, angular, and dry, splitting into 2–4 nutlets; flowers in globular heads—RUBIACEAE (*Cephalanthus*)
         K. Flowers and fruits not in heads or compact headlike cymes.
            M. Some sepals becoming greatly enlarged (7–10 cm long) and creamy to pink and petal-like so the inflorescence is especially showy; petioles connected by a stipular line—RUBIACEAE (*Pinckneya*)

131

M. Sepals not as above.
  N. Leaf margins entire.
    O. Leaves granular-farinose beneath—LOGANIA-CEAE (*Buddleia*)
    O. Leaves various beneath, but not granular-farinose.
      P. Leaves acuminate at the apex.
        Q. Perianth segments 10 or more, undifferentiated into a distinct calyx and corolla; receptacle urnshaped, hollow, narrow at the mouth, enclosing a number of 1-seeded achenes—CALYCANTHACEAE (*Calycanthus*)
        Q. Perianth segments 5 or less or absent; receptacle not as above; fruit a drupe or drupelike.
          R. Flowers unisexual; corolla lacking; fruit more than 1 cm in diameter—SANTALACEAE
          R. Flowers bisexual; corolla present; fruit less than 1 cm in diameter.
            S. Inflorescence axillary—LYTHRA-CEAE (*Decodon*)
            S. Inflorescence terminal.
              T. Flowers usually 5-merous; fruit crowned with 5 minute, persistent sepals—CAPRI-FOLIACEAE
              T. Flowers usually 4-merous; fruit crowned by 4 sepals—CORNACEAE
      P. Leaves obtuse to acute at the apex, not acuminate.
        U. Flowers conspicuous, blue (rarely white), corolla large, salverform, the limb 2.5 cm wide; stems somewhat woody, trailing, and forming mats—APOCYNACEAE (*Vinca*)
        U. Flowers inconspicuous, not blue; plants not mat forming.
          V. Leaf venation penniveined—APOCYNACEAE (*Nerium*)
          V. Leaf venation not penniveined.
            W. Stamens numerous, 10 or more; fruit a capsule; plants often glandular dotted—HYPERIACEAE
            W. Stamens 2–5; fruit a berry, drupe, or composed of 4 nutlets.

X. Stems obscurely 4-angled; fruit of 4 nutlets; plants aromatic—LABIATAE/LAMIACEAE

X. Stems terete; fruit a berry or drupe; plants not conspicuously aromatic.

    Y. Ovary inferior; stamens usually 5; epipetalous; inflorescence cymose—CAPRIFOLIACEAE

    Y. Ovary superior; stamens 2, not epipetalous; inflorescences racemose or paniculate—OLEACEAE

N. Leaf margins toothed.

  Z. Stems obscurely 4-angled; fruit of 4 nutlets inside the persistent calyx—LABIATAE/LAMIACEAE

  Z. Stems terete, if somewhat 4-angled fruit not composed of 4 nutlets.

    AA. Inflorescences in axillary clusters.

      BB. Stamens inserted on the edge of a staminal disk—CELASTRACEAE

      BB. Stamens not inserted on a staminal disk.

        CC. Stamens 2; flowers actinomorphic—OLEACEAE

        CC. Stamens 4; flowers zygomorphic—VERBENACEAE (*Lantana*)

    AA. Inflorescences terminal at branch ends.

      DD. Small shrub of coastal shell mounds and hammocks; leaf blades 2–4 cm long and 1–2 cm wide—RHAMNACEAE (*Sageretia*)

      DD. Larger shrub of inland rich woodlands and bluffs; blades 4–10 cm long, 2–8 cm wide—HYDRANGEACEAE (*Philadelphus*)

KEY II. SHRUBS WITH ALTERNATE COMPOUND LEAVES

A. Leaves decompound (twice or thrice compound).
   B. Stems coarsely prickly.
      C. Leaflets 3 cm or more broad; fruit a purple to black drupe—ARALIACEAE (*Aralia*)
      C. Leaflets less than 2 cm broad; fruit a legume—MIMOSACEAE
   B. Stems not prickly.
      D. Flowers pink or yellow, due to colored filaments, corolla inconspicuous; fruit a legume—MIMOSACEAE
      D. Flowers with white corollas; filaments not colored; fruit a red berry—BERBERIDACEAE (*Nandina*)
A. Leaves once compound.
   E. Teeth of leaflets bearing a conspicuous green gland on the central undersurface of each tooth; plants ill-smelling, colonizing extensively by root sprouts—SIMAROUBACEAE (*Ailanthus*)
   E. Teeth of leaflets lacking conspicuous glands beneath; plants not as above.
      F. Leaves predominately trifoliate or pinnately compound with only 3 leaflets.
         G. Stems spiny.
            H. Petioles winged; midrib of leaflets not spiny—RUTACEAE
            H. Petioles wingless; midrib of leaflets often spiny—ROSACEAE
         G. Stems not spiny.
            I. Mature leaves conspicuously glandular above—RUTACEAE
            I. Mature leaves not glandular above.
               J. Leaflets obtuse, mucronate; fruit a legume—FABACEAE
               J. Leaflets acuminate, not mucronate; fruit a drupe—ANACARDIACEAE
      F. Leaflets pinnately compound, predominately with more than 3 leaflets.
         K. Plants generally unbranched with monopodal stems; wood and flowers yellow; flowering December to March; berries blue; escaped ornamental—BERBERIDACEAE (*Mahonia*)
         K. Plants without the above combination of features.
            L. Leaflets borne on a wide, flat phyllodelike rachis—CAESALPINACEAE (*Parkinsonia*)
            L. Leaflets not borne on a phyllodelike rachis but rachis may be slightly winged.
               M. Leaflets entire.
                  N. Inflorescence axillary—FABACEAE
                  N. Inflorescence terminal.

        O.   Fruit a legume; flowers conspicuous, yellow—
            CAESALPINACEAE (*Cassia*)

        O.   Fruit drupelike; flowers inconspicuous, white
            to greenish—SAPINDACEAE (*Sapindus*)

M. Leaflets toothed or lobed.

    P.   Terminal leaflet of at least some of the leaves lobed.

        Q.   Fruit a follicle; corolla lobes much shorter than
            the calyx; wood of root yellow—RANUN-
            CULACEAE (*Xanthorhiza*)

        Q.   Fruit a drupe; corolla lobes longer than calyx;
            root not yellow—ANACARDIACEAE

    P.   Terminal leaflets not lobed; leaflets may be serrate.

        R.   Stamens more than 10; flowers not in cat-
            kins—ROSACEAE

        R.   Stamens 10 or less, or staminate flowers borne
            in catkins.

            S.   Terminal leaflets entire—ANACARDIA-
                CEAE

            S.   Terminal leaflets serrate—RUTACEAE

KEY III. SHRUBS WITH ALTERNATE SIMPLE EVERGREEN LEAVES
(or semi-evergreen at the northern end of our range).

A. Twigs with stipular rings at the nodes; flowers white with numerous spirally arranged perianth parts; stamens and carpels on an elongate receptacle—MAGNOLIACEAE (*Magnolia*)
A. Twigs without stipular rings at the nodes; flowers not as above.
    B. Leaves scalelike to acicular.
        C. Flowers yellow, sessile or pedicellate on tips of short branches—CISTACEAE (*Hudsonia*)
        C. Flowers pink to off-white, numerous in racemes 1–8 cm long—TAMARICACEAE (*Tamarix*)
    B. Leaves broad, not scalelike to acicular.
        D. Foliage, flowers, and fruits notably aromatic when crushed or broken.
            E. Leaves irregularly serrate on their upper margins; blades punctate with resinous dots—MYRICACEAE
            E. Leaves entire, not lobed nor serrate.
                F. Petiole winged; fruit a large hesperidium, similar in appearance to cultivated citrus—RUTACEAE (*Citrus*)
                F. Petiole not winged; fruit not citruslike.
                    G. Midribs and principal lateral veins of the leaves prominent; large insect galls usually present along margins of blade—LAURACEAE (*Persea*)
                    G. Midribs of the leaves prominent but lateral veins scarcely evident; insect galls not present along margins—ILLICIACEAE (*Illicium*)
        D. Foliage not strongly aromatic.
            H. Leaf blades with silvery, often overlapping scales, at least beneath.
                I. Fruit a fleshy drupe; plant an escaped ornamental—ELAEAGNACEAE (*Elaeagnus*)
                I. Fruit a 3-lobed capsule; native plant of limited distribution in specialized habitats—EUPHORBIACEAE (*Croton alabamensis*)
            H. Leaf blades glabrous to pubescent, but without silvery scales beneath.
                J. Leaves succulent; branches recurving; fruit a berry; low-spreading plant of coastal sand dunes, shell mounds and salt marshes—SOLANACEAE (*Lycium*)
                J. Leaves not succulent; plant not as above.
                    K. Anthers opening by terminal pores; flowers urceolate or campanulate—ERICACEAE
                    K. Anthers not opening by terminal pores; flowers various but not urceolate nor campanulate.
                        L. Fruit a woody capsule; stamens numerous and united to petals; flowers large and showy—THEACEAE
                        L. Fruit not a woody capsule; plants without the

above combination of characteristics.

M. Stems semiwoody, 1–2 dm long, dying the second spring, low-growing plants with long rhizomes, the evergreen leaves crowded toward the summit of the erect stems; leaves dark green (or brownish purple in winter) mottled with light green (especially during the winter)—BUXACEAE (*Pachysandra procumbens*)

M. Stems definitely woody, plants not as above—

    N. Ovary inferior; fruit a red to orange pome; corolla of 5 small white petals borne with the stamens on a hypanthium; spiny-stemmed escaped ornamental—ROSACEAE (*Pyracantha*)

    N. Ovary superior; plants without above combination of characteristics.

        O. Style attached basally to ovary; low (4 dm or less) stoloniferous shrub of sand ridges and high pinelands—CHRYSOBALANACEAE (*Licania*)

        O. Style terminally attached to ovary; plants not as above.

            P. Flowers white, including the hypanthium, arranged in axillary racemes; leaves with bitter almond odor; fruit a black drupe; native to Coastal Plain, uncommon Piedmont escape—ROSACEAE (*Prunus caroliniana*)

            P. Plants without the above combination of features.

                Q. Flowers in terminal or lateral narrow racemes or raceme-like panicles; fruit dry, terete or winged nutlike drupes—CYRILLACEAE

                Q. Flowers in axillary clusters; fruits not as above.

                    R. Plants with milky sap; stems with thorny branches often supporting epiphytic lichens—SAPOTACEAE (*Bumelia*)

                    R. Plants without milky sap; stems not thorny, normally not supporting epiphytic lichens—AQUIFOLIACEAE

KEY IV. SHRUBS WITH ALTERNATE SIMPLE DECIDUOUS LEAVES

A. Fruit a hollow fleshy receptacle with achenes (a fig), or a rounded aggregate fruit, or multiple fruit; sap milky—MORACEAE
A. Fruit not as above; sap may be milky.
  B. Flowers unisexual.
  C. Pistillate flowers in spiny involucres; seed surrounded by spiny involucres—FAGACEAE (*Castanea*)
  C. Pistillate flowers and seed not in spiny involucres.
    D. Male flowers in erect catkins; plants dioecious; rare, treelike shrub of limited distribution in wet habitats—LEITNERIACEAE (*Leitneria*)
    D. Male flowers not in erect catkins; plants not as above.
    E. Flowers of at least one sex in spherical heads or clusters.
      F. Sap milky; female flowers in globular clusters—MORACEAE
      F. Sap not milky; male flowers in globular clusters—NYSSACEAE
    E. Flowers not in spherical heads or clusters.
      G. Flowers of at least one sex in elongate catkins or catkinlike structures.
      H. Leaves velvety; sap milky—MORACEAE (*Broussonetia*)
      H. Leaves not velvety; sap not milky.
        I. Fruit an acorn; buds and leaves clustered at twig ends; pith star-shaped in cross section—FAGACEAE (*Quercus*)
        I. Fruit not an acorn; buds and leaves not as above.
        J. Fruit a 1-seeded nut; seeds without a tuft of hairs; ovary inferior; staminate flowers not subtended by a cuplike disk—BETULACEAE
        J. Fruit a capsule; seeds with a conspicuous tuft of hairs; ovary superior; staminate flowers subtended by a cuplike disk—SALICACEAE (*Salix*)
      G. Flowers not in catkins or catkinlike structures.
      K. Leaf bases oblique; fruit an evenly winged samara or a hardy, globular blackish drupe—ULMACEAE
      K. Leaf bases not oblique; fruit not an evenly winged samara; if a drupe, leaf bases not at all oblique.
        L. Fruit a 3-lobed capsule; pistillate flowers borne at the base of a raceme, spike, or spikelike thyrse with staminate flowers located above; seeds white or light brown—EUPHORBIACEAE
        L. Fruit various, but not a 3-lobed capsule; plants not as above.
          M. Staminate flowers in racemes; drupes plumlike, dangling, obvious in fruit—SANTALACEAE (*Pyrularia*)
          M. Staminate flowers not in racemes; fruit not as above.
          N. Plant strongly aromatic; flowers light yellow; perianth of 6 relatively short sepals—LAURACEAE
          N. Plants not strongly aromatic; flowers white or yellow, if yellow, then blooming in the fall; perianth, if present, of both calyx and corolla.
            O. Fruit a red drupe; flowers small, in axillary clusters; corolla white—AQUIFOLIACEAE
            O. Fruit a brown capsule; flowers in spikes or axillary clusters; corolla yellow, or if absent, with prominent white filaments—HAMAMELIDACEAE

138

B. Flowers bisexual.
   P. Lower leaf surface covered by silvery scales—ELAEAGNACEAE
   P. Lower leaf surface glabrous to pubescent but not covered with silvery scales.
      Q. Fruit a legume; petioles swollen at their bases; flowers purple to pink in clusters on old wood or stems from previous season; leaf blades cordate—CAESALPINACEAE (*Cercis*)
      Q. Fruit not a legume; plants not as above.
         R. Base of stamens fused in a staminal column or cylinder surrounding the style; plants with stellate trichomes; seed ciliate—MALVACEAE (*Hibiscus*)
         R. Base of stamens variously attached but not forming a staminal collumn; plants without above characteristics.
            S. Pistil with 3 styles attached laterally, oblique to one side of the ovary; fruit an oblique 1-sided drupe; leaves relatively broadly ovate; flowers in panicles 2–3 dm long with feathery branches—ANACARDIACEAE (*Cotinus*)
            S. Pistils with terminally attached styles; plants without above characteristics.
               T. Petals crisped, colorful, and showy; flowers in terminal panicles; bark smooth but peeling in age in thin flakes; cultivated and persistent at old house sites—LYTHRACEAE (*Lagerstroemia*)
               T. Petals not crisped; plants not as above.
                  U. Stems with aborted terminal buds, the latters role assumed by upper axillary buds which become the leaders; fruit a tart, fleshy, mushy berry with several large brown seeds—EBENACEAE (*Diospyros*)
                  U. Plants not as above.
                     V. Inner bark of stem bright yellow; sepals and petals each 6; usually with 2 glands near the base of each petal; leaves borne on short spur shoots subtended by a thorn—BERBERIDACEAE (*Berberis*)
                     V. Inner bark of stem not bright yellow; if light yellow, plants without preceding characteristics.
                        W. Sap of leaves and twigs milky; spur shoots present, bearing most of the leaves and flowers; thorns often present, of 2 types, naked or leafy; plants often with many lichens on twigs—SAPOTACEAE (*Bumelia*)
                        W. Sap of leaves and twigs not milky; twigs not as above.
                           X. Stamens numerous. (11 or more).
                              Y. Leaves thickish, sweet-tasting, somewhat pubescent; flowers yellow, in compact axillary fascicles—SYMPLOACEAE (*Symplocos*)
                              Y. Leaves not thickish nor sweet-tasting; plants not as above.
                                 Z. Perianth showy, arranged in at least 3 series of 3 parts each; pith diaphragmed—ANNONACEAE (*Asimina*)
                                 Z. Perianth arranged in only 1 or 2 series.
                                    AA. Fruit a woody capsule; stamens more or less united basally and with the base of the petals—THEACEAE
                                    AA. Fruit a follicle, drupe, or pome; stamens distinct, attached to the hypanthium—ROSACEAE

139

X.   Stamens 10 or fewer.
   BB.   Corolla absent; sepals petaloid and corollalike, funnelform, or cylindrical; stamens inserted on tube; ovary superior on the base of the receptacular cup; fruit drupelike—THYME-LAEACEAE
   BB.   Corolla present; plants without above characteristics.
      CC.   Anthers opening by terminal pores; flowers urceolate or campanulate; fruit a capsule or berry; stamens usually twice the number of petals, i.e., 8 or 10, but sometimes only 4 or 5—ERICACEAE
      CC.   Anthers not opening by terminal pores; plants without the above characteristics.
         DD.   Fruit with 2 deeply furrowed vertical sutures.
            EE.   Fruit an elongated capsule; flowers and fruits borne on cylindrical, terminal racemes—SAXIFRAGA-CEAE (*Itea*)
            EE.   Fruit a small, beadlike drupe only slightly elongate; flowers and fruits borne on racemelike panicles in spreading clusters—CYRILLACEAE
         DD.   Fruit without 2 deeply furrowed vertical sutures.
            FF.   Ovary inferior.
               GG.   Fruits nutlike, winged—STYRACACEAE (*Halesia*)
               GG.   Fruits not nutlike, nor winged.
                  HH.   Fruit a globose, pulpy, reddish to purple, brown, or green berry crowned by a persistent calyx; stems and fruit spiny—GROSSU-LARIACEAE (*Ribes*)
                  HH.   Fruit a depressed, globose, blue to black drupe 8–10 mm wide crowned by a persistent style; stems and fruit not spiny—CORNACEAE (*Cornus alternifolia*)
            FF.   Ovary superior.
               II.   Stamens positioned opposite to the conspicuously concave petals and basally attached to a staminal disk; fruit dry, splitting into mericarps; pubescence not stellate—RHAMNACEAE
               II.   Stamens not as above; petals not concave; fruit not splitting into mericarps; pubescence stellate.
                  JJ.   Flowers borne in axillary clusters; corollas 8–20 mm long—STRYACACEAE (*Styrax*)
                  JJ.   Flowers borne in erect terminal racemes or panicles of racemes; corollas 5–8 mm long—CLETHRACEAE (*Clethra*)

Key to Families of Woody Vines

A. Leaves compound.
    B. Leaves opposite.
        C. Leaflets entire, 2 per leaf—BIGNONIACEAE
        C. Leaflets toothed or lobed, 3 or more per leaf.
            D. Leaflets 3 per leaf—RANUNCULACEAE
            D. Leaflets 5 or more per leaf—BIGNONIACEAE
    B. Leaves alternate.
        E. Leaflets with small notch in the rounded apex—LARDIZABA-LACEAE
        E. Leaflets with an acute or obtuse apex, without notch.
            F. Plants climbing by aerial roots; leaflets 3; fruit a drupe—ANACARDIACEAE
            F. Plants climbing by twining or tendrils; leaflets 3—many; fruit a legume or berry.
                G. Stems twining; plants without tendrils; fruit a legume—FABACEAE
                G. Stems not twining; plants with tendrils; fruit a berry—VITACEAE
A. Leaves simple.
    H. Leaves opposite.
        I. Stems climbing by aerial roots—HYDRANGACEAE
        I. Stems climbing by twining.
            J. Corolla zygomorphic; fruit a berry—CAPRIFOLIACEAE
            J. Corolla actinomorphic; fruit a follicle or capsule.
                K. Leaves evergreen, leathery; fruit a capsule; seeds without hairy tufts—LOGANIACEAE
                K. Leaves not evergreen and leathery; fruit a follicle; seeds with hairy tufts.
                    L. Corolla yellow; fruit a follicle less than 5 mm in diameter—APOCYNACEAE
                    L. Corolla not yellow; fruit a follicle more than 5 mm in diameter—ASCLEPIADACEAE
    H. Leaves alternate.
        M. Tendrils in pairs from the petioles; stems without a distinct central pith; vascular bundles scattered; prickles sometimes present on stem—SMILACACEAE
        M. Tendrils absent, or if present not arising in pairs from the petioles; stems with pith or rarely hollow vascular bundles in a ring; prickles not present.
            N. Stems climbing by growing in cypress bark fissures—ERICACEAE (*Pieris*)
            N. Stems climbing by tendrils, aerial roots, or by twining or by sprawling on other plants.
                O. Plants climbing by twining or sprawling.
                    P. Inflorescence of disk and ray flowers surrounded by an

involucre; plant climbing by sprawling—COMPOSI-TAE (*Aster*)

P. Inflorescence not of disk and ray flowers surrounded by an involucre; plant climbing by twining.

    Q. Leaves pinnately veined.

        R. Lateral veins of leaves nearly straight, evenly spaced and parallel—RHAMNACEAE (*Berchemia*)

        R. Lateral veins of leaves variously arranged.

            S. Petioles of largest leaves 3–5 cm long—SCHIZANDRACEAE

            S. Petioles of largest leaves normally less than 2 cm long—CELASTRACEAE

    Q. Leaves palmately veined.

        T. Fruit a drupe; flowers small, unisexual, regular in shape—MENISPERMACEAE

        T. Fruit a capsule; flowers large, bisexual, s-shaped or pipe-shaped—ARISTOLOCHIA-CEAE

O. Plants climbing by tendrils or aerial roots.

    U. Plants climbing by aerial roots—ARALIACEAE (*Hedra*)

    U. Plants climbing by tendrils.

        V. Leaves entire, not lobed; ocrea present; tendrils terminal—POLYGONACEAE (*Brunnichia*)

        V. Leaves toothed or lobed; ocrea not present; tendrils lateral, attached opposite leaves—VITACEAE

Keys to Genera

KEY TO *AESCULUS*

A. Flowers white, in erect terminal spikes resembling a bottle brush; stamens exserted, 3 or more times longer than the petals—*A. parviflora*

A. Flowers cream to scarlet, in short terminal panicles; stamens equaling or less than 2 times the length of the petals—
  B. Flowers scarlet; stamens longer than the lateral petals; petals stipitate-glandular on margins; capsule usually more than 4 cm broad—*A. pavia**
  B. Flowers cream, yellow, or pinkish; stamens equal to or usually shorter than the lateral petals; petals without marginal glands; capsule less than 4 cm broad—*A. sylvatica**

KEY TO *ACACIA*

A. Spines usually present.
  B. Leaflets reticulate; plants of southern Florida north along the east coast to barrier islands of Georgia—*A. farnesiana*
  B. Leaflets not conspicuously reticulate; plants of western Florida panhandle, Gulf Coast to Texas, California, and Mexico—*A. smallii*

A. Spines absent—*A. angustissima*

*May hybridize where the two species occur together, yielding progeny with a blend of colors.

KEY TO *AMELANCHIER*

A. Top of ovary glabrous.
  B. Racemes drooping; petals 10–20 mm long, narrowly oblong or cuneate—*A. arborea*
  B. Racemes erect; petals 4–10 mm long, obovate or oblong-obovate.
    C. Plant commonly a shrub or tree with a vaselike form, not stoloniferous; racemes 2.5–6 cm long; pedicels 10–20 mm long—*A. canadensis*
    C. Plant a colonial shrub, without vaselike form, not stoloniferous; racemes 1–3 cm long; pedicels 2–5 mm long—*A. obovalis*

A. Top of ovary tomentose.
  D. Plant stoloniferous; leaf blades toothed to slightly below the middle; racemes lax—*A. spicata*
  D. Plant usually not stoloniferous; leaf blades toothed nearly to the base; racemes upright.
    E. Leaves coarsely dentate, 3–6 teeth per cm of margin—*A. sanguinea*
    E. Leaves finely serrate, 6–10 teeth per cm of margin—*A. canadensis*

KEY TO *AMORPHA**

A. Leaves short-petiolate, petiole typically shorter than the width of the lowest leaflet; shrubs usually less than 1 m tall.
  B. Mucro at tip of leaflets included in notch, or if exserted, tip of mucro conspicuously swollen—*A. herbacea*
  B. Mucro at tip of leaflets exserted, tip of mucro tapered.
    C. Plant of coastal plain of Carolinas and Georgia; smallest calyx lobes usually 0.4–0.8 (1.3) mm long; plants not conspicuously canescent—*A. georgiana*
    C. Plant of the central United States; smallest calyx lobes 1–1.5 mm long; plants conspicuously canescent—*A. canescens*
A. Leaves with petioles longer than the width of the lowermost leaflet; shrubs usually more than 1.2 m tall.
  D. Calyx lobes not well developed, less than 0.8 mm long—*A. glabra*
  D. Calyx lobes well developed, more than 0.8 mm long.
    E. Calyx lobes about half as long or as long as the calyx tube, all acute or acuminate.
      F. Plants of the Carolinas and Georgia; secondary venation of the leaflets slightly to moderately elevated beneath, but not conspicuously reticulate; leaflets 2–3 cm long—*A. schwerinii*
      F. Plants of Louisiana and Texas; secondary venation of leaflets conspicuously elevated and forming a striking reticulum; leaflets 4–6 cm long—*A. paniculata*
    E. Calyx lobes, at least some of them, less than half as long as the calyx tube; some of the lobes rounded.
      G. Calyces and pedicels blackening upon drying; calyx tube without glands or only sparingly punctate-glandular—*A. nitens*
      G. Calyces and pedicels not blackening upon drying; calyx tube usually conspicuously punctate-glandular.
        H. Petiolules conspicuously pustulate-glandular; plants of Arkansas and Oklahoma—*A. ouachitensis*
        H. Petiolules not pustulate-glandular or with only inconspicuous glands.
          I. Shrub less than 1 m tall; petioles much shorter than the width of the lowest leaflets—*A. georgiana*
          I. Shrub 1.5–6 m tall; petioles longer than the width of the lowest leaflets—*A. fruticosa*

*Adapted from Wilbur, 1975.

KEY TO *AMPELOPSIS**

A. Leaves compound.
    B. Leaves bipinnate or partly tripinnate—*A. arborea*
    B. Leaves palmately 3–5 parted—*A. aconitifolia*
A. Leaves simple.
    C. First year stem glabrous; leaf blade usually not lobed—*A. cordata*
    C. First year stem pubescent, sometimes almost glabrous near the end of the year; leaf blade usually lobed—*A. brevipedunculata*

*From Duncan, 1967

KEY TO *ACER*

A. Inflorescences in terminal corymbs; shrubs or small trees of lower elevations of Piedmont, Ridge and Valley, Cumberland and Coastal Plain; leaves yellowish green beneath, lobed but not finely to coarsely serrate—*A. leucoderme*
A. Inflorescences in terminal racemes or panicles; large shrubs or small trees of high elevations of Appalachian Mountains; leaves greenish beneath, coarsely to finely serrate—
    B. Leaves finely serrate; inflorescence a pendulous raceme; bark striped—*A. pensylvanicum*
    B. Leaves coarsely serrate; inflorescence an erect panicle; bark not striped— *A. spicatum*

KEY TO *ASCYRUM*

A. Styles 3–4; inner sepals slightly smaller than outer.
    B. Outer sepals acute to acuminate, resembling the leaf blades in shape—*A. tetrapetalum*
    B. Outer sepals rounded, unlike the leaf blades in shape—*A. stans*
A. Styles 2; inner sepals very small, petal-like or obsolete.
    C. Decumbent or mat-forming shrubs
        D. Pedicels reflexed at maturity; leaf blades linear-oblanceolate, 1–4 mm wide—*A. pumila*
        D. Pedicels erect at maturity; leaf blades oblanceolate, to elliptic, 4–6 mm wide—*A. hypericoides* var. *multicaule*
    C. Erect, ascending shrubs—*A. hypericoides* var. *hypericoides*

145

KEY TO *ASIMINA*

A. Leaf blades membranous, obovate, tips acuminate to acute; flowers reddish, arising from previous year's twigs prior to or during emergence of current season's leaves; shrubs of rich woods or bottoms.
  - B. Flowers 2–3 cm or more broad; peduncles 1 cm or longer at flowering—*A. triloba*
  - B. Flowers 1–1.7 cm broad; peduncles less than 1 cm long at flowering, the flowers appearing subsessile—*A. parviflora*
A. Leaf blades coriaceous, oblong to oval, tips not acuminate; flowers reddish to white or yellow, appearing before, during or after leaf emergence; plants of pine flatwoods or sandy scrub.
  - C. Flowers arising from wood of previous season's growth prior to or during emergence of leaves—*A. incana*
  - C. Flowers arising after emergence of present season's leaves, axillary to new leaves or terminal to new shoot growth.
    - D. Shrubs seldom more than 0.5 m tall with decumbent to arching, sparsely branched shoots—*A. pygmaea*
    - D. Shrubs usually more than 1 m tall with erect to suberect shoots—*A. longifolia*

KEY TO *BERBERIS*

A. Leaves with entire margins; thorns unbranched, simple, usually solitary, rarely with a pair of small prickles at the base; flowers solitary or in small umbels; berry dry—*B. thunbergii*
A. Leaves with toothed margins; thorns usually branched, without small prickles at base; flowers in racemes; berry juicy.
  - B. Twigs brown and rough-warty; leaves coarsely spinulose-dentate; petals notched at the apex; racemes mostly 5–10 flowered—*B. canadensis*
  - B. Twigs gray, not rough-warty; leaves finely spinulose-denticulate; petals entire; racemes mostly 10–15 flowered—*B. vulgaris*

KEY TO *BUMELIA*

A. Leaf blades copiously pubescent beneath.
  - B. Pubescence lustrous, creamy white, becoming tawny or coppery—*B. tenax*
  - B. Pubescence woolly, greenish to slightly tawny—*B. lanuginosa*
A. Leaf blades glabrous, or with scattered hairs or slightly cobwebby beneath.
  - C. Leaf blades 5–12 cm long, broadly elliptic—*B. lycioides*
  - C. Leaf blades 4 cm or less in length, obovate to obovate-elliptic or obovate-spatulate.
    - D. Leaves obovate-elliptic; rare Georgia endemic—*B. thornei*
    - D. Leaves obovate to obovate-spatulate; widespread coastal plain species—*B. reclinata*

146

KEY TO *CEANOTHUS*

A. Leaves entire (occasionally with 4–6 glandular teeth), fleshy; inflorescences paniculate—*C. microphyllus*
A. Leaves toothed, membranous; inflorescences of thyrses.
    B. Inflorescences axillary on new growth; peduncles elongate—*C. americanus*
    B. Inflorescences terminal on new growth, with several leaves below inflorescences—*C. herbaceous*

KEY TO *CONRADINA*

A. Calyx tube densely pubescent with short hairs.
    B. Short 2-leaved branches present in most axils; leaf blades glabrous above—*C. verticillata*
    B. Short 2-leaved branches absent from most axils; leaf blades pubescent on both sides—*C. canescens*
A. Calyx tube essentially glabrous—*C. glabra*

KEY TO *CORNUS**

A. Leaves alternate but crowded near the stem tips, appearing opposite or whorled—*C. alternifolia*
A. Leaves opposite.
    B. Flowers greenish yellow in a dense headlike cluster surrounded by 4 large white or pink, petal-like, showy bracts; fruit scarlet.
        C. Small, low semiwoody shrub, 1–2.5 dm tall—*C. canadensis*
        C. Shrub or small tree to 15 m tall—*C. florida*
    B. Flowers white or creamy white in an open, broad, cymose inflorescence not surrounded by showy bracts.
        D. Pith of 2nd year and older stems white.
            E. Mature fruit white—*C. stolonifera*
            E. Mature fruit blue.
                F. Leaves glabrous beneath, or with a few appressed trichomes—*C. foemina*
                F. Leaves pubescent beneath, the trichomes various—*C. aspirifolia*
        D. Pith of 2nd year and older stems brown.
            G. Mature fruit white (rarely faintly bluish in *C. drummondi*) on red pedicels.

*The cymose dogwoods often are difficult to identify.

<dl>
<dd>

H. Lower leaf surface woolly, upper surface scabrous—*C. drummondi*

H. Lower leaf surface glabrous or inconspicuously hairy with minute trichomes, upper surface more or less smooth—*C. racemosa*

</dd>
</dl>

G. Mature fruit blue.

I. Leaves narrowly ovate to broadly elliptic; twigs and branchlets dull purple; young twigs silky; leaves usually with 3–5 pairs of veins—*C. amomum*

I. Leaves broadly ovate to rounded; twigs and branchlets green or reddish blotched with purple; young twigs smooth; leaves usually with 6–8 pairs of veins—*C. rugosa*

KEY TO *CRATAEGUS**

A. Leaves rounded, truncate or cordate at the base.

B. Leaves thickly coated with short appressed hairs on the upper surface and densely white tomentose beneath, especially on the veins—*C. mollis*

B. Leaves glabrous to glabrate but not as above.

C. Veins running to the sinuses as well as to the lobe apices.

D. Leaves lobed; inflorescences glabrous or essentially so—*C. phaenopyrum*

D. Leaves dissected; inflorescences pubescent—*C. marshallii*

C. Veins not running to the sinuses.

E. Petioles and bases of blades conspicuously glandular-serrate—*C. flava*

E. Petioles not glandular-serrate or only remotely so.

F. Sepals evenly glandular-serrate—*C. coccinea*

F. Sepals entire or remotely glandular-serrate—*C. flabellata*

A. Leaves cuneate to attenuate at the base.

G. Sepals serrate, persisting on fruit.

H. Leaves with black-gland-tipped teeth.

I. Teeth extending to base of blade; flowers usually in groups of 2–3—*C. flava*

I. Teeth not extending to base of blade; flowers solitary, rarely 2—*C. uniflora*

H. Leaves without black-tipped teeth.

J. Nutlets (seed) mostly 2–3 in each fruit, deeply pitted—*C. calpodendron*

J. Nutlets (seed) 3–5 in each fruit, smooth or only slightly pitted—*C. punctata*

G. Sepals entire or with a few remote teeth, and persisting on fruit, or deciduous.

K. Leaves 3-lobed near apex—*C. spathulata*

K. Leaves not 3-lobed, at least not near the apex.

*Adapted from Radford et al, 1968.

L. Nutlets (seed) deeply pitted—*C. succulenta*
L. Nutlets (seed) not, or only slightly, pitted.
    M. Leaves dull above, often lobed—*C. viridis*
    M. Leaves lustrus above, rarely lobed.
        N. Fruit blue and glaucous—*C. brachyancantha*
        N. Fruit red to greenish red.
            O. Inflorescence compound, usually more than 3-flowered; nutlets (seed) mostly 2 in each fruit—*C. crus-galli*
            O. Inflorescence simple, 1–3-flowered; nutlets (seed) mostly 3–5 in each fruit—*C. aestivalis*

KEY TO *DIERVILLA*

A. Leaf blades petiolate—*D. lonicera*
A. Leaf blades sessile.
    B. Young branchlets and lower leaf surfaces more or less glabrous—*D. sessifolia*
    B. Young branchlets and lower leaf surfaces pubescent—*D. rivularis*

KEY TO *ELAEAGNUS*

A. Leaves evergreen, blades wavy margined—*E. pungens*
A. Leaves deciduous.
    B. Fruit on slender stalks 2–2.5 cm long; leaves elliptic to obovate or oval—*E. multiflora*
    B. Fruit short stalked, the stalks much less than 2 cm; leaves elliptic or linear lanceolate.
        C. Leaves linear-lanceolate; fruit yellow when mature—*E. angustifolia*
        C. Leaves elliptic; fruit scarlet when mature—*E. umbellata*

KEY TO *EUONYMUS*

A. Flowers 4-merous; petioles of the terminal leaves on the branches more than 5 mm long; mature capsules smooth—*E. atropurpureus*
A. Flowers 5-merous; petioles of the terminal leaves on the branches less than 5 mm long; mature capsules tuberculate.
    B. Erect and ascending shrubs; uppermost leaves ovate to lanceolate—*E. americanus*
    B. Decumbent and trailing shrubs, rooting at the nodes; uppermost leaves obovate—*E. obovatus*

KEY TO *FORESTIERA*

A. Leaves evergreen, margins entire; often on small hammocks in or at salt-marsh edge—*F. segregata*
A. Leaves deciduous, margins serrate or minutely so; not a plant of salt-marsh hammocks.
    B. Leaf blades uniformly pubescent beneath—*F. godfreyi*
    B. Leaf blades glabrous beneath, or nearly so, sometimes pubescent on veins.
        C. Plants flowering before the leaves expand; fruits slender, their length 2 or more times their width—*F. acuminata*
        C. Plants flowering after the leaves have expanded; fruits broad, their length less than twice their width—*F. ligustrina*

KEY TO *GAYLUSSACIA*

A. Leaves evergreen, coriaceous, without resinous glands, margins remotely toothed; drupe blue with bloom—*G. brachycera*
A. Leaves deciduous, thin, with resinous glands at least beneath, margins mostly entire.
    B. First-year stems with stalked glands (use a 10× lens).
        C. First-year stems with long silvery gland-tipped hairs more than 1 mm long—*G. mosieri*
        C. First-year stems with short gland-tipped hairs about 0.1 mm long—*G. dumosa*
    B. First-year stems without stalked glands; sessile glands may be present.
        D. Leaves glandular on both surfaces—*G. baccata*
        D. Leaves glandular on lower surface only.
            E. Leaves with a short, abrupt, mucronate to cuspidate tip at least 0.5 mm long; mountain species—*G. ursina*
            E. Leaves with a small glandular tip 0.1–0.2 mm long or with a small notch at the apex; coastal plain species.
                F. Corolla about 4 mm long; sepals about ⅓ rd as long as the corolla tube—*G. frondosa*
                F. Corolla about 3 m long; sepals about ½ as long as the corolla tube—*G. nana*

KEY TO *HALESIA*

A. Corolla lobes longer than the tube; fruit 2-winged—*H. diptera*
A. Corolla lobes shorter than the corolla tube; fruit 4-winged.
    B. Styles of mature flowers exserted ⅓rd to ½ their length; corollas 7–10(12) mm long; anthers at or slightly exceeding the corolla tube—*H. parviflora*
    B. Styles of mature flowers essentially equalling the corolla; corollas (12)15–20 mm long; anthers included in the corolla tube—*H. carolina*

KEY TO WOODY *HYPERICUM**

A. Sepals and petals 4, the inner much reduced—*H. microsepalum*
A. Sepals and petals 5.
  B. Inflorescences usually only 1–3 flowered; petals more than 15 mm long—*H. frondosum*
  B. Inflorescences predominately more than 3-flowered; petals usually less than 15 mm long.
    C. Midstem leaves ovate-triangular, cordate basally and somewhat clasping—*H. myrtifolium*
    C. Midstem leaves not ovate-triangular, not cordate basally.
      D. Leaves all linear-subulate, needlelike, with parallel margins.
        E. Largest leaves usually not exceeding 10 mm long.
          F. Plant decumbent, rarely over 5 dm tall; stems 6-angled—*H. reductum*
          F. Plant erect, up to 15 dm tall; stems 2-winged—*H. brachyphyllum*
        E. Largest leaves usually more than 10 mm long.
          G. Plant decumbent—*H. lloydi*
          G. Plant erect.
            H. Largest leaves 20–40 mm long; species of the folded Appalachians and Plateaus—*H. dolabriforme*
            H. Largest leaves 10–20 mm long; species of the Coastal Plain.
              I. Bark of older stems thin and relatively tight, brown, reddish brown or grayish, exfoliating in thin flakes or strips; larger leaves variable in size, the longest 13–20 mm in length—*H. nitidum*
              I. Bark of older stems readily exfoliating into papery plates exposing red bark beneath; larger leaves uniformly 10–13 mm long—*H. fasciculatum*
      D. Leaves not linear-subulate, the margins not parallel, narrowed basally, dialated distally.
        J. Mat-forming species of high elevations in southern Appalachians—*H. buckleyi*
        J. Erect species.
          K. Capsules, excluding beak, 8–13 mm long—*H. prolificum*
          K. Capsules, excluding beak, less than 8 mm long.
            L. Leaf blades with a narrow articulation at the extreme base, this showing as a narrow horizontal line.
              M. Crown of plant bushy-branched, the branchlets slender, flexuous, and usually spreading; larger leaves thinnish and flexuous—*H. galioides*

*Adapted from Godfrey and Wooten (1981).

151

M. Crown of plant with stiffish, erect-ascending branches; larger leaves thickish and stiffish—*H. densiflorum*

L. Leaf blades without an articulation at the base.
    N. Main stem leaves usually with short leafy branches in their axils—*H. cistifolium*
    N. Main-stem leaves without short leafy branches in their axils—*H. nudiflorum*

KEY TO *ILEX*
Contributed by Greg Krakow

A. Leaves coriaceous, evergreen.
    B. Leaves crenate throughout, margins without spines—*I. vomitoria*
    B. Leaves serrate, entire or crenate only toward the tip, often with spines.
        C. Drupe black.
            D. Leaves dull green, sparsely crenate at the tip, margins without spines—*I. glabra*
            D. Leaves glossy green, essentially entire, but remotely spinulose—*I. coriacea*
        C. Drupe red, orange, or yellow.
            E. Mature leaves ovate to lanceolate, usually at least 1.5 cm wide, entire to sharply serrate—*I. cassine*
            E. Mature leaves narrow, less than 8 mm wide, margins usually entire—*I. myrtifolia*
A. Leaves not leathery, deciduous.
    F. Floral parts and nutlets mostly 4-and 5-merous; nutlets more or less ribbed on back.
        G. Leaf blades oblanceolate (rarely narrowly elliptic in *decidua*) narrowly cuneate, margins usually distally crenate.
            H. Fruiting pedicels 2–8 mm long—*I. decidua*
            H. Fruiting pedicels 1–2.3 cm long—*I. longipes*
        G. Leaf blades round to elliptic, obovate, the bases rounded, margins entire or serrate.
            I. Leaves with conspicuous reticulate raised veins beneath, plant of swamp and river margins—*I. amelanchier*
            I. Leaves not conspicuously reticulate-veined beneath; plants of high banks of streams, upland areas.
                J. Fruiting pedicels more than 1 cm long—*I. longipes*
                J. Fruiting pedicels less than 8 mm long.
                    K. Largest leaves less than 6.5 cm long; drupe usually 4–7 mm in diameter—*I. ambigua*
                    K. Largest leaves more than 6.5 cm long; drupe usually 8–12 mm in diameter—*I. montana*
    F. Floral parts and nutlets mostly 6- to 8-merous; nutlets smooth on back.
        L. Sepals ciliate; plant of stream and swamp borders—*I. verticillata*
        L. Sepals without cilia; plant of uplands—*I. laevigata*

KEY TO *KALMIA*

A. Flower clusters terminal; corolla over 2 cm wide—*K. latifolia*
A. Flower clusters lateral; corolla 1.5 cm in width or less.
    B. Leaf blades 1 cm or less in length—*K. hirsuta*
    B. Leaf blades 2 cm or more in length.
        C. Leaves deciduous, alternate; corolla white to pinkish—*K. cuneata*
        C. Leaves evergreen, whorled; corolla reddish purple to rose pink.
            D. Leaves glabrous beneath—*K. angustifolia*
            D. Leaves pale velvety pubescent beneath—*K. carolina*

KEY TO *LEUCOTHOE*

A. Leaves evergreen.
    B. Leaf blades long-acuminate—*L. fontanesiana*
    B. Leaf blades acute or short-acuminate or mucronate—*L. axillaris*
A. Leaves deciduous.
    C. Anthers 2-awned; racemes usually recurved; seeds winged; mountain species—*L. recurva*
    C. Anthers 4-awned; racemes usually straight or nearly so; seeds wingless; Piedmont and Coastal Plain species—*L. racemosa*

KEY TO *LIGUSTRUM*

A. Leaves definitely evergreen, blades usually 4–15 cm long.
    B. Leaf blades acuminate; corolla tube as long as the lobes; panicles to 25 cm long—*L. lucidum*
    B. Leaf blades obtuse to short-acuminate; corolla tube slightly longer than the lobes; panicles to 15 cm long—*L. japonicum*
A. Leaves deciduous or semi-evergreen, blades usually 2–5 cm long.
    C. Corolla tube shorter than the lobes; petiole pubescent—*L. sinense*
    C. Corolla tube 1.5 times as long as the lobes; petiole glabrous—*L. ovalifolium*

KEY TO *LINDERA*

A. Leaf blades thick, coriaceous, elliptic-obovate—*L. subcoriacea*
A. Leaf blades thin, not coriaceous, elliptic-oblong to elliptic or elliptic-obovate.
    B. Leaf blades drooping, rounded or obtuse at the curved base; rare shrub— *L. melissaefolium*
    B. Leaf blades erect, narrowed to an acute or wedge-shaped base; common shrub—*L. benzoin*

KEY TO *LONICERA*

A. Erect shrubs.
    B. Peduncles much longer than the flowers.
        C. Stems hollow; bractlets obvious at bases of ovaries; introduced species—*L. tatarica*
        C. Stems solid; bractlets at bases of ovaries minute, not obvious; native species—*L. canadensis*
    B. Peduncles shorter than the flowers.
        D. Leaves spinulose-mucronate at the apex—*L. fragrantissima*
        D. Leaves short-acuminate, not mucronate at the apex—*L. maackii*
A. Vines climbing or sprawling by twining stems.
    E. Inflorescences axillary; leaves not connate; flowering in pairs with connate ovaries; introduced species—*L. japonica*
    E. Inflorescences terminal; leaves connate below the inflorescences; ovaries separate, not connate; native species.
        F. Corolla deep red outside, 3.5–4 cm long, the 5 lobes more or less equal, scarcely bilabiate—*L. sempervirens*
        F. Corolla orange, yellow, cream, white, brick red or purplish, 1.5–3 cm long, strongly bilabiate.
            G. Upper surface of uppermost connate leaves strongly glaucous, the connate upper leaves more or less circular—*L. prolifera*
            G. Upper surface of uppermost connate leaves green or barely glaucous, the connate leaves longer than broad, not circular in outline.
                H. Lower surface of leaves conspicuously whitened or silvery blue; corolla tube slightly enlarged on one side at the base; corolla yellow to greenish yellow tinged with purple, rose or brick red, 1.5–2.3 cm long—*L. dioica*
                H. Lower surface of leaves slightly gray-green or pale but not noticeably whitened; corolla tube not enlarged at the base; corolla orange, or creamy yellow, 2–3 cm long—*L. flava*

KEY TO *LYONIA*

A. Leaves evergreen.
    B. Lower leaf surfaces lepidote.
        C. Flowers borne on twigs of the season—*L. fruticosa*
        C. Flowers borne on twigs of the previous season—*L. ferruginea*
    B. Lower leaf surface not lepidote, more or less glabrous—*L. lucida*
A. Leaves deciduous.
    D. Corolla 3–4 mm long, globose, about twice as long as the calyx, white—*L. ligustrina*
    D. Corolla 7–14 mm long, subcylindical, several times as long as the calyx, white to pink—*L. mariana*

KEY TO *MALUS*

A. Hypanthium pubescent—*M. pumila*
A. Hypanthium glabrous.
    B. Pome 1 cm or less in diameter; petals white, oblong; leaves glabrous, acuminate—*M. baccata*
    B. Pome 2–3.5 cm in diameter; petals pink or rose fading to white; leaves acute or blunt.
        C. Leaf blades round or cordate at base, those of fertile branches broadly lanceolate, oval or ovate, acute—*M. coronaria*
        C. Leaf blades tapering to base, those of fertile branches oblong or narrowly elliptic, blunt or short-mucronate—*M. angustifolia*

KEY TO *MYRICA*

A. Leaves pinnatifid; stipules slightly clasping; fruit in a bristly involucre—*M. asplenifolia*
A. Leaves entire, dentate or incised; stipules absent; fruit not in a bristly involucre.
    B. Bracts subtending staminate flowers longer than the stamens; fruit not covered with white wax; pistillate bractlets persistent—*M. gale*
    B. Bracts subtending staminate flowers shorter than the stamens; fruit usually covered with white wax; pistillate bractlets deciduous.
        C. Crushed leaves without scent or aroma; margins entire; staminate flowers with 8 stamens; leaves smooth—*M. inodora*
        C. Crushed leaves aromatic; margins of leaves toothed; staminate flowers with less than 7 stamens; leaves scurfy.
            D. Leaves densely glandular on both surfaces; blades usually oblanceolate—*M. cerifera*
            D. Leaves densely glandular below, sparcely glandular above; blades obovate to elliptic.
                E. Fruit pubescent at first, more than 4.5 mm in diameter; leaves deciduous, blades distinctly revolute—*M. pensylvanica*
                E. Fruit usually not pubescent, less than 4.5 mm in diameter; leaves evergreen, blades not distinctly revolute—*M. heterophylla*

KEY TO *PHILADELPHUS*

A. Flowers terminal; bark of branchlets loose.
    B. Pedicels and peduncles usually glabrous; stigmas distinct; petals 2–3 cm long—*P. inodorus*
    B. Pedicels and peduncles pubescent; stigmas united; petals 1–2 cm long—*P. hirsutus*
A. Flowers in a raceme of 2 or more nodes; bark of branchlets tight—*P. pubescens*

A. Leaves evergreen; mature fruit with a dry, hard exocarp; flowers in axillary racemes—*P. caroliniana*
A. Leaves deciduous; mature fruit with a pulpy, soft exocarp; flowers in umbellate clusters in terminal racemes.
    B. Flowers pink, sessile or nearly so; ovary velvety; stone coarsely wrinkled or pitted—*P. persica*
    B. Flowers white, pedicellate; ovary glabrous; stone not wrinkled or pitted.
        C. Flowers and fruits in racemes terminating branches of the current season's growth.
            D. Sepals soon deciduous; calyx lobes obtuse; leaf margins with triangular, ascending teeth—*P. virginiana*
            D. Sepals persistent under the fruit; leaf margins with short, appressed teeth.
                E. Leaves glabrous beneath except near veins, the apex of the blades mostly acuminate; rachis of inflorescence glabrous—*P. serotina*
                E. Leaves pubescent beneath; apex of blades mostly obtuse; rachis of inflorescence pubescent—*P. alabamensis*
        C. Flowers and fruits in umbellate clusters arising laterally from scaly buds of the previous season's growth.
            F. Stone globose or subglobose; cherries.
                G. Clusters of fruits and flowers leafy bracted at base—*P. mahaleb*
                G. Clusters of fruits and flowers not leafy bracted, subtended only by bud scales.
                    H. Margins of sepals glandular-serrulate; fruit nearly black; teeth at middle of leaf blade margin 1–4 mm apart, more or less the same size—*P. pumila*
                    H. Margins of sepals not glandular-serrulate; fruit bright red; teeth at middle of leaf blade margin 0.5–1 mm apart, irregular in size—*P. pensylvanica*
            F. Stone flattened to turgid, 2-edged; plums.
                I. Margins of leaves with glandular or gland-tipped teeth.
                    J. Mature leaf blades usually 2 cm or less in width; calyx lobes without glands or toothed margins—*P. angustifolia*
                    J. Mature leaf blades usually 2.5 cm or more in width; calyx lobes with glandular toothed margins.
                        K. Flowers opening before the leaves have expanded; leaf margins with low and almost pointless teeth, the gland facing the indented lower side of the margin; fully grown leaves more or less flat—*P. munsoniana*
                        K. Flowers opening as the leaves are about one-half grown; leaf margins with triangular and ascending teeth, the gland arising from the tip of each tooth; fully grown leaves more or less folded lengthwise—*P. hortulana*

I. Margins of leaves without glandular or gland-tipped teeth.
    L. Mature leaves velvety pubescent beneath, sometimes only slightly so.
        M. Leaves gradually acuminate—*P. alleghaniensis*
        M. Leaves abruptly acuminate—*P. mexicana*
    L. Mature leaves more or less glabrous beneath, sometimes pubescent on the veins.
        N. Flowers 2–2.5 cm across; the larger leaves 7–11 cm long—*P. americana*
        N. Flowers about 1 cm across; the larger leaves 4–7 cm long—*P. umbellata*

KEY TO *RHAMNUS*

A. Flowers apetalous—*R. alnifolia*
A. Flowers with petals.
    B. Flowers 4-merous; seeds deeply grooved on the back—*R. lanceolata*
    B. Flowers 5-merous; seeds not grooved.
        C. Fruits 3-carpellate; cymes pedunculate; pedicels pubescent—*R. caroliniana*
        C. Fruits 3-carpellate; cymes sessile; pedicels glabrous—*R. frangula*

KEY TO *RHODODENDRON**

A. Leaves evergreen; stamens 10.
   B. Leaves lepidote and punctate, scurfy-dotted beneath.
      C. Flowers appearing before the leaves; plants endemic to Florida panhandle—*R. minus* var. *chapmanii*
      C. Flowers opening after the leaves; plants of N.C., S.C., Ga., Ala.—*R. minus*
   B. Leaves not lepidote or punctate beneath.
      D. Capsules and pedicels stipitate-glandular; calyx lobes mostly 2–4 mm long; flowers rose to white—*R. maximum*
      D. Capsules and pedicels pubescent; calyx lobes mostly less than 1 mm long; flowers lilac-purple—*R. catawbiense*
A. Leaves deciduous; stamens 5–7.
   E. Stamens usually (5)6–7; corolla tube less than ¼th as long as the lobes; corolla rotate or rotate-campanulate, slightly 2-lipped; flowers pink or white, orange-spotted, opening before the leaves—*R. vaseyi*
   E. Stamens 5; corolla tube more than ¼th as long as the lobes; corolla funnelform; flowers yellow to orange, scarlet, red, white, or pink.
      F. Early to midseason flowering, the flowers opening with or before the leaves but before winter buds have formed.
         G. Flowers white to pink, usually without a blotch on largest lobe.
            H. Corolla bearing glands in prominent rows along largest veins of lobes.
               I. Shrubs less than 0.5 m tall; petioles with short-stipitate glands; corolla white to flushed with pink; plant stoloniferous—*R. atlanticum*
               I. Shrub more than 0.5 m tall; petioles without glands; corolla white, sometimes with a pink blush.
                  J. Styles glabrous, purple to red; branchlets glabrous, smooth; plant not stoloniferous—*R. arborescens*
                  J. Styles pubescent, not colored; branchlets hirsute, pubescent with bristlelike setae; plant sometimes stoloniferous—*R. viscosum*
            H. Corolla without prominent rows of glands along veins of lobes.
               K. Filaments about 2 times as long as corolla tube.
                  L. Corolla white; plant stoloniferous; flowers sweetly fragrant; corolla lobes equalling the tube—*R. alabamense*
                  L. Corolla pink; plant not stoloniferous; flowers clovescent fragrant; corolla lobes shorter than the tube—*R. roseum*
               K. Filaments about 3 times as long as corolla tube.
                  M. Leaves strigose or hirsute along the midvein beneath; flowers not fragrant; corolla lobes equal-

---

*Adapted from Galle (no date).

ling the tube; pedicels without glands—*R. peri-clymenoides*

    M. Leaves canescent beneath; flowers fragrant; corolla lobes half as long as the tube; pedicels hoary, with or without glands—*R. canescens*

  G. Flowers scarlet, red, orange, yellow, or salmon, often with a yellow blotch or flush on the largest lobe.

    N. Winter buds pubescent; lobes yellow, flowers fragrant; plant of Gulf Coastal Plain—*R. austrinum*

    N. Winter buds glabrous; lobes yellow to red, flowers not fragrant; plants of Piedmont and Mountains.

      O. Flowers average 40 mm broad; tube without glands, but pubescent, longer than lobes—*R. flammeum*

      O. Flowers average 48 mm broad; tube with glandular setae, equal to, or shorter than the lobes—*R. calendulaceum*

F. Late flowering, the flowers appearing after the winter buds are at least partly developed.

  P. Corolla white; flowers fragrant.

    Q. Branchlets densely strigose; winter buds with aristate mucronate scales; leaves often pubescent beneath; corolla tube glandular, pilose, and sparingly villous outside; style usually not colored, glabrous to minutely pubescent at base—*R. serrulatum*

    Q. Branchlets glabrous, smooth; winter buds glabrous; leaves glabrous; corolla tube pubescent inside, slightly glandular outside; style purple to red, glabrous—*R. arborescens*

  P. Corolla scarlet to yellow or salmon.

    R. Flowers salmon to scarlet; plant stoloniferous; branchlets with stiff bristles; plant of the Appalachian region—*R. bakeri*

    R. Flowers yellow to scarlet, without yellow spot; plant not stoloniferous; branchlets glabrous and smooth; plant of southwest Ga. and southeast Ala.—*R. prunifolia*

KEY TO *RHUS*

A. Leaves ternately compound with 3 leaflets; flowers in catkinlike clusters appearing on old wood before the leaves—*R. aromatica*

A. Leaves pinnately compound; flowers in terminal panicles appearing on new wood after the leaves.

  B. Leaflets entire or nearly so; rachis of leaf winged—*R. copallina*

  B. Leaflets toothed; rachis of leaf not winged.

    C. Stems glabrous—*R. glabra*

    C. Stems pubescent.

      D. Leaflets glaucous beneath—*R. typhina*

      D. Leaflets not glaucous but greenish beneath—*R. michauxii*

KEY TO *RIBES*

A. Flower stalks jointed beneath ovary; berry separating from pedicel—*R. glandulosum*
A. Flower stalks not jointed beneath ovary; berry not separating from pedicel.
    B. Stamens included; sepals shorter than the free portion of the hypanthium—*R. cynosbati*
    B. Stamens exserted; sepals longer than the free portion of the hypanthium.
        C. Ovary and fruit prominately spiny; leaves glabrous above—*R. echinellum*
        C. Ovary and fruit not spiny; leaves finely pubescent above.
            D. Filaments pubescent; sepals 6–10 mm long—*R. curvatum*
            D. Filaments glabrous; sepals 4–5 mm long—*R. rotundifolia*

KEY TO *ROBINIA*

A. Twigs and leaf rachises conspicuously hispid with hairs 1–5 mm long—*R. hispida* (in part)
A. Twigs and leaf rachises not conspicuously hispid.
    B. Twigs and peduncles viscid, with sessile or raised glands, or young growth and peduncles densely glandular-pubescent—*R. viscosa*
    B. Twigs and peduncles lacking sessile glands, the young growth and peduncles without glandular pubescence—*R. hispida* (in part)

KEY TO *ROSA*

A. Hypanthium and upper part of pedicel conspicuously prickly, the largest prickles (1.7) 2–4 (7.5) mm long; some prickles with a glandular tip—*R. laevigata*

A. Hypanthium and upper part of pedicel glabrous to stipitate-glandular but not conspicuously prickled.

    B. Styles much exserted, united into a column, protruding from the orifice of the hypanthium.

        C. Leaflets mostly 3; flowers 4–8 cm broad, pink; native plant—*R. setigera*

        C. Leaflets mostly 7–9; flowers 2–5 cm broad, white; introduced.

            D. Leaflets membraneous; stipules fimbriate-pectinate; styles glabrous; commonly planted, often escaping and naturalizing—*R. multiflora*

            D. Leaflets firm; stipules jagged-dentate; styles pubescent; an uncommon escape—*R. wichuraiana*

    B. Styles not exserted or only slightly so, distinct, not united into a column, forming a dense brush at the orifice of the hypanthium.

        E. Stipules divided nearly to their base into linear-attenuate segments, not adnate to the petiole for more than ⅓rd of this length—*R. bracteata*

        E. Stipules not divided as above, adnate to the petiole ⅓rd to ⅔rd of their length.

            F. Leaflets conspicuously glandular dotted beneath—*R. eglanteria*

            F. Leaflets not conspicuously glandular dotted over the entire lower leaf surface, sometimes glandular along midrib.

                G. Large erect shrub of swamps or wet places—*R. palustris*

                G. Plants mainly of well-drained habitats.

                    H. Pedicels of the solitary flowers subtended by a bract.

                        I. Infrastipular prickles straight; low shrub; common native species—*R. carolina*

                        I. Infrastipular prickles curved downward; tall shrub; escaped species—*R. canina*

                    H. Pedicels of the solitary flowers not subtended by a bract—*R. gallica*

KEY TO *RUBUS*

A. Leaves simple; petals deep red-purple; plant unarmed—*R. odoratus*
A. Leaves pinnately or palmately compound; petals white or pink; plants usually armed with bristles, prickles or thorns.
   B. Petals shorter than sepals; mature fruit separating from the receptacle which is persistent on the pedicel. RASPBERRIES
      C. Corolla pink to rose or light purple, petals appressed to stamens; stem densely hispid with gland-topped reddish hairs—*R. phoenicolasius*
      C. Corolla white, petals erect and ascending; stems not densely hispid with gland topped reddish hairs.
         D. Fruits usually black; pedicels not stipitate-glandular; stems thorny—*R. occidentalis*
         D. Fruits usually red; pedicels not stipitate-glandular; stems hispid and bristly—*R. idaeus* var. *canadensis*
   B. Petals longer than sepals; mature fruit separating from the pedicel with the receptacle included. BLACKBERRIES
      E. Blades of leaflets white-tomentose beneath.
         F. Leaflets distinctly oblanceolate to obovate, broadest well above the middle—*R. cuneifolius*
         F. Leaflets ovate, broadest at the middle—*R. bifrons*
      E. Blades of leaflets not white-tomentose beneath.
         G. Stems arching or erect, seldom rooting at the tip.
            H. Glandular hairs abundant on the pedicels—*R. allegheniensis*
            H. Glandular hairs absent.
               I. Leaflets deeply dissected—*R. laciniatus*
               I. Leaflets not deeply dissected.
                  J. Leaflets velvety pubescent beneath—*R. argutus*
                  J. Leaflets more or less glabrous beneath.
                     K. Inflorescence leafy throughout—*R. betulifolius*
                     K. Inflorescence usually leafy only at the base—*R. canadensis*
         G. Stems prostrate and trailing, often rooting at the tips. DEWBERRIES
            L. Bristles stout, stiff, with expanded bases—*R. flagellaris*
            L. Bristles mostly of slender, small-based prickles or glandular bristles.
               M. Flowers normally solitary at the end of each branch—*R. trivialis*
               M. Flowers racemose—*R. hispidus*

KEY TO *SALIX**

A. Leaves mostly alternate, but at least some opposite or subopposite—*S. purpurea*
A. Leaves always alternate.
    B. Apex of buds sharp-pointed, bud scale margins free and overlapping—*S. caroliniana*
    B. Apex of buds blunt, bud scale margins fused.
        C. Leaves green or pale beneath.
            D. Leaves lanceolate or elliptic-lanceolate, margins serrate—*S. lucida*
            D. Leaves linear, margins distinctly glandular-denticulate—*S. exigua*
        C. Leaves glaucous beneath.
            E. Leaf margins serrulate or serrate.
                F. Leaves densely short-sericeous beneath; stipules of small glands or absent—*S. sericea*
                F. Leaves glabrous to glabrate beneath; stipules prominent—*S. eriocephala*
            E. Leaf margins entire or crenate.
                G. Leaves glabrate, margins not revolute, young leaves usually sparcely pubescent.
                    H. Branches persistently pubescent; leaves rugose-veiny beneath, lacking ferruginous hairs—*S. bebbiana*
                    H. Branches glabrate; leaves not rugose-veiny beneath, young leaves with some ferruginous hairs—*S. discolor*
                G. Leaves permanently pubescent, at least beneath, margins sometimes revolute, younger leaves densely villous or tomentose.
                    I. Leaf margins entire and undulate; leaf blades oblong to oblanceolate or narrowly so—*S. humilis*
                    I. Leaf margins crenate or irregularly serrate, rarely subentire; leaf blades elliptic, obovate to oblanceolate.
                        J. Leaf margins not revolute; stipules small, less than 2 mm long, soon falling away—*S. bebbiana*
                        J. Leaf margins revolute; stipules conspicuous, to 15 mm long, persistent—*S. cinerea*

*Adapted from Argus (1986)

KEY TO *SATUREJA*

A. Corolla more than 2.5 cm long, scarlet—*S. coccinea*
A. Corolla less than 2 cm long, white to pink to purple.
    B. Leaf blades prominently revolute, linear to linear-elliptic—*S. ashei*
    B. Leaf blades flat, elliptic-ovate or -obovate.
        C. Leaves subsessile, minutely and densely pubescent—*S. dentata*
        C. Leaves petiolate, glabrous—*S. georgiana*

KEY TO WOODY *SMILAX*

A. Stems and lower leaf surfaces densely pubescent—*S. pumila*
A. Stems and lower leaf surfaces glabrous or nearly so.
    B. Leaves thick, oblong to oblanceolate; lower leaf surface midvein raised; lateral veins not evident—*S. laurifolia*
    B. Leaves thin, not oblong; midvein no more evident than lateral veins.
        C. Leaves glaucous and whitish or grayish beneath—*S. glauca*
        C. Leaves light green beneath.
            D. Fruit red to reddish when mature—*S. walteri*
            D. Fruit black to blue-black when mature.
                E. Leaf blades lanceolate to ovate, apex tapering to an acute or acuminate tip—*S. smallii*
                E. Leaf blades ovate, ovate-oblong, suborbicular, hastate or fiddle shaped, apex of blade rounded, obtuse, or abruptly acuminate.
                    F. Stalks of umbels distinctly longer than petiole of subtending leaf.
                        G. Margin of leaf blade with thickened band; stem with rigid, broad-based prickles—*S. bona-nox*
                        G. Margin of leaf blade not thickened; stem with weak bristlelike prickles—*S. hispida*
                    F. Stalks of umbells not exceeding petiole of subtending leaf.
                        H. Leaf blades ovate, or rarely ovate-lanceolate, thin and pliant, without marginal vein—*S. rotundifolia*
                        H. Leaf blades variable in shape, at maturity, stiff and thick, with a marginal vein—*S. auriculata*

KEY TO *SPIRAEA*

A. Inflorescence flattened, broader than long.
    B. Flowers pink—*S. japonica*
    B. Flowers white—
        C. Leaves broadly oblong, margins coarsely toothed, not glaucous—*S. betulifolia*
        C. Leaves oblong to oblanceolate, margins entire or nearly so, glaucous beneath—*S. virginiana*
A. Inflorescence elongate, generally longer than wide.
    D. Leaves densely covered beneath with a white to tawny tomentum—*S. tomentosa*
    D. Leaves green beneath, without a white to tawny tomentum.
        E. Branches of the inflorescence pubescent—*S. alba*
        E. Branches of the inflorescence glabrous—*S. latifolia*

KEY TO *TOXICODENDRON*

A. Leaves pinnately compound with 5 or more leaflets—*T. vernix*
A. Leaves ternately compound with 3 leaflets.
    B. Plant climbing or trailing; aerial rootlets present when climbing; middle (terminal) leaflet acute or acuminate; leaves scattered along the stem; fruit mostly glabrous—*T. radicans*
    B. Plant not climbing or trailing; aerial rootlets absent; middle leaflet with rounded or blunt tip; leaves mostly clustered near the stem tip; fruit pubescent—*T. quercifolia*

KEY TO *VACCINIUM*

A. Corolla 4-lobed, the lobes longer than the tube; the lobes recurved at the time of flowering.
    B. Stem erect; leaves deciduous; margins somewhat serrate, ciliate—*V. erythrocarpon*
    B. Stems trailing; leaves evergreen; margins entire.
        C. Pedicels with a pair of green, leaflike bracts 2–4 mm long attached above the middle of the pedicel—*V. macrocarpon*
        C. Pedicels with a pair of red scalelike bracts 1.5 mm or less long attached at or below the middle of the pedicel—*V. oxycoccos*
A. Corolla 4–5 lobed, the lobes shorter than the tube.
    D. Anthers conspicuously awned.
        E. Corolla open in bud, the anthers exserted beyond the corolla at time of flowering; margins of leaves entire—*V. stamineum*
        E. Corolla closed in bud, the anthers included within the corolla at time of flowering; margins of leaves bearing occasional glands, entire or with small teeth—*V. arboreum*
    D. Anthers not conspicuously awned.
        F. Leaves distinctly evergreen and coriaceous; margins thickened; leaf blades less than 1.5 mm long.
            G. Corolla campanulate; plant trailing—*V. crassifolium*
            G. Corolla cylindrical to urceolate, longer than wide.
                H. Stalked glands present on the undersurface of leaves; hypanthium and fruit nonglaucous—*V. myrsinites*
                H. Stalked glands absent from the undersurface of leaves; hypanthium and fruit glaucous—*V. darrowi*
        F. Leaves deciduous, membranous to coriaceous, or a few leaves persistent toward ends of vigorous shoots, or if appearing persistent, leaves more than 2 cm long.
            I. Corolla and hypanthium thickly pubescent—*V. hirsutum*
            I. Corolla and hypanthium essentially glabrous—.
                J. Lower leaf surfaces with stipitate glandular hairs—*V. tenellum*
                J. Lower leaf surface not glandular; the margin may be glandular-serrulate.
                    K. Plants low-bush type, 0.5–1 m tall.
                        L. Leaves bright green on both sides—*V. angustifolium*
                        L. Leaves pale green or glaucous beneath—*V. pallidum*
                    K. Plants high-bush type, more than 1 m tall—*V. corymbosum*

KEY TO *VIBURNUM*

A. Marginal flowers sterile with a greatly enlarged, slightly irregular corolla; leaves scurfy-stellate beneath, blades definitely heart shaped—*V. lantanoides*

A. Marginal flowers not sterile, all flowers uniformly fertile and similar to each other; leaves not scurfy-stellate beneath, blades of various shapes including slightly heart shaped.

    B. Leaves (or most of them), distinctly 3-lobed—*V. acerifolium*

    B. Leaves not lobed.

        C. Leaf blades oblanceolate to spatulate—*V. obovatum*

        C. Leaf blades elliptic, ovate, or slightly cordate.

            D. Leaf margins coarsely dentate; lateral veins simple or 1–2 forked, each extending into a tooth.

                E. Leaves glabrous or slightly pubescent beneath, margins with 4–22 pairs of teeth; petioles usually 6 mm or more long—*V. dentatum*

                E. Leaves of velvety pubescent beneath, margins with 4–10 pairs of teeth; petioles usually less than 6 mm long—*V. rafinesquianum*

            D. Leaf margins finely serrate or nearly entire; lateral veins branching and anastomosing before reaching the leaf margin.

                F. Inflorescences on peduncles 0.5–5 cm long; lateral twigs mostly long and flexible—*V. nudum*

                F. Inflorescences sessile or nearly so; lateral twigs mostly short and stiff.

                    G. Few or no rusty short scurfy hairs on younger leaves, on the petiole or lower leaf surface (a few petioles below the inflorescence may have some rusty pubescence); leaf blades dull above—*V. prunifolium*

                    G. Rusty, short, scurfy hairs appearing on younger leaves, on the petiole, on the lower leaf surface and midvein; leaf blades glossy above—*V. rufidulum*

KEY TO *VITIS*
Contributed by Mike Moore

A. Tendrils simple; bark closely adherent; lenticels prominent; pith continuous through nodes—*V. rotundifolia*

A. Tendrils forked; older bark shredding; lenticels absent or inconspicuous; pith interrupted at nodes.

    B. Leaves densely tomentose beneath, concealing the leaf undersurface; tendrils continuous or absent at every third node.

        C. Tendrils or inflorescences present at three or more consecutive needs; tendrils usually bifid—*V. labrusca*

        C. Tendrils or inflorescences present at only two consecutive nodes; tendrils usually trifid.

            D. Stipules 2–3 mm long; Ala. to La. species—*V. mustangensis*

            D. Stipules 1 mm or less long; Fla. species—*V. shuttleworthii*

    B. Leaves variously pubescent beneath but never so deep as to conceal the leaf undersurface; tendrils absent at every third node.

        E. Leaves distinctly glaucous beneath, the glaucescence partially obscured in individuals with arachnoid pubescence; nodes frequently glaucous—*V. aestivalis*

        E. Leaves not glaucous beneath, nodes never glaucous.

            F. Tendrils, if present, confined to uppermost leaves; leaves reniform, conduplicately folded; sprawling vines or subshrubs, rarely climbing—*V. rupestris*

            F. Tendrils present at most nodes, absent every third node; leaves cordate to cordate-ovate, not conduplicately folded; low- to high-climbing vines.

                G. Branchlets of the season densely pubescent with short, straight hairs which lie perpendicular to the surface of the branchlet; branchlets distinctly angled in cross section; leaves pubescent beneath with both cobwebby and short, straight trichomes—*V. cinerea* var. *cinerea*

                G. Branchlets pubescent with varying degrees of appressed cobwebby trichomes or glabrous; branchlets terete or angled in cross section; leaves variously pubescent or glabrous beneath.

                    H. Nodes banded with red pigmentation, the remainder of the stem green; branchlets cobwebby, often densely so; leaves cobwebby beneath, often densely so; branchlets slightly angled in cross section—*V. cinerea* var. *floridana* (NOTE: Individuals corresponding to *V. baileyana* Munson, generally regarded in synonymy with *V. vulpina*, will key here.)

                    H. Nodes not banded with red pigmentation; branchlets mostly green or with a complete covering of purplish red pigmentation; branchlets generally glabrous to thinly cobwebby; leaves glabrous or with only short, straight trichomes along the veins and in their axils, varying to very thinly cobwebby branchlets more or less terete in cross section.

I.   Branchlets entirely purplish red; nodal diaphrams 2–5 mm thick; leaves generally 3-lobed, the terminal lobe long-acuminate—*V. palmata*

I.   Branchlets generally green or with red pigmentation only on the upper surface; nodal diaphrams 2 mm or less thick; leaves unlobed to 3-lobed, the terminal lobe mostly acute.

    J.   Nodal diaphram less than 1 mm thick; leaves generally 3-lobed, the two lateral lobes pointing forward; leaf teeth mostly with concave apicular margins; Va. and Tenn. and northward species—*V. riparia*

    J.   Nodal diaphrams greater than 1 mm thick; leaves generally unlobed, but if 3-lobed, the lateral lobes divergent; leaf teeth mostly with convex apicular margins; throughout our range—*V. vulpina*

KEY TO *WISTERIA*

A.   Legumes and ovary glabrous; pedicels 6–10 mm long; native species—*W. frutescens*

A.   Legumes and ovary with velvety pubescence; pedicels 1–2.5 cm long; introduced species.

    B.   Flowers 1.5–2 cm long, opening gradually from base of inflorescence; leaflets 13–19; racemes slender, 2–5 dm long—*W. floribunda*

    B.   Flowers 2.3–2.6 cm long, opening almost simultaneously along inflorescence; leaflets 7–13; racemes stout, 1.5–2 dm long—*W. sinensis*

KEY TO *YUCCA*

A.   Leaves with margins having fraying filamentous fibers; fruit erect; stem usually less than 3 dm tall—*Y. filamentosa*

A.   Leaves with margins not fraying into filamentous fibers; fruit pendant; stem usually more than 3 dm tall.

    B.   Margins of leaves entire or sometimes scabrous—*Y. gloriosa*

    B.   Margins of leaves serrate—*Y. aloifolia*

Glossary

Accuminate tapering gradually to a drawn-out point.
Achene a hard, dry, indehiscent, 1-seeded fruit, 1-locular.
Acicular needle shaped.
Actinomorphic set of flower parts that can be cut through the center into similar parts along 2 or more planes; radially symmetrical.
Acute sharp-pointed at apex.
Adnate fusion of unlike structures or parts.
Adventitious buds developing without pattern, or roots from some structure other than a root.
Aggregate a number of separate fruits from a single flower clustered together.
Ament a tassel-like group of unisexual flowers.
Anther the pollen-bearing portion of the stamen.
Anthesis time at which a flower is open; when plant is in bloom.
Apetalous lacking petals.
Apomictic reproducing without sexual reproduction; seed production without a sexual process.
Aril enlarged raphe, an appendage on the seed.
Aristate having a bristlelike appendage, awned.
Ascending directed or rising upward obliquely.
Attenuate tapering, elongate.
Auricle an ear-shaped lobe.
Auriculate furnished with auricles.
Awn a stiff bristlelike appendage.
Axil the point between two structures, as leaf and stem.
Angiosperm plant bearing true flowers, fruit, and seed; seed covered by carpels which give rise to fruit; plant with covered seed.
Axillary in an axil.

Bald mountaintop without trees: a grassy bald, grass covered; a shrub bald, shrub covered, often by heaths.
Beak a long, thick projection.
Berry a fleshy fruit from a single ovary with 1 to many embedded seeds, as the tomato or grape.
Bifid having two lobes or segments, forked.
Bifurcate forked, as two-pronged.
Bipinnate twice pinnate.
Bisexual an individual flower having both male and female parts.
Blade the expanded part of a leaf, petal, or other structure.
Bloom white, waxy or powdery covering, often on leaves or fruit.
Bract a reduced leaf usually subtending a flower.
Bristle stiff, strong but slender hair or trichome.
Bundle-scar ends of vascular bundles showing in leaf scars.

Caducous falling or dropping early.
Calyx the outer part of the perianth or floral envelope.
Cambium a sheath of generative tissue in a woody stem.

Campanulate bell shaped.

Canescent gray-pubescent and hoary.

Capillary very slender, threadlike.

Capitate headlike.

Capsule a dry, dehiscent fruit originating from 2 or more fused carpels.

Carpel one member of a compound pistil, or a single pistil.

Catkin a scaly-bracted pendulous spike bearing asexual flowers.

Caudate with a tail or tail-like appendage.

Caudex persistent woody base of a perennial plant.

Cilia marginal hairs or trichomes.

Ciliate marginally fringed with hairs.

Clasping base that partly or wholly surrounds another structure.

Clavate club shaped.

Claw a petiolelike base of some petals and sepals.

Clonal pertaining to a group of plants all descending from a single individual.

Colonial a group of plants with a clonal relationship where all plants are from one rootstock, rhizome, stolon, or root system.

Compound composed of two or more similar or united parts.

Coppice a thicket; to regenerate shrubs by cutting back to near the ground so new stems arise as sprouts from stump or roots.

Cordate heart shaped, with a sinus and rounded lobes.

Coriaceous leathery.

Corolla the inner whorl of the perianth; all of the petals.

Corymb short, broad, flat inflorescence, outer flowers blooming first.

Crenate with shallowly rounded teeth, scalloped.

Crest an elevated ridge or appendage on an organ.

Crisped curled or twisted in relation to a horizontal plane.

Cuneate wedge shaped, narrow end at point of attachment.

Cuspidate tipped with a short, rigid point.

Cyme a broad, flat-topped determinate inflorescence, the central flowers blooming first.

Cymule a diminutive cyme.

Deciduous not persistent; falling after completion of the normal function as autumn leaves or flowers after anthesis.

Decumbent lying on the ground, usually with the tip ascending.

Dehiscent opening of fruit or anther to shed seed or pollen.

Deltoid triangular.

Dentate marginal teeth pointing outward, not forward.

Determinate inflorescence where the terminal flower matures first, limited in number and extent.

Dichotomous forking in pairs.

Dicotyledon angiosperm with two cotyledons; flowers usually 4–5 parted or multiples thereof; vascular cambium usually present; vascular bundles usually arranged in a ring; leaves usually net-veined.

Digitate fingered, several members rising from one point.

Dioecious staminate and pistillate flowers on separate plants.

Distal farthest away from the center, the point of attachment.

Doubly serrate with small serrations on larger sawlike teeth.

Drupe fleshy, usually 1-seeded, indehiscent fruit with seed enclosed in a stony endocarp.

Echinate bearing prickles.
Eglandular without glands.
Ellipsoid three-dimensional ellipse.
Elliptic narrowed to rounded ends; widest at the middle.
Emarginate leaves or other structures notched at the apex.
Endemic species restricted to a limited geographic section.
Endocarp innermost layer of the pericarp.
Entire margins smooth, without lobes, divisions or teeth.
Epipetalous said of stamens inserted on the corolla.
Erose unevenly toothed, eroded, finely or minutely torn.
Exfoliating peeling off in thin layers or shreds.
Exserted projecting out of or beyond.

Falcate sickle shaped.
Farinose a surface with a mealy or scurfy coating.
Fascicle a bundle or close cluster.
Filament the stalk bearing the anther.
Filiform threadlike, usually round in cross section.
Fimbriate fringed; having filiform appendages.
Floricane stem at flowering and fruiting stage.
Foliate leaflike in texture and appearance.
Follicle dry fruit from one carpel, dehiscent on one suture.
Fusiform narrow ellipse with pointed ends, spindle shaped.

Gamopetalous having fused petals.
Gibbous swollen, usually on one side.
Glabrate becoming glabrous with age.
Glabrous without pubescence.
Gland a secreting organ or appendage.
Glandular having secreting organs or trichomes, glands.
Glandular-pubescent bearing secreting capitate trichomes.
Glaucous having a whitened bloom.
Globose spherical or globular.
Gymnosperm plant bearing seed borne on ovulate scales without true flowers or fruit; literally, a plant with naked seed.
Gynophore stipe of stalk of a pistil.

Hammock southern mixed forest broadly mesic with deciduous hardwoods, southern magnolia, spruce pine. Often on river bluffs or uplands protected from fire.
Hastate arrowhead shaped, basal lobes narrow, turned outward.
Hesperidium berry with a tough, leathery rind, e.g., a citrus fruit.
Hirsute bearing long, shaggy hairs, rough to the touch.
Hisutulous slightly hirsute.
Hispid bearing rough hairs or bristles.
Hoary grayish white with fine, close pubescence.

Hyaline translucent.

Hypanthium floral cup or tube formed either from the receptacle or from fusion of the bases of the petals, sepals, and stamens, or both.

Imbricate overlapping, as shingles.

Imperfect flower with one of the sexes wanting.

Included not protruding beyond the surrounding organ.

Incised irregularly cut or slashed, often deeply.

Indehiscent not opening by regular lines.

Indeterminate inflorescence where flowers open progressively from the base upward or outside of the cluster inward toward the center.

Inferior ovary lies below attachment of perianth and stamens.

Inflorescence the flower cluster.

Infrastipular below the stipules.

Inserted attached to another part or organ.

Internode part of a stem between two successive nodes.

Involucre whorl of bracts around a flower or flower cluster.

Involute rolled inward.

Keeled with a keel or ridge.

Lacerate irregularly torn or cut.

Laciniate divided into long, narrow, equal divisions or segments.

Lanate woolly.

Lanceolate lance shaped.

Lateral on or at the side.

Lax loose and open.

Leaflet a single division of a compound leaf.

Leaf scar mark on stem where leaf was attached.

Lenticular lens shaped.

Lenticel corky spots on young bark, arising in relation to epidermal stomates.

Lepidote scurfy, with small scales.

Liguliform strap shaped.

Limb expanded flat part of gamopetalous corolla, distince from the tube or throat.

Limesink a depression formed by collapse of a cavern; a sink hole.

Linear long and narrow with parallel margins.

Lobulate divided into small lobes.

Locular having one or more locules.

Locule compartment of ovary, anther, or fruit.

Lunate crescent shaped.

Membranous thin and pliable.

Mericarp one of two seedlike carpels of an umbelliferous fruit.

Mesic pertaining to conditions of medium moisture supply.

Midrib center rib of leaf or similar structure.

Monocotyledon an angiosperm with one cotyledon; flowers usually three-parted or multiples thereof; vascular cambium usually lacking and bundles scattered; leaves usually parallel veined.

Monoecious bearing both male and female unisexual flowers on the same plant.

Mucro a short, abrupt spur or spiny tip.
Mucronate bearing a short, abrupt spur or spiny tip.
Muricate rough with sharp, hard points.

Naturalized of foreign origin but reproducing.
Nerved having simple or unbranched veins or slender ribs.
Node place on the stem bearing a leaf and one or more buds.
Nut dry, indehiscent 1-seeded fruit with a bony or woody cover.
Nutlet diminutive of nut.

Obcordate inverted heart-shaped.
Obovate ovate with broader end toward the apex.
Obovoid egg shaped with broad end uppermost.
Obtuse rounded to blunt at the end.
Ocrea sheath or tabular structure formed by union of 2 stipules.
Orbicular flat with a circular outline.
Ovary basal part of the pistil enclosing the ovules.
Ovate egg shaped with broader end lowermost.
Ovoid oval in outline.
Ovule the body which after fertilization becomes the seed.

Pale a small, thin scale or bract; a receptacle scale or bract in Compositae.
Palmate with 3 or more lobes, veins, or leaflets arising from one point.
Panicle loose, irregularly compound inflorescence; a highly branched raceme.
Papilionaceous butterflylike, composed of standard, wings, and keel petals, found
    in many legumes.
Papillose having short, rounded wartlike protuberances.
Pectinate comblike.
Pedicel the stalk of a single flower.
Peduncle a primary stalk, supporting a cluster or a single flower.
Pendulous hanging downward.
Penniveined veined in a pinnate manner.
Perfoliate having the stem apparently passing through the leaf.
Perianth corolla and calyx, the floral envelope.
Pericarp the wall of a mature ovary, i.e., that part of a fruit outside the seed.
Persistent remaining attached; not falling off.
Petal a division of the corolla.
Petiole the stem of a leaf.
Petiolule the stem of a leaflet, a small petiole.
Phyllode an expanded bladeless petiole.
Pilose pubescence of scattered long, slender hairs.
Pine barren a site usually of longleaf pine with a groundcover of wire grass, herbs,
    and low shrubs.
Pinna a leaflet or primary division of a compound leaf.
Pinnate leaflets or pinnae of compound leaf placed on either side of the rachis,
    featherlike.
Pinnatifid pinnately cleft.
Pinniparallel finely parallel, as the barbs in a feather.
Pinnule secondary pinna or leaflet.

Pistil female flower organ when complete, consisting of ovary, stigma, and style.

Pistillate female; having pistils, lacking fertile stamens.

Pith soft tissue at the center or a stem.

Plicate fan-folded.

Plumose with hairlike branches, feathery.

Pocosin bog formed in a shallow, undrained depression with evergreen shrubs.

Polygamous bearing unisexual and bisexual flowers on the same individual plant.

Polymorphic with 3 or more forms.

Polypetalous having separate petals.

Polyploid having the number of chromosomes in the somatic cells more than twice the haploid number, multiplication of the chromosome set.

Pome a fleshy fruit formed from an inferior ovary with several locules as the apple or pear.

Prickle spinelike body originating from the epidermis.

Primocane first-year nonflowering cane of a bramble.

Procumbent prostrate, trailing or lying flat.

Prostrate lying flat on the ground.

Puberulent minutely pubescent.

Pubescent covered with short, soft trichomes.

Punctate dotted with depressions, translucent internal glands or colored dots.

Pustulate bearing pustules or blisters.

Pyrene the nutlet of a drupe.

Pyriform pearshaped.

Raceme a simple elongated, indeterminate inflorescence with pedicelled or stalked flowers.

Rachis an axis of flowers or leaflets.

Receptacle expanded apex of floral axis bearing floral parts.

Recurved curved downward or backward.

Reflexed abruptly recurved downward.

Reniform kidney shaped.

Repand undulate or wavy.

Resinous glandular dotted; with appearance of resin.

Reticulate netted.

Retrorse turned backward or downward.

Revolute rolled downward, the margin turned toward the lower side.

Rhizome a horizontal underground stem.

Rostrate beaked, narrowed to a slender point.

Ruderal growing in disturbed sites or waste places; weeds of old fields, roadsides; weedy plant often introduced.

Rufous reddish brown.

Rugose wrinkled, as leaf surfaces with sunken veins.

Sagittate arrowhead shaped, with two acute basal lobes pointing downward.

Salverform corolla form of cylindrical tube and spreading lobes.

Samara indehiscent winged fruit.

Savanna a generally treeless area of grasses, sedges, and forbs, usually rather wet during spring.

Scabrous rough and harsh to the touch; with short, bristly hairs.

Scandent climbing.

Scape a leafless flowering stem rising from the ground sometimes bearing bracts or scales.

Scarious thin, dry, and membranaceous, not green.

Schizocarp fruit that splits into 1-seeded portions, mericarps.

Scurfy with scalelike or branlike particles.

Sepal a separate part of the calyx.

Septate partitioned by walls.

Sericeous silky with closely appressed soft pubescence.

Serotinous produced late in the season; or cones not opening for several years.

Serrate having sharp teeth pointing forward.

Serrulate minutely serrate.

Sessile not stalked.

Seta a bristle.

Setose having bristles.

Shrub woody perennial, smaller than a tree, usually several stemmed.

Sinuate with a deep, wavy margin.

Sinus the cleft or recess between two lobes.

Slough a wet place with deep mud and sluggish channel.

Spathe a large bract enclosing an inflorescence.

Spatulate spoon shaped.

Spicate arranged in or resembling a spike.

Spiculose a surface covered with fine points.

Spike an elongated, simple, indeterminate inflorescence with sessile flowers.

Spine a sharp, woody outgrowth from the stem, usually a modified stem, sometimes a petiole or stipule.

Spinulose with small spines.

Spur a tubular projection from petal or sepal; a very short compact branch with little internodal development.

Squarrose spreading or recurved at the tip.

Stamen pollen-bearing organ; usually an anther and filament.

Staminate having stamens and no functional pistils.

Staminode a sterile stamen.

Standard the upper broad petal of a papilionaceous corolla.

Stellate starlike.

Stigma the part of the pistil that receives the pollen.

Stipe stalk that supports the pistil or carpel.

Stipitate borne on a short stalk, as stipitate glands.

Stipule basal-paired appendages of a leaf, sometimes fused.

Stolon a sucker, runner, or basal branch that is disposed to root.

Stramineous straw colored.

Striate marked with longitudinal lines, streaks, or ridges.

Strigillose provided with small, firm, slender bristles.

Strigose bearing sharp, stiff, straight appressed trichomes.

Style part of the pistil between ovary and stigma.

Subulate awl shaped.

Sulcate grooved or furrowed lengthwise.

Superior ovary ovary with perianth or floral envelope inserted below it.

Swamp a wooded or brushy area usually having surface water.

Syncarp multiple or fleshy aggregate fruit, as a mulberry.
Synonym a superceded or discarded name.

Teeth a marginal serration or dentation, usually sharp pointed.
Tendril a slender twining or clasping appendage for climbing.
Terete round in cross section.
Terminal at the end.
Ternate in threes.
Thorn a spine, usually a simple or branched stem.
Thyrse a compact compound panicle.
Tomentose densely pubescent with matted soft wool-like hairs.
Tomentulose finely tomentose.
Trailing prostrate, not rooting.
Trichome any hairlike outgrowth of the epidermis.
Trifoliate with three leaflets.
Trifurcate three-pronged; having three forks as branches.
Truncate ending abruptly, the base or apex cut nearly straight across.
Tubercle a little tuber; thickened growth on roots due to symbiotic fungi.
Turbinate top shaped; inversely conical.

Umbel indeterminate inflorescence of several pedicellate flowers rising from a common point of attachment.
Undulate wavy, repand.
Unisexual an individual flower having only male or female parts, not both.
Urceolate urn shaped.
Utricle small bladder; a one-seeded indehiscent fruit.

Valve one portion of a split capsule.
Vein strand of vascular tissue in a flat organ such as a leaf or other structure.
Velutinous velvety; a coating of fine, soft hairs.
Verrrucose bearing a wartlike or nodular surface.
Verticil a whorl or circular arrangement of parts about an axis.
Villous having long, fine hairs, not matted.
Virgate wand shaped, twiggy.
Viscid sticky, glutinous.

Whorl three or more leaves or flowers at one node.
Woolly clothed with long and tortuous or matted hairs.

Xeric dry.

Zygomorphic corolla or calyx when divisible into equal parts in one plane only; bilaterally symmetric.

Bibliography

Alabama Natural Heritage Program. 1984. An Initial Prioritization of Alabama's Natural Heritage Elements. 32 p. U. of Ala. University, Ala.

Allard, .H. A. 1943. The Eastern False Mistletoe (*Phorodendron flavescens*): When does it flower? Castanea 8:72–78

Anderson, L. C. *Forestiera godfreyi* (Oleaceae), a New Species from Florida and South Carolina. Sida 11:1–5.

Anonymous 1986. Louisiana Natural Heritage Program: List of Special Plants. 11 p. mimeo. Dept. of Nat. Res., Coastal Mgmt. Div. Baton Rouge.

Anonymous No Date. Plant Species Monitored by Wildlife/Heritage Data Base. 7 p. mimeo. W.Va. Dept. Nat. Res. Wildlife Res. Div.

Argus, G. W. 1986. The genus *Salix* (Salicaceae) in the Southeastern United States. Syst. Bot. Monog. 9:1–170.

Bailey, V. L. 1962. Revision of the Genus *Ptelea* (Rutaceae). Brittonia 14:1–45.

Brizicky, G. K. 1962. The Genera of Rutaceae in the Southeastern United States. J. Arnold Arb. 43:1–22.

_____ 1963. The Genera of Sapindales in the Southeaster United States. J. Arnold Arb. 44:462–501.

_____ 1964. The Genera of Celastrales in the Southeastern United States. J. Arnold Arb. 45:206–234.

_____ 1964. The Genera of Cistaceae in the Southeastern United States. J. Arnold Arb. 45:346–357.

_____ 1964. The Genera of Rhamnaceae in the Southeastern United States. J. Arnold Arb. 45:439–463.

_____ 1965. The Genera of Vitaceae in the Southeastern United States. J. Arnold Arb. 46:48–67.

Campbell, C. S., C. W. Greene, and S. E. Bergquist. 1987. Apomixis and Sexuality in Three Species of *Amelanchier*, Shadbush (Rosaceae, Maloideae). Amer. Jour. Bot. 74:321-328.

Carvell, W. N., and W. H. Eshbaugh. 1982. A systematic study of the Genus *Buckleya* (Santalaceae). Castanea 47:17–37.

Chaudhri, M. M. 1980. Draft Index of Author Abbreviations. H. M. Stationary Office, London.

Clark, Ross C. 1971. The Woody Plants of Alabama. Ann. Mo. Bot. Garden 58(2): 90–242.

_____ 1974. *Ilex collina*, a second species of *Nemopanthus* in the Southern Appalachians. J. Arnold Arb. 55:435–440.

Clarkson, Roy B. 1960. Note on the distribution of *Alnus crispa* in Eastern North America. Castanea 25:83–85.

Coker, W. C. 1944. The woody Smilaxes of the United States. Jour. Elisha Mitchell Sci. Soc. 60:27–69.

Coon, Nelson. 1963. Using Plants for Healing. 272 p. Hearthside Press.

Davis, H. A., Albert M. Fuller, and Tyreeca Davis. 1967–1970. Contributions toward revision of the *Eubati* of Eastern North America. I Castanea 32:20–37; II 33:50–70; III 33:206–241: IV 34:157–179: V 34:235–266; VI 35:176–194.

Dean, Blanche E., and Amy Mason. 1968. Trees and Shrubs. 250 p. So. Univ. Press. Birmingham, Ala.

Duncan, Wilbur H. 1967. Woody Vines of the Southeastern States. Sida 3(1):1–76.
_____ & T. M. Pullen. 1962. Lepidote Rhododendrons of the Southeastern United States. Brittonia 14:290–298.

Ebinger, J. E. 1974. Systematic study of the Genus *Kalmia*. Rhodora 76:315–398.

Elias, T. S. 1971. The Genera of Myricaceae in the Southeastern United States. J. Arnold Arb. 52:305–381.

Ernst, W. R. 1963. The Genera of Hamamelidaceae and Platanaceae in the Southeastern United States. J. Arnold Arb. 44:193–210.

_____ 1964. The Genera of Berberidaceae, Lardizabalaceae and Menispermaceae in the Southeastern United States. J. Arnold Arb. 45:1–35.

Eyde, R. H. 1966. The Nyssaceae in the Southeastern United States. J. Arnold Arb. 47:117–125.

Farmer, J. A., and J. L. Thomas. 1969. Disjunction and Endemism in *Croton alabamensis*. Rhodora 71:94–103.

Ferguson, I. K., 1966. The Genera of Caprifoliaceae in the Southeastern United States. J. Arnold Arb. 47:33–59.

Fernald, Merritt Lyndon. 1950. Gray's Manual of Botany. 8th Ed. 1632 p. American Book Co. N.Y., N.Y.

Galle, Fred. No Date. Native and Some Introduced Azaleas for Southern Gardens. Booklet No. 2. Ida Cason Galloway Foundation, Pine Mt., Georgia. 28 p.

_____ 1985. Azaleas. 438 p. Timber Press. Portland Ore.

Godfrey, Robert K., and Jean W. Wooten. 1981. Aquatic and Wetland Plants of Southeastern United States. Dicotyledons. 933p. Univ. Ga. Press. Athens.

Gonsoulin, G. J. 1974. A revision of *Styrax* (Styracaceae) in North America, Central America, and the Caribbean. Sida 5:191–258.

Graham, S. A. 1966. The Genera of Araliaceae in the Southeastern United States. J. Arnold Arb. 47:126–136.

Grimm, William Carey. 1957. The Book of Shrubs. 522p. Telegraph Press. Harrisburg, Pa.

Gunn, Scott C., 1986. Personal communication. Rare Plant List of Tennessee. July 8.

Halls, Lowell K. 1977. Southeastern Fruit-Producing Woody Plants used by Wildlife. U.S.D.A. Forest Service. Gen. Tech. Rept. SO-16. 235p.

Hardin, J. W. 1971. Studies of the Southeastern United States Flora. II. The Gymnosperms. Jour. Elisha Mitchill Sci. Soc. 87:43–50.

_____ 1973. The Enigmtic Chokeberries (*Aronia*, Rosaceae). Bull. Torrey Bot. Club 100:178–184.

_____ 1974. Studies of the Southeastern Flora. IV. Oleaceae. Sida 5:274–285.

Harlow, William M. 1941. Fruit Key and Twig Key to Trees and Shrubs. 50 p., 56 p. Dover Publications. N.Y., N.Y.

Harper, Francis. 1958. The Travels of William Bartram. Yale Univ. Press, New Haven, Ct. 727 p.

Harshberger, J. W. 1899. The Botanists of Philadelphia. Pub. by the Author. Philadelphia, Pa.

Heinrich, Bernd. 1987. Thermoregulation in winter moths. Sci. American 256(5):104–112. March.

Horn, D. D., and P. Somers. 1981. *Neviusia alabamensis* in Tennessee. Sida 9:90–91.

Jaynes, R. A. 1971 The Kalmias and their hybrids. Quart. Bull. Amer. Rhod. Soc. July. pp. 1–5.

179

Jennison, H. M. 1933. A new species of *Conradina* from Tennessee. Jour. Elisha Mitchell Soc. 48:268–269.

Jones, S. B., and A. E. Luchsinger. 1986. *Plant Systematics* (2nd ed.) McGraw–Hill Book Co., N.Y.

Judd, Walter. 1979. Generic Relationships in the *Andromedeae (Ericaceae)*. Jour. Arn. Arb. 60:477–503.

———— 1981. A monograph of *Lyonia* (Ericaceae). Jour. Arnold Arb. 62:63–128.

———— 1982. A Taxonomic Revision of *Pieris* (Ericaceae). Jour. Arnold Arb. 63:103–144.

Keener, C. S. 1977. Studies in the Ranunculaceae of the Southeastern United States. IV. Miscellaneous Genera. Sida 7:1–12.

Kral, R. 1960. A Revision of *Asimina* and *Derringothamnus* (Annonacee). Brittonia 12:233–278.

Krochmal, Arnold, Russell S. Walters, and Richard M. Doughty. 1969. A Guide to Medicinal Plants of Appalachia. U.S.Forest Service Res. Paper NE-138. 291 p.

Little, Elbert L., Jr. 1976. Atlas of United States Trees, Volume 4, Minor eastern hardwoods. U. S. Dept. Agric. Misc. Publ. 1342, 17 p., 230 maps.

McClintock, Elizabeth 1957. A Monograph of the Genus *Hydrangea*. Proc. Calif. Acad. 29:147–256.

McClure, F. A. in T. R. Soderstrom. 1973. Genera of Bamboos Native to the New World (Gramineae: Bambusoideae). Smithsonian Contribution to Botany, No. 9.

McCollum, Jerry L., and David R. Ettman. 1977. Georgia's Protected Plants. 64 p. mimeo. Ga. Dept. Nat. Res. Atlanta.

McKell, Cyrus M., James P. Blaisdell, and Joe R. Goodin (Eds.) 1972. Wildland Shrubs-Their Biology and Utilizaton. U.S. Forest Service Gen. Tech. Rept. INT-1. 494 p. August.

Martin, Alexander C., Herbert S. Zim, and Arnold L. Nelson. 1951. American Wildlife and Plants. A Guide to Wildlife Food Habits. 500 p. Dover Publications. N.Y., N.Y.   ·

Muenscher, W. C. 1936. Keys to Woody Plants. 105 p. Pub. by the Author. Ithica, N.Y.

Nevling, L. I. 1962. The Thymelaeaceae in the Southeastern United States, J. Arnold Arb. 43:428–434.

Nicely, K. A. 1965. A Monographic Study of the Calycanthaceae. Castanea 30:38–81.

Nicholson, Robert G. 1986. To the Arks with Rabbitbane: Plant Conservation at the Arnold Arboretum. Arnoldia 46(3):23–25.

North Carolina Natural Heritage Program. 1985. Special Plants List. 12 p. mimeo.

Phillips, H. R. 1985. Growing and Propagating Wild Flowers. The Univ. of N.C. Press, Chapel Hill.

Pilatowski, R. E. 1982. A Taxonomic Study of the *Hydrangea arborescens* Complex. Castanea 47:84–98.

Porter, Duncan M., 1979. Rare and Endangered Vascular Plant Species in Virginia. 52 p. mimeo. U. S. Fish and Wildlife Service and V. P. I. Blacksburg, Va.

Prance, G. T. 1970. The Genera of Chrysobalancceae in the Southeastern United States. J. Arnold Arb. 51:521–528.

Radford, Albert E., Harry E. Ahles, and C. Ritchie Bell. 1968. Manual of the Vascular Flora of the Carolinas. 1183 p. Univ. N. C. Press. Chapel Hill, N.C.

Rayner, Douglas A., et al. No Date. Native Vascular Plants-Rare, Threatened or Endangered, in South Carolina. 25 p. mimeo. Heritage Trust Program. Columbia, S. C.

Reveal, J. L., and J. J. Seldin. 1976. On the identity of *Halesia carolina* L. (Styracaceae). Taxon 25:123–140.

Roane, Martha K., and Josephine DeN. Henry. 1983. The Species of *Rhododendron* Native to North America. Jour. Am. Rhododendron Soc. 37(3):137–145;164–168. Summer, July. Also pub. in Va. Jour. Sci. 32(2):50–68. 1981.

Robertson, K. R. 1974. The Genera of Rosaceae in the Southeastern United States. J. Arnold Arb. 55:303–401; 611–662.

Shinners, Lloyd H. 1952. *Ceanothus herbaceus* Raf. for *C. ovatus:* a correction of name. Field and Labratory 19:33–34.

―――― 1962. *Rhododendron nudiflorium* and *A. roseum* (Ericaceae): Illegitimate names. Castanea 27:94–95.

Shuey, A. G., and R. P. Wonderlin. 1977. The Needle Palm, *Rhapidophyllum hystrix.* Principes 21:47–59.

Skog, J. T., and N. H. Nickerson. 1972. Variation and speciation in the genus *Hudsonia.* Ann. Missouri Bot. Gard. 59:454–464.

Small, John Kunkel. 1933. Manual of the Southeastern Flora. 1554 p. Pub. by the Author. The Science Press, Lancaster Pa.

Southall, R. M., and J. W. Hardin. 1974. A Taxonomic Revision of *Kalmia* (Ericaceae). J. Elisha Mitchell Sci. Soc. 90:1–23.

Spongberg, S. A. 1971. The Staphyleaceae in the Southeastern United States. J. Arnold Arb. 52:196–203.

―――― 1974. A Review of Deciduous-leaved Species of *Stewartia* (Theaceae). J. Arnold Arb. 55:182–214.

Strausbaugh, P. D., and Earl L. Core. 1970, 1971, 1973, 1977. Flora of West Virginia. Second Ed. W. Va. Univ. Bull. Series 70(7–2); 71(12–3); 74(2–1); 77(12–3).

Tehon, Leo R. 1942. Fieldbook of Native Illinois Shrubs. Manual 3. 307 p. Ill. Nat. Hist. Surv. Urbana.

Thieret, J. W. 1966. Habit Variation in *Myrica pensylvanica* and *M. cerifera.* Castanea 31:183–185.

Thomas, J. L., 1960. A Monographic Study of the Cyrillaceae. Contr. Gray Herb. 186:1–114.

U.S.D.A. Forest Service. 1974. Seeds of Woody Plants in the United States. U.S.D.A. Agric. Handb. 450. U.S. Govt. Printing Office. Washington, D.C.

U.S. Fish and Wildlife Service. 1984. Endangered and Threatened Wildlife and Plants. U.S.F and W. Ser., 50 CFR 17.11 and 17.12.

Van Dersal, William R. 1938. Native Woody Plants of the United States. U.S.D.A. Misc. Pub. 303. 362 p. maps.

Vander Kloet, S. P. 1980. The taxonomy of the highbush blueberry, *Vaccinium corymbosum.* Can. Jour. Bot. 58:1187–1201.

―――― 1983. The Taxonomy of *Vaccinium: Cyanococcus:* a summation. Can. Jour. Bot. 61:256–266.

―――― 1983. The Taxonomy of *Vaccinium* Subgen. Oxycoccus. Rhodora 85:1–43.

Webster, G. L. 1967. The Genera of Euphorbiaceae in the Southeastern United States. Rhodora 48:303–430.

Wiggington, B. F. 1963. Trees and Shrubs for the Southeast. 280 p. Univ. Ga. Press. Athens.

Wilbur, R. L. 1975. A Revision of the North American Genus *Amorpha* (Leguminosae-Psoraleae) Rhodora 77:337–409.

Wilson, James S. 1965. Variation of Three Taxonomic Complexes of the Genus *Cornus* in Eastern United States. Trans. Kans. Acad. Sci. 67:747–817.

Wilson, K. A., and C. E. Wood. 1959. The Genera of Oleaceae in the Southeastern United States. J. Arnold Arb. 40:369–384.

Wofford, B. E. 1983. A New *Lindera* from North America. J. Arnold Arb. 64:325–331.

Wood, C. E. 1958. The Genera of Woody Ranales in the Southeastern United States. J. Arnold Arb. 39:296–346.

_____ 1959. The Genera of Theaceae of the Southeastern United States. J. Arnold Arb. 40:413–419.

_____ 1961. The genera of Ericaceae in the Southeastern United States. Jour. Arnold Arb. 41:10–80.

Yates, I. E., and W. H. Duncan. 1970. Comparative Studies of *Smilax* Section *Smilax* of the Southeastern United States. Rhodora 72:290–312.

Appendix A

SHRUBS AND WOODY VINES OF "SPECIAL SIGNIFICANCE," BY STATES

SPECIES	La.	Ala.	Tn.	Ga.	S.C.	N.C.	Va.	W.Va.
Acacia angustissima	X							
Aesculus parviflora					X			
Alnus crispa			X					
Amelanchier bartramiana								X
A. sanguinea			X					
Ampelopsis arborea								X
A. cordata								X
Andromeda glaucophylla								X
Arctostaphlos uva-ursi							X	
Aristolochia macrophylla					X			
A. tomentosa					X			
Brunnichia cirrhosa							X	
Buckleya distichophylla			X	X		X		
Bumelia tenax						X		
B. thornei				X				
Calycanthus floridanus var. laevigatus							X	
Celastras scandens	X							
Chrysobalanus oblongifolius[1]	X							
Comptonia peregrina[2]			X					
Cornus canadensis							X	
C. foemina var. racemosa					X			
C. rugosa								X
Crataegus harbisoni			X					
Croton alabamensis		X						
Decodon verticillatus								X
Diervilla lonicera			X					
D. sessilifolia var. rivularis			X					
Elliottia racemosa				X				
Euonymus atropurpureus					X			
E. obovatus			X					
Forestiera ligustrina	X				X			
F. segregata					X			
Fothergilla gardenii		X		X				
F. major		X	X		X			
Gaultheria procumbens					X			
Gaylussacia brachycera							X	X

1=Licania michauxii
2=Myrica peregrina

SPECIES	La.	Ala.	Tn.	Ga.	S.C.	N.C.	Va.	W.Va.
					STATE			
G. dumosa			X					X
G. mosieri					X			
Halesia diptera					X			
H. parviflora					X			
Hudsonia ericoides					X			
H. montana						X		
H. tomentosa							X	X
Hydrangea arborescens	X							
Hypericum species		X	X		X		X	
Ilex amelanchier	X	X						
I. cassine	X							
I. coriacea							X	
I. myrtifolia	X							
Iva imbricata							X	
Juniperus communis var. depressa					X			
Kalmia angustifolia var. caroliniana			X					
K. cuneata					X			
K. hirsuta		X						
K. latifolia	X							
Leucothoe populifolia³					X			
L. racemosa			X					
L. recurva								X
Licania michauxii					X			
Lindera melissifolia					X			
L. subcoriacea	X					X		
Litsea aestivalis				X	X	X		
Lonicera dioica			X					
L. flava		X			X			
Lyonia ferruginea					X			
L. mariana	X							
Lythrum curtissii				X				
Menziesia pilosa			X					
Myrica gale						X		
M. inodora	X							
Nemopanthus collina		X	X	X		X	X	X
Nestronia umbullula		X	X	X		X	X	
Neviusia alabamensis		X	X					
Nyssa ogechee					X			
Osmanthus americana							X	
Paxistima canbyi						X	X	X
Pieris floribunda						X	X	X
P. phillyreifolia		X			X			
Pinckneya pubens⁴					X			
Prunus allegheniensis								X
P. angustifolia								X

3=Agaristra populifolia
4=Pinckneya bracteata

SPECIES	STATE							
	La.	Ala.	Tn.	Ga.	S.C.	N.C.	Va.	W.Va.
P. gracilis	X							
P. pumila							X	X
Pyrularia pubera		X						
Rhamnus alnifolia			X					X
R. lanceolata	X							
Rhapidophyllum hystrix					X			
Rhododendron arborescens							X	
R. atlanticum		X						
R. bakeri		X				X		
R. cumberlandense							X	
R. flammeum					X			
R. prunifolia				X				
R. roseum						X		
R. vaseyi						X		
Rhus michauxii					X	X		
R. toxicodendron[5]								X
R. vernix[6]								X
Ribes curvatum	X	X						
R. cynosbati		X						
R. echinellum					X			
R. glandulosum						X		
R. hirtellum								X
R. lacustre								X
R. triste								X
Rosa acicularis								X
R. blanda								X
Rubus idaeus var. canadensis						X		
Sageretia minutiflora					X			
Schisandra coccinea		X	X	X		X		
Smilax laurifolia		X						
Spirea alba		X						
S. corymbosum		X					X	
S. virginiana		X					X	
Stewartia malacodendron		X					X	
S. ovata		X			X		X	
Stillingia aguatica					X			
Symplocos tinctoria			X					
Taxus canadensis			X					
Torreya taxifolia				X				
Vaccinium caesium								X
V. macrocarpon			X			X	X	
V. sempervirens					X			
V. tenellum			X					
Viburnum bracteatum		X	X	X				
V. obovatum		X						

5=Toxicodendron quercifolia
6=Toxicodendron vernix

SPECIES				STATE				
	La.	Ala.	Tn.	Ga.	S.C.	N.C.	Va.	W.Va.
V. rafinesquinum		X						
V. trilobium								X
Vitis cinerea								X
V. munsoniana		X						
V. rotundifolia								X
V. rupestris			X					
Zanthoxylum americanum	X							

Appendix B

RETAIL NURSERIES OFFERING NATIVE SHRUBS AND VINES FOR LANDSCAPING

Ben Pace Nursery
Rt 1, Box 925
Pine Mountain, GA 31822
404-663-2346

Camellia Forest Nursery
125 Carolina Forest Rd
Chapel Hill, NC 27514
919-967-5529

Carroll Gardens
444 East Main St
Westminster, MD 21157
301-848-5422

Eco-Gardens
PO Box 1227
Decatur, GA 30031
404-294-6468

Gardens of the Blue Ridge
PO Box 10
Pineola, NC 28662
704-733-2417

Griffey's Nursery
1670 Hwy 25-70
Marshall, NC 28753
704-656-2334

James Harris
538 Swanson Dr.
Lawrenceville, GA 30245
404-963-7468

Holbrook Farm and Nursery
Rt 2 Box 2238
Fletcher, NC 28732
704-891-7790

Louisiana Nursery
Rt 7, Box 43
Opelousas, LA 70570
318-948-3696

Magnolia Nursery
Rt 1, Box 87
Chunchula, AL 36521
205-675-4696

Mountain Ornamental Nursery
PO Box 83
Altamount, TN 37301
615-692-3424

Native Gardens
Rt 1, Box 494
Greenback, TN 37742
615-856-3350

Native Nurseries
1661 Centerville Rd
Tallahassee, FL 32308
904-386-8882

Native Plant Nursery
Sanibel-Captiva Conservation
    Foundation
Drawer S
Sanibel, FL 33957
813-472-1932

Niche Gardens
Rt 1, Box 290
Chapel Hill, NC 27514
919-967-0078

Oak Hill Farm
204 Presley St
Clover, SC 29710
803-222-4245

Salter Tree Farm
Rt 3, Box 1332
Madison, FL 32340
904-973-6312

Thomasville Nurseries
PO Box 7
Thomasville, GA 31799
912-226-5568

Transplant Nursery
Parkertown Rd
Lavonia, GA 30553
404-356-8947

Winterthur Museum
Winterthur, DE 19735
302-656-8591

Woodlanders, Inc.
1128 Colleton Ave
Aiken, SC 29801
803-648-7522

Index A

COMMON NAMES

189

Index B

SCIENTIFIC NAMES

Numbers in italic indicate a page number in the keys; boldface numbers indicate a plate.

197